Key Concepts in Social Research

Recent volumes include:

Key Concepts in Medical Sociology
Jonathan Gabe, Mike Bury and Mary Ann Elston

Fifty Key Concepts in Gender Studies
Jane Pilcher and Imelda Whelahan

Forthcoming titles include:

Key Concepts in Leisure Studies
David Harris

Key Concepts in Critical Social Theory
Nick Crossley

Key Concepts in Urban Studies
Mark Gottdiener

The SAGE Key Concepts series provide students with accessible and authoritative knowledge of the essential topics in a variety of disciplines. Cross-referenced throughout, the format encourages critical evaluation through understanding. Written by experienced and respected academics, the books are indispensable study aids and guides to comprehension.

GEOFF PAYNE AND JUDY PAYNE

Key Concepts in
Social Research

SAGE Publications
London • Thousand Oaks • New Delhi

SAGE Publications Ltd
55 City Road
1 Oliver's Yard
London EC1Y 1SP

SAGE Publications Inc
2455 Teller Road
Thousand Oaks, California 91320

SAGE Publications India Pvt Ltd
B-42 Panchsheel Enclave
Post Box 4109
New Delhi 100 017

British Library Cataloguing in Publication data

A catalogue record for this book is available from the British Library

ISBN 0 7619 6542 4
ISBN 0 7619 6843 2

Library of Congress control number: 2003112276

Typeset by M Rules
Printed in Great Britain by The Cromwell Press Ltd, Trowbridge, Wilture

contents

introduction

please start here

There are lots of good books on social research methods, so why choose this one? Five good reasons.

First, if you have just begun to look at this book, please do start here. It explains the way we have presented the information. **Many research methods books are too complicated**. Some take you through the whole of the research process as if you were doing a piece of research – which is fine if that is what you are actually doing. Others go into far too much detail. That can be useful if you are working through a project, or are training to be a social research worker. But that doesn't apply to most students, most of the time.

It certainly doesn't apply if 'social research methods' is only one module in the programme you are taking, or part of a subsidiary subject. Too much information makes it hard to find your way around, and to sort out the more useful parts. Most students don't need all that. If you have a class presentation or term test to prepare for, what you need to get started are the basic important points. If you want to go further or are tackling a dissertation, we give suggestions for other reading, and enough coverage to provide a solid base for the ambitious or more advanced reader to get started. But what this book aims to do is to start you off with the core elements: it keeps it short and to the point.

Second, **the way many other books explain things is not always straightforward**. Experts often assume that you know a lot more than you do. Researchers tend to write in a way that is fine for the specialist, extra keen or very bright student (because that is the kind of student they were themselves). Most students aren't like that. You have other, wider interests and calls on your time. You are faced with assessment deadlines. You need a straight answer. We have been teaching research methods for many years, and that's something we have learned. We know what explanations are clear, and what works for students, how much previous learning to expect, and what to emphasise and what to leave out. We have kept it simple.

Third, **this book is easy to use and focused**. It sticks to 50 key concepts (that is, both ideas and techniques) that come up most often in social research methods courses and research. We have also included some topics to help with particular confusions some students have reported to us in the past. It is a book of '50 key concepts', not '*the* 50 key concepts' (universal agreement on a top 50 is an impossible dream).

For example, we have not found space for 'statistical inference' techniques, 'multivariate analysis' and details of software packages, or for the research styles of some important schools of sociology like post-modernism, symbolic interactionism and constructivism, or certain research techniques like discourse analysis and graphical displays. There are lots of other specialist textbooks that deal with such issues, and you can't please everyone! Our choice of 50 concepts has been made with the needs of social science students, not professional researchers, in mind. The selection is also influenced by our accumulated experience over several decades as empirical researchers ourselves. We see real life research as being untidy, bedevilled with practical problems, and seldom living up to the remarkably high standards of theoretical textbooks. This book is for you.

Fourth, **the concepts treated in this book are easy to locate and well cross-referenced**. You can find the main entry for the topic you are seeking in the Contents list. The concepts are listed in alphabetic order, and are cross-referenced in each section by 'links' to related topics. Each section is written in simple language, with as few technical terms as possible. Where we *have* used technical terms that you need to know, they are usually marked in the text by single inverted commas (e.g. 'in-depth interviews'). Other significant words or terms are highlighted by italics. This should help you quickly spot the key points when they are mentioned only briefly or contained in longer sentences. We give concrete examples as we go along, to illustrate each concept and ground it in direct experience.

Fifth, each section has been **designed to give you enough information to get started, without being too long**. We aim to give you more than a dictionary or encyclopaedia would, so that you get straight to the basics. If you then want to follow up the concept in another source, you will be better equipped to do so.

In case you do want to go further, we include some references to other sources in each section. Each References section is divided into two parts: the first offering mainly general information and alternative explanations, and second, those publications that mainly give examples, some 'classics' and some very recent and easily available. In fact, the two types often overlap. We include some internet sources (and discuss using them), but as web addresses change so rapidly, there is little point in trying to produce a print technology address book listing electronic sites.

We do, however, highlight terms and ideas in each summary, so that you check your own understanding as you go along. Immediately following this Preface, there is a User's Guide to explain the layout of each section. It is worth looking at this before you go on to look at the individual sections. We want the book to do what you want.

We hope you find this book useful. It is a book for 'dipping into' rather than reading from cover to cover. You can tailor your reading of the different sections to suit your own needs and what is required by the modules you are taking. Although social research methods is a technical subject, it doesn't have to be a dry one. There is little point in treating research as just a set of practical skills, or alternatively as involving a lot of abstract theory. We have tried to connect a description of what researchers *do* with an outline of the ideas that explain *why* they do things that way. Each concept contributes towards building a fuller picture: as you grasp each one, they will slowly fit together into a whole.

What matters most is that once you have read a section, you feel confident about the particular concept that you have to deal with. The overall picture will take care of itself while you concentrate on gaining that confidence with each concept. Understanding the social sciences is easier, and a lot more fun, when you begin to see the way people actually do their research. 'Knowledge' about the social world comes from studying it. The credibility of that knowledge depends on how well that 'studying' is carried out – which is what social research methods is all about.

user's guide

One sentence definition

Evaluation Studies: Evaluation Studies assess the processes and consequences of innovation in social policy or organisations.

Summary **Outline** of points covered in the section

Section Outline: *Evaluation studies as applied social research. Measuring and explaining social change. Problems with 'external' evaluators. Programme specifications driven by evaluation: 'measurable outcomes'. Focusing on 'process' or 'outcome'? Working with evaluatees. Evaluating programmes: who is involved; how are they involved; did it work? Power and politics in evaluation. Example: the Health Education Authority.*

Detailed discussion in about 1250 words (in this example, only part is shown)

Evaluative research is undertaken to assess the *worth* or *success* of something: a programme, a policy, or a project. Social evaluation is *not* a method or technique like social surveys or participant observation. It is a particular and increasingly common type of applied social research that might employ any of the other research methods discussed in this book. What distinguishes it is its purpose: its action orientation to support or introduce change (Clarke and Dawson, 1999).

Links to other sections in the book highlighted

Evaluation studies focus on measurements (numeric or descriptive, but usually the former) of social *inputs*, *outputs*, and *processes*: it typically studies *change*. At their most basic, evaluations replicate classic scientific experimental methods (**Experiments**). Thus observations of people are made before and after something is done to them, and the two observations are compared. If there are differences in the observations, this is likely to be attributed to what was done. However, human behaviour involves more factors than can easily be controlled in a laboratory experiment. Was it the intervention or some other factor that produced the observed differences? Few evaluations include a 'control group' (**Experiments**), which weakens their credibility.

Key words or terms, to check your own understanding

Key Words

collaborative evaluation
social inputs and outputs
measurable outcomes
processual evaluation
stakeholders

Links

Action Research
Experiments

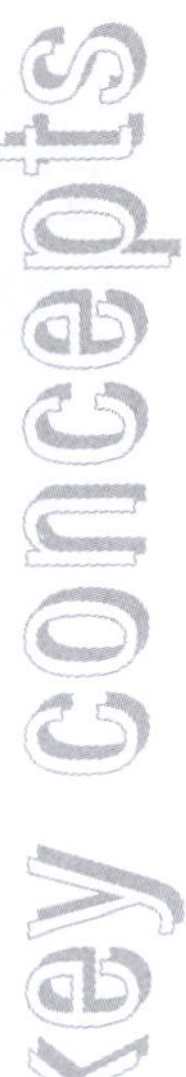

References to sources, other longer accounts and examples of use

REFERENCES

General

Clarke, A. and Dawson, R. (1999) *Evaluation Research*. London: Sage.

House, E. and Howe, K. (1999) *Values in Evaluation and Social Research*. London: Sage.

Examples

Curtice, L. (1993) 'The WHO Healthy Cities Project in Europe' in J. Davies and M. Kelly (eds), *Healthy Cities: Research and Practice*. London: Routledge.

6

Key Concepts in Social Research

Action Research

Action research is research which, identifying a social problem, is primarily designed to provide an empirical test of a possible solution: it contains an innovation to produce the change in policy or procedure, monitored by social research methods.

Section Outline: *Action research as social experiment. Understanding versus changing the world. Applied disciplines: practice skills and social research skills. Example: the Community Development Project. Recent models. Tensions between researching and achievement of change. Problems of control and interpretation in social experiments.*

There are two main reasons why people do social research. One is because there is an intellectual challenge: we want to fill a gap in our knowledge, or we believe that currently accepted theories should be tested against new evidence. An alternative reason is that we want to change the world. This second kind of *applied* research may be sponsored by a private organisation (e.g. the managers of the Hawthorne factory, who wanted to improve productivity: see **Hawthorne Effect**) or by public bodies concerned with tackling social problems like crime, health or social exclusion. Action research is one type of applied research that is essentially a social experiment, introducing some new policy and then monitoring its effects.

In the first kind of research, the researcher normally stands back from the subject of the research, taking an objective, detached view (**Positivism and Realism**). The goal is not to change the thing that is being studied, but to *explain* it. The measure of good research is how well it helps us to understand what we are studying. We would not like our research work to be judged solely on how far it changed the world.

So in studying poverty or racism, for example, our task is not to abolish poverty or prevent racism. It is true that researchers often do tackle topics that concern them as citizens. If their research does end up improving the conditions of the poor or the position of minority ethnic groups, then that is welcomed. However, even here, the original motives for the research are also likely to be intellectual questions about the topic.

Some disciplines such as social policy, public health or social work, are more applied in nature. They tend to have more practical concerns than, say, sociology. Their students are trained to engage with the social world and to change it for the better. While these disciplines do carry out a great deal of conventional research in a purely investigative manner, they have also promoted research directly linked to achieving social change: 'action research'.

In early action research, social researchers were teamed up with professional practitioners trying new ways of tackling social problems. The researchers would provide an initial description of social conditions, the practitioners would implement a policy response, and the researchers would then study the resulting change. There would be continued feedback and flow of information between the two, so that new adaptations could be developed. The purpose of the research was to support the intervention, providing the information the practitioners needed. The emphasis was on the

> dynamic interaction between the social scientist and the practitioners as part of the ongoing experimental process . . . adaptive rather than controlled, with changes evolving out of increasing awareness and emerging opportunities (Lees 1975: 4–5).

Action research in this view is a kind of social experiment, in which interventions could be tested and successively modified on the basis of what was being achieved (**Experiments**).

This arrangement recognised two problems. First, most practitioners had not been trained as researchers. They therefore needed help from experts in social research to monitor what was actually happening. Second, those who are sponsoring a change have a vested interest in seeing it succeed. By using independent researchers, there was less chance of any accusation of bias when the success or failure of the intervention came to be evaluated.

One of the most extensive action research projects was Britain's 'Community Development Project' (CDP) in the early 1970s (Home Office 1971). In 12 areas with high levels of social need, 'project' or 'action' teams were to be hired by local authorities to intervene. Research teams based in universities or polytechnics provided the research back-up.

The CDP was not a success. With several governmental institutions involved, there was no agreement on priorities. Staff turn-over weakened continuity of work. The belief that 'experimental action and the "superior vision" of research will somehow identify the magic ingredient' (Smith 1975: 191) led to over-optimistic expectations, and so caused a sense of failure. In some cases the researchers became closely associated with the interventions, and so lost their independent vision. In other cases the action team and the research team fell out (see Payne et al. 1981 for more details).

A more recent model of action research excludes separate social researchers. Modern-day practitioners are more likely to be trained in social research skills, and certainly have better access to research reports and sources that provide advice on how to do research. Their training is also more likely to stress the importance of using evidence – 'evidence-based practice' – than simply following basic training and accepting conventional wisdom. More pragmatically, few projects can afford to employ both practitioners and full-time researchers. Action researchers are now often single workers or at best in very small teams.

This later approach to action research goes some way to avoiding the problem of 'expertise' that we noted the earlier version tried to address. However, it is unrealistic to expect practitioners to be as expert at social research as research specialists (Clarke et al. 2002). The training of practitioners must necessarily concentrate on much more than just social research skills, and after qualification their daily professional routines are unlikely to include much hands-on research activity (see **Community Profiles**). Nor does the merging of research and practice help to solve the second issue noted above, that the credibility of the intervention is enhanced by it being separated from the research monitoring it.

Thus we have a tension between two approaches. 'Pure' research has sometimes been criticised for being 'academic' in the worst sense, i.e. too detached, theoretical, and concerned only with a dialogue between people in universities. Concerned citizens, or professional practitioners dealing directly with social problems like racism, can feel disappointed when researchers stand back from personal involvement in problem-solving. However, such research can claim to bring an independence of judgement. The very lack of involvement is what merits its claim to objective findings (see **Ethical Practice** and **Feminist Research** for an alternative argument).

Critics of action research focus on two issues. First, the research element tends to be subordinated to the intervention. It is not an equal partnership. Indeed, as in the CDP case, researchers and practitioners find it impossible to maintain their relationships, slipping into either conflict or too close an association. When there is only a single action researcher, these tensions are experienced at the personal level. There is always the suspicion that practitioners' career orientations to their professions will outweigh their concerns for reliable social research. Unless anticipated outcomes and definitions of 'success' are defined in advance, and the measurement of them are scrupulously adhered to (**Indicators and Operationalisations**), the research element will be undermined (Sapsford and Abbott 1992: 101–7). Working in the health field and generally supportive of action interventions, Grbich (1999: 193–214) gives a good account of action research which stresses this need for proper evaluations (**Evaluation Studies**).

Second, whereas a chemistry experiment in the lab operates with a small number of factors in a controlled environment, social life and therefore social experiments are more complicated. Many more factors are involved and cannot be controlled. It is not logically possible to be sure that events outside of the social experiment have not come into play. In particular, without a comparable separate situation, where there has been no intervention, how are we tell what produced any changes? Just because something happens *after* a policy intervention, it does not mean that it has been *caused* by the intervention. (See **Association and Causation** on confounding variables.)

Key Words

bias and objectivity
'pure' and 'applied' research
social experiment
social intervention

Links

Association and Causation
Community Profiles
Ethical Practice
Evaluation Studies
Experiments
Feminist Research
Hawthorne Effect
Indicators and Operationalisations
Positivism and Realism

REFERENCES

General

Grbich, C. (1999) *Qualitative Research in Health*. London: Sage.
Lees, R. (1975) *Research Strategies for Social Welfare.* London: Routledge & Kegan Paul.
Payne, G., Dingwall, R., Payne, J. and Carter, M. (1981) *Sociology and Social Research*. London: Routledge & Kegan Paul.
Sapsford, R. and Abbott, P. (1992) *Research Methods for Nurses and the Caring Professions.* Buckingham: Open University Press.

Examples

Clarke, S., Byatt, A., Hoban, M. and Powell, D. (2002) *Community Development in South Wales.* Cardiff: University of Wales Press.
Home Office (1971) *CDP: An Official View.* London: HMSO.

Association and Causation

Association is a connection between two social phenomena, demonstrated by one tending to vary according to variations in the other, whereas causality is a special case of association, when changes in one systematically result in direct changes in the other.

Section Outline: *Association and imprecise connections. Example: church-going and age. Association and correlation. Direction of connection: narratives. Spurious relationships. Examples: class and political attitudes; explaining illness. Necessary and sufficient conditions. Causality in quantitative and qualitative methods.*

Research provides descriptions of what it studies. Some descriptions connect two social phenomena, making it possible to say that they *tend* to happen together, or rarely happen together, or that when one comes first, the other usually follows. These connections or 'relationships' are referred to as *associations*. A special kind of strong association, which uses one thing to explain why another thing happens, is a causal relationship. Because we want to know why society is like it is (particularly if our philosophical orientation points us towards explanations, see **Positivism and Realism**) a common error is to mistake an association for causation.

A useful starting point is trying to guess something about people in a room. Our accuracy, based on no prior information, would be low. But if we knew something related to what we were guessing about, it would help. Rose and Sullivan (1993: 21–31) show how we could improve on our guesses about people's politics by knowing, first, if they own or rent their homes and, second, to which social class they belong.

In social science, connections between social phenomena are generally imprecise. First we need to decide how we will recognise each of the things we are seeking to study (**Indicators and Operationalisations**). Next, we will have many more associations between them than causal relationships, because the things we study are complex and rarely produced by a single cause. Our research methods are also imperfect, inevitably summarising and simplifying the real world. Even if there are causal relationships to discover, we have difficulty in identifying them.

The most common level of association between two social phenomena or variables is one in which *more, but not all,* cases of the second are found when the first is present. For example, there is an association between age and Christian church attendance in Britain. A higher proportion of older people go to church than do young adults: 28 per cent against 14 per cent (Gill 1999). However, the association between age and church attendance is less than perfect. The most striking thing is that most people of all ages do not attend church. Then, not *every* older person goes to church, while *some* younger people go to church as well. We can say that the probability of an older person being a church-goer is about 3 in 10. This kind of imprecise, 'probabilistic' association is typical of sociological findings.

Our interpretation will be influenced by the empirical data, e.g. the *levels* of church attendance among the elderly, and the extent of the *difference* between them and the church attendance rates of younger people. An initial step in evaluating the evidence of an association is to inspect the data as a contingency table (**Contingency Tables**). We could also use some of the statistical techniques for measuring the strength of associations in standardised ways (e.g. 'correlation'), and whether the apparent connection could have happened by chance (e.g. 'chi-square test'). Correlation is a type of association: to say that there is a correlation between two things does *not* mean that one 'causes' the other. We should also ask whether some third factor might have produced the pattern of association or correlation between the two (Rose and Sullivan 1993); a question of the **Validity** of the findings.

If there is a causal relationship, it must be that 'being elderly' causes 'higher church attendance', rather than church-going making people older. Knowing the *direction* of an association, we can explore the reasons for it. Do elderly people fear death more, predisposing them to need religious comfort? Are older people more isolated, and thus likely to use the church congregation for company? Are more elderly people churchgoers because they grew up at a time when church attendance was common, and they have retained the habit? These kinds of 'narratives' or 'rationales' can be further explored empirically. Showing correlations, even large numbers of correlations between similar variables, is not enough. We need the narrative or explanatory theory to tell us why we can go beyond a correlational association to talk about a causal relationship (Hage and Foley-Meeker 1988; Blalock 1970: 63–78).

Narratives help to clarify the direction of causality, and prevent silly interpretations. *The Guardian* (3 March 2003) reported that men who do not 'shave daily are 70 per cent more likely to suffer a stroke than those who do'. What narrative could possibly explain this? In fact the study had found that manual workers, and particularly those unmarried and who smoked, shaved less. In other words, those in disadvantaged lower socio-economic positions, and whose diet and lifestyle were unhealthy, tend to be more prone to strokes. Chin stubble is simply a by-product of the true cause.

When an apparent connection between two variables (stubble and strokes) is actually due to a third variable (unhealthy lifestyle) this is called a 'spurious relationship'. Whereas in formal experiments (**Experiments**), it is easier to manipulate one variable (the 'cause', or 'independent variable') and see what happens to another (the 'effect' or 'dependent variable'), 'cross-sectional' survey and field research simply measures what is happening without being able to make things vary. Unless we have data from repeated studies ('replications') or a longitudinal study (**Longitudinal Studies**), it is hard to show that one thing happened *before* another; one requirement of demonstrating causality.

However, the fact that an outcome seems to have several associations does not make them automatically spurious. Suppose we were investigating how people's own socio-economic positions affect their opinions about government spending on hospitals and schools. We would find more, but not all, lower social class people favour high spending, but that some in the higher social classes also favour it. Class tends to be *associated* with political attitudes, only in a particular, limited way. We could not claim a strong causal relationship, because we do not have the classic kind of open-and-shut case of causality: if one thing is present (low social class), then always and only is the other thing present (favours government spending).

Our finding that the class/attitude causal relationship is weak should not be surprising. Other factors influence attitudes, like a person's gender or membership of an ethnic group. Education, age, health, family circumstances (young children) and employment (in the public or private sector) are also plausible sources of attitude influences. For example, teachers and nurses (not members of the lower classes), aged in their 30s (the child-rearing phase of life) are strong advocates of higher government expenditure. Teachers and nurses are predominantly female occupations: is their support for government spending more a product of their gender, or due more to their employment and family circumstances?

Another problem, equally typical of sociological explanation, is the distribution of illness and early death. Explanations include social inequalities in life experience and access to health services; low socio-economic position of parents (impacting through pregnancy and childhood); genetic predispositions to certain illnesses; adult lifestyle (smoking, alcohol and diet); type of employment; and education (knowledge about symptoms and treatments) (Payne and Payne 2000). All of these predispose people to ill health, but it makes a great difference for social policy where the emphasis is placed. Sapsford's discussion (1999: 27–33) of the antecedents and consequences of women's drinking in research by Wilsnack and others gives a concrete sociological example of cause and effect in health research. Evidence-based practice makes causality of more than just academic interest.

Some causes or 'prior conditions' are said to be 'necessary': the outcome cannot happen without them, but the outcome does not *always* happen because other factors also have to be present. Other conditions are 'sufficient': if they are present, the outcome happens *regardless* of other factors. However, the outcome might still happen without the prior condition. To establish causality, one needs both 'necessary and sufficient' rules to apply. It is often difficult to establish this, or to tell which 'causes' are the stronger. Wickham-Crowley's work (1992) on Latin American guerrilla movements and revolutions demonstrates how events are connected, but that the connections are complex and multiplex. Multivariate analysis is one group of statistical methods for showing how sets of variables interact in their effects on a dependent variable.

In designing research, it is good practice to consider all the factors that one's prior theoretical model suggests might be associated with the outcome. Of course, not everything can be included: we often end up with a rather simple set of associated factors. As a result, sociologists commonly play safe, using the term 'association' rather than 'cause'. The problem of causality is particularly important in quantitative research, with its aim of identifying and explaining social regularities (**Quantitative Methods** and **Qualitative Methods**). It is less pressing in those kinds of qualitative research which seek only to interpret context-specific meanings.

Key Words

causal diretion
correlation
cross-sectional
dependent variable
independent variable

narrative
necessary and sufficient
rationale
spurious

Links

Contingency Tables
Experiments
Indicators and, Operationalisations
Longitudinal studies and cross-sectional studies
Positivism and Realism
Qualitative Methods
Quantitative Methods
Validity

REFERENCES

General

Blalock, H. (1970) *An Introduction to Social Research*. Englewood Cliffs, NJ: Prentice-Hall.
Hage, J. and Foley-Meeker, B. (1988) *Social Causality*. London: Unwin Hyman.
Rose, D. and Sullivan, O. (1993) *Introducing Data Analysis for Social Scientists*. Buckingham: Open University Press.
Sapsford, R. (1999) *Survey Research*. London: Sage.

Examples

Gill, R. (1999) *Church-Going and Christian Ethics*. Cambridge: Cambridge University Press.
Payne, J. and Payne, G. (2000) 'Health', in G. Payne, (ed.) *Social Divisions*. Basingstoke: Palgrave.
Wickham-Crowley, T. (1992) *Guerrillas and Revolution in Latin America*. Princeton, NJ: Princeton University Press.

Attitude Scales

Attitude scales provide a quantitative measurement of attitudes, opinions or values by summarising numerical scores given by researchers to people's responses to sets of statements exploring dimensions of an underlying theme.

Section Outline: *Tapping meanings in quantitative research. Agreement and disagreement with statements. Example: Islamic religiosity. Objective meanings. Scale characteristics. Piloting for uni-dimensionality, presentation and layout. Scales: Likert; Thurstone; Bogardus; Guttman; Semantic Differential. Advantages and disadvantages of scales.*

Although quantitative research is often said to be less interested in the *meanings* that people attach to their actions, many surveys do in fact enquire into this area. Market research in particular asks about *evaluations* of products and services. The main survey method used to tap meanings is attitude scaling.

'Attitude scales' (or 'indexes' or 'ratings': see Schutt 1999: 75–81; Hoinville et al. 1982: 33–37 for examples of construction) consist of asking informants to respond to a statement (or a question) in terms of a fixed range of levels. For example, a study of religiosity, citizens' rights, and gender among Islamic groups sought levels of agreement or disagreement with statements like:

- Islam does not separate politics and religion.
- All Muslims must work together to face the Western challenge against Islam.
- Families should insist that women wear veils.
- Western clothing is more practical than traditional clothing.

Each statement was linked to an issue, like religiosity, women's political rights, or 'traditionalism' forming a set of attitudes (Rizzo et al. 2002: 651).

The characteristic difference between this and qualitative research is that the categories are more obviously determined by the researcher than by the informants. 'Meanings' are explored in an objective framework set externally by the research. In contrast, subjective meanings are believed to emerge from the informants' lengthy and detailed communication with the qualitative researcher (**Qualitative Methods**; **Quantitative Methods**).

The logic behind attitude scales, drawing on social psychology, is that people are assumed to discriminate systematically in their views (Eysenck 1953). Responding to suitable statements enables respondents to express their views. Their discriminations form a continuum from positive to negative orientations to the statements. Combinations of their discriminations can be brought together in a way that reflects underlying attitudes, which relate to other sociological variables.

It is important to differentiate between a simple 'opinion' or 'reaction' to a single issue (e.g. 'I think very rich people should pay higher taxes') and an attitude set (e.g. holding progressive views about politics and social issues in general). Sociological questionnaires often include questions about specific opinions, when the research is concerned with the answers themselves. Attitude scales are less interested in the specific answers, except as a means of identifying the supposed underlying attitude set. A whole range of issues can be addressed in this single issue way. The annual British Social Attitudes surveys have typically produced collections of articles covering the environment, gender, employment, class, race, the family, morality and religion: the current survey includes transport, money loans, education, drugs and tolerance of others (Park et al. 2002). Although this kind of work talks about 'attitudes' and sometimes contains questions very similar in format to those used in attitude scaling (see the questionnaires in the British Social Attitude series; Ashford and Timms 1992; Hoinville et al. 1982), it makes fewer assumptions about underlying attitude sets and rarely combines single answers into scales.

There are several different types of scale, of varying complexity and purpose (Kumar 1999: 127–35). Their common features are:

- the presentation of a series of stimuli (usually *statements*);
- a requirement that the response to each must be one selected from a fixed and *limited* choice (e.g. 'strongly agree; 'agree'; 'undecided'; 'disagree'; or 'strongly disagree');
- the *scoring* of responses into a numerical value (e.g. 1 to 5 on each statement; and
- some *combination* of these numerical scores into a *single number* on a 'scale').

Conventionally, a small sample of people complete 'pilot interviews' by answering 'open-ended questions'. This discovers the range of opinions, beliefs, and views held. These are translated into statements, which are then tested out on another sample. The statements chosen for the main study are sets, each of which relates to a single concept and sometimes referred to as 'sub-scales'. This test of 'unidimensionality' is usually based on statistical analyses such as factor analysis in the first instance, and by simple inspection and logic where the tests do not produce clear answers. Any statements that receive almost complete agreement or disagreement are then discarded, because they fail to discriminate between people. The remaining components of each set are expected to be highly correlated with each other, showing 'internal consistency'.

The phrasing and presentation of the stimulus statements are guided by the same rules that apply to good questionnaire design (**Questionnaires**). The language should be simple and avoid technical jargon. Words with loaded significance or particular meaning should be excluded, including 'never', 'always', 'only' and 'almost'. Statements should be short (as a rule of thumb, not more than 20 words), each consisting of a single, uncomplicated sentence. Double negatives should be avoided.

Each statement must be clear and unambiguous. It should cover a single topic. Our earlier example, 'Families should insist that women wear veils' actually covers two topics: whether *women should wear veils*, and whether *families should insist on it*. It is therefore not a sound choice. Statements need to be self-contained, dealing with only one feature, covering its aspects without overlapping into other ideas.

Instructions, particularly in 'self-completion questionnaires', need to be clear. An example is usually given before the first statement task. Sets of statements need to be grouped together, and not run over the page, because this can sometimes confuse respondents.

Bryman recommends that where space allows, it is better to offer the alternative answers in a vertical layout (2001: 134–5). This reduces the chances of informants accidentally picking responses that do not reflect their views, and makes coding the answers (**Social Surveys**) easier and quicker, e.g.:

Islam does not separate politics and religion.

strongly ☐ agree	agree ☐	undecided ☐	disagree ☐	strongly ☐ disagree

Islam does not separate politics and religion.

strongly agree	☐
agree	☐
undecided	☐
disagree	☐
strongly disagree	☐

However, it is obvious from this example that a vertical layout takes up much more space, and there will be resource limitations to this.

Particularly when a horizontal layout is inevitable, not all statements should take the same format, i.e. with agreements always listed on the left and disagreements on the right of the page (or coming first or last in the sequence). This is because respondents can lapse into a fixed pattern of ticking the boxes. By reversing the thrust of some statements, informants have to respond to each stimulus on its own terms (when we score such reversed statements, we also reverse the numbering system: e.g. 1 becomes 5 so that all statements then count in the same way).

The most widely used attitude scale is the Likert Scale, which uses five levels of agreement/disagreement. Although many of its construction rules are often ignored, in its strict format it calls for an extensive list of statements (around 100) from a much larger list of 'possibles', and rigorous testing for internal consistency. This degree of preparation is impractical where the attitude scale is only one element of a larger survey, and small sets of statements work almost as effectively.

The forerunner of the Likert Scale was the Thurstone Scale, which differed in two main ways. In construction, its statements were initially evaluated by expert 'judges' into degrees of positivity, and where there was consensus among them, these were given a middle scale value. Other statements were scored by the researcher to give a range around the average. Respondents were asked simply to agree or disagree with each statement, the extent of their overall agreement (or 'expression of attitude') coming from the initial evaluation by the judges and the researcher. This cumbersome process was barely sustainable in psychological experiments on attitudes, and proved unsuitable for the complexities of sociological work.

Two other scales work on the basis of a hierarchy of attitudes, in which 'agreement' at one level implies agreement at all lower levels of the statement set. For instance, in race relations research, hypothetical acceptance of someone from a minority ethnic group as a marriage partner presupposes acceptance as a friend, a neighbour and a work colleague, whereas acceptance as a neighbour presupposes only acceptance as a work colleague. In the Bogardus Social Distance Scale, this is presented as variations on the same statement, and distance is calculated on the basis of group mean values. In the Guttman Scale, informants respond to different but related statements previously sorted into hierarchical order.

A final type of scale is the Semantic Differential Scale. Pairs of opposite concepts (strong/weak; democratic/authoritarian) are offered as being associated with groups or processes. A score, usually between 6 and 0, covers the spread between each pair. Respondents choose the numbers that best represent their views. Scores are combined, or compared as profiles. The best and fullest descriptions of these scales and their practical construction can still be found in older textbooks: Goode and Hatt 1952; Festinger and Katz 1954; and Moser 1958: 235–41.

The advantages of attitude scales are that they simplify complexity into a single score, easily collected from a sample, and capable of statistical manipulation. They have good reliability (**Reliability**). Students like them because they access 'issues' like drugs, gender or inequality, rather than just 'facts'. However, they assume consistent attitudes rather than uncertainty, general attitudes rather than reactions in specific contexts, and that hypothetical statements are congruent with real actions. The numerical values attributed to responses are treated as uniformly spaced (**Levels of Measurement**) and fail to capture the complexity of meaning as claimed by qualitative methods.

Key Words

Bogardus Social Distance Scale
Guttman Scale
internal consistency
Likert Scale
Semantic Differential Scale
stimulus
Thurstone Scale

Links

Levels of Measurement
Qualitative Methods
Quantitative Methods
Questionnaires
Reliability
Social Surveys

REFERENCES

General

Bryman, A. (2001) *Social Research Methods.* Oxford: Oxford University Press.
Eysenck, H. (1953) *Uses and Abuses of Psychology.* Harmondsworth: Penguin.
Festinger, L. and Katz, D. (eds) (1954) *Research Methods in the Behavioural Sciences.* London: Staples Press.
Goode, W. and Hatt, P. (1952) *Methods in Social Research*. New York: McGraw-Hill.
Hoinville, G., Jowell, R. and Associates (1982) *Survey Research Practice.* London: Heinemann.
Kumar, R. (1999) *Research Methodology.* London: Sage.
Moser, C. (1958) *Survey Methods in Social Investigation*. London: Heinemann.
Schutt, R. (1999) *Investigating the Social World* (2nd edn). Thousand Oaks, CA: Pine Forge Press.

Examples

Ashford, S. and Timms, N. (1992) *What Europe Thinks: a Study of Western European Values*. Aldershot: Dartmouth.
Park, A., Curtice, J., Thomson, K., Jarvis, L. and Bromley, C. (eds) (2002) *British Social Attitudes: the 19th Report.* London: Sage
Rizzo, H., Meyer, K. and Ali, Y. (2002) 'Women's Political Rights: Islam, Status and Networks in Kuwait'. *Sociology*, 36 (3): 639–62.

Auto/biography and Life Histories

Life histories are records of individuals' personal experiences and the connections between them and past social events, while auto/biography treats these accounts not as established facts but as social constructions requiring further investigation and re-interpretation.

Section Outline: *Snapshots versus histories. Collecting life histories. Wide content of life histories: world views. Oral history. Individuals in historical settings. Conflicting accounts. Collective life histories. Auto/biography: artifice; fabrication; reflexivity and creative inconsistencies.*

Most social research has focused on very limited periods of time. Survey research normally concentrates on the state of things at the time of the interviews. While observation and depth interviews often follow events in a social process, they generally cover quite short sequences of action. In contrast, the people being studied actually live from cradle to the grave, in their own unique historical times. Our research snapshots can only snatch a short cross-section of their full lives and personal histories, and will often take them out of the context of their times (**Longitudinal Studies**). 'Sociology without history resembles a Hollywood set: great scenes, sometimes brilliantly painted, with nothing and nobody behind them' (Tilley 1992: 1).

Life history research attempts to address this problem by seeking to reconstruct the events in respondents' lives (Denzin 1981; Plummer 1983). In interviews, respondents are invited to talk about their pasts, giving their own personal and unique version of their experiences. The interviews are usually 'unstructured', although good practice is to start at one point and work systematically either forward or backwards. This makes it easier for respondents to proceed from one reminiscence to the next, and also makes subsequent analysis easier. However, a life history is not just a simple chronological list of events. Lewis reports how he tried

> to cover systematically a wide range of subjects: their earliest memories, their dreams, their hopes, fears, joys, and sufferings; their jobs; their relationship with friends, relatives, employers; their sex life; their concepts of justice, religion and politics; their knowledge of geography and history; in short their total world view of the world (Lewis 1961: xxi).

Although life histories sometimes concentrate on particular sections of the respondents' lives, they are not necessarily organised around stages of the 'life course', such as childhood, middle age and old age. The purpose of the historical perspective is more often to see how experiences and events come together with reference to some particular issue, such as one of Lewis's topics listed above, rather than to explore the life course itself.

The life history approach is one type of 'narrative interview'. In addition to data collected from interviews (**Interviewing**), information may also be drawn from diaries, letters, photographs, newspaper cuttings, administrative records and even census returns. Other names for life histories are 'biographical method' and 'oral history'. Oral history is usually associated with collecting spoken histories on particular topics from people whose experiences would otherwise go unrecorded, such as manual workers in dying industries, older people or residents in rural communities.

Rather than treating society as disembodied 'structures' or the accounts of individual 'actors' or 'agents', life history research often sets the personal recollections of individuals into the context of other groups and events. This attempts to bring structure and agency together. Miller (2000) calls individuals' personal versions of their own lives 'life stories'. He reserves the term 'life histories' for the linking of such stories to other sources like letters, to be understood in the context of other people of the same age at the same point in time who make up the individuals' unique cohort. This linkage is very important, since it rounds out the personal history with its setting, so creating a broader and genuinely *social* history.

The intention of the life history method is normally to explore 'what happened' according the eye witness, but also to discover 'the inner experience of individuals, how they interpret, understand, and define the world around them' (Faraday and Plummer 1979: 776). The respondent or biographical 'author' presents us with both a perception of self and the social world. We can concentrate either on the actors' points of view and identity, or on what this tells us about how the social environment influences both experiences and their narration. These subjective impressions, based in personal retrospection, shape our collective depictions of social processes. They may, however, also conflict with other 'histories' created by historians or politicians. We need, in Blaikie's reversal of the usual phrase, to see ourselves, not just to see ourselves as others see us (Blaikie 2003).

Collections of life histories can be analysed in several different ways. These include drawing together what each says about a particular topic; using selections from each separately as concrete illustrations of more theoretical points; organising the recordings into categories to provide a classification or typology; or applying quantitative techniques to explore the statistical associations (**Association and Causation**) between cases and variables. Each of these is based on a search through the set, using some kind of content analysis (**Content Analysis**).

Despite the obvious attractions of this method, it was not widely used until the last decade. Even the invention of portable tape-recorders did little to stimulate its use, and the three best-known examples of life history research are all now very old. Thomas and Znaniecki's (1958) *Polish Peasant* is based on the experiences of Central European immigrants to America, collected almost a hundred years ago and originally published just after the First World War. *The Jack Roller,* the personal story of a mugger, came out three-quarters of a century ago (Shaw 1930), while Oscar Lewis's (1961) description of a life in poverty for one family, *The Children of Sanchez*, dates from the 1950s.

The lack of life history research for many years is partly due to the rival attractions of other methods, and partly to doubts about whether personal reminiscences could be treated as 'accurate' accounts (**Objectivity**). More recently, this concern for 'accuracy' has been replaced by a much more sophisticated approach. What is usually termed the 'auto/biographical methodology' questions the notion of truth about the world 'out there', being much more concerned with the *process of telling the story*, its significance for the teller, and the unreliability, in a strict sense, of *all* historical accounts.

Auto/biography draws heavily on two traditions, post-modernism and feminism. From the former it takes the idea that all texts are socially constructed, and rather than being statements that directly tell us about the world, are themselves something to be investigated. Thus a conventional autobiography, just as much as a biography, is a selection and interpretation of a life. Both should be treated

> as works of artifice and fabrication, drawing analytic attention to their use of genre conventions, temporal and other structuring, rhetoric and authorial 'voice'. Here, rather than treating biography and auto-biography as unproblematic resources, they are instead conceptualised as topics of investigation in their own right (Stanley 1993: 2).

Accounts of reality and reality itself are taken to be inextricably linked together. Sources – and in this approach, we are just as likely to be dealing in an unobtrusive way with written documents (**Unobtrusive Methods**; **Documentary Methods**) as with unstructured interviews – are seen neither as purely individual accounts of social action, nor exclusively as aspects of social structure.

Auto/biography is also concerned to stay close to the lived day-to-day experience, for example the way memory 'plays tricks', expanding and contracting recollection of time periods. Personal lives provide a rich resource for sociological reflection, and it is here that the feminist tradition plays a significant part. 'Reflexivity' (with regard to gender) is central to feminist methodology, involving challenges to claims for objectivity against subjectivity, and the division between public and private lives (**Feminist Research**). The auto/biographical emphasis is to see the recalled life in all its complexity, bringing to its consideration all the subtlety of the reader's own personal experience.

Key Words

chronological events
life course
narrative interview
oral history
reflexivity

Links

Association and Causation
Content Analysis
Documentary Methods
Feminist Research
Interviewing
Longitudinal and cross-sectional Studies
Objectivity
Unobtrusive Methods and Triangulation

REFERENCES

General

Denzin, N. (ed.) (1981) *Biography and Society.* Beverly Hills, CA: Sage.
Faraday, A. and Plummer, K. (1979) 'Doing Life Histories'. *Sociological Review,* 27 (4): 773–98.
Lewis, O. (1961) *The Children of Sanchez.* New York: Vintage.
Miller, R.L. (2000) *Researching Life Stories and Family Histories.* London: Sage.
Plummer, K. (1983) *Documents of Life.* London: Allen & Unwin.

Stanley, L. (1993) 'Editorial Introduction'. *Sociology*, 27 (1): 1–4 (Special Issue on Auto/biography in Sociology).
Tilley, C. (1992) *History and Sociological Imagining.* Working Paper Series No. 134. New York: New School of Social Research.

Examples

Blaikie, A. (2003) *Scottish Lives in Modern Memory.* Edinburgh: Edinburgh University Press.
Shaw, C. (1930) *The Jack Roller.* Chicago: University of Chicago Press.
Thomas, W. and Znaniecki, F. (1958) *The Polish Peasant in Europe and America.* New York: Octagon Books.

Bias

Bias is a systematic error in data collection or analysis, caused by inadequate technical procedures (for instance in sampling, interviewing or coding).

Section Outline: *Bias and objectivity. Bias as errors of procedure. Sample bias: representative samples and setting. Interviewer bias: data distortion. Selectivity bias: analytic failings. Transparency and reflexivity. Lack of objectivity leads to bias.*

Bias is a concept that is often linked to lack of objectivity (**Objectivity**). At first sight, bias and objectivity seem like opposite ends of the same principle. Bias suggests that personal judgements particular to the observer have been involved, favouritism displayed, distortions in the evidence introduced. Objectivity suggests a lack of involvement, a scrupulousness in reporting and interpreting, an independence and neutrality of judgement. Bias in research makes it invalid, objectivity produces a better kind of 'knowledge'. However, such reactions draw on unspoken assumptions about *how* and *what kinds* of research should be done. When we look more closely, the picture is not so clear.

Although the terms 'bias' and 'objectivity' are often used to refer to the same issues (e.g. Hammersley 1998; Hoinville et al. 1982; Shipman 1997), it is helpful to reserve them for different dimensions of the problems they address. In this discussion, we will use bias to refer to *errors of procedure*, and objectivity (or lack of it) to refer to questions of *research orientation and interpretation*. It is not possible to insist that this dichotomy is strictly maintained, particularly as we move from quantitative to qualitative research, but we shall at least be able to appreciate why and where the two terms overlap.

The credibility of research largely depends on the absence of obvious errors in the way it has been carried out (**Reliability**; **Validity**). We can illustrate this most easily in quantitative research. When settings are selected for study, they should represent all other settings to which findings might apply. Thus a study done in Chicago might be generalised to *all* large cities, large *American* cities, or it might be *unique* to that city: e.g. the debate about inner-city economies and the ghetto (Massey and Denton 1993; Waldinger 1996; Wilson 1978, 1987, 1997). Does the choice of Chicago 'bias' the conclusions drawn, so that they do not apply to other cities? The test here is what claims to generalisation are being made. Any claim of bias is a technical matter and is nothing to do with personal preferences.

A particular case of this is the representativeness of samples. A sample must be designed so that it represents the universe of objects from which it is drawn (**Sampling: Types**), drawn accurately from its sampling frame, and fully covered by the *fieldwork* (all of the sample elements correctly included). For example, if an incomplete 'sample frame' (the telephone directory) were used, some people (ex-directory or mobile phone users) would not be included. This would be a poor sample design because non-listed people are different from those listed. Second, if the selection of names is not done carefully and checked, sections could be omitted. If data are not collected from all members of a sample, this introduces a further source of bias, because those included are likely to differ from those who were left out.

These failings are usually called 'sampling bias'. Sampling bias is the result of poor procedures, and not to be confused with 'sampling error'. The latter refers to the total difference (from various sampling biases) between the sample and the universe it is supposed to represent.

One particular kind of sampling bias can arise from interviewer behaviour. Systematic biases – such as not contacting those who work unsocial hours, or distortions in the completion of 'quota samples' – distort findings (**Sampling: Types**). Interviewers tend to fill their quotas with people who look approachable, respectable, and who are available at the time and in the place the interviewer is working. Quota samples therefore tend to over-represent women with children and leave out those at the extremes of society. Although the effect is produced by the actions of the interviewer, this is usually referred to as 'sample bias' because it is the sample units that are wrong. Systematic sampling biases undermine research findings because results are then drawn from 'completed' samples that fail to reflect the universes that they were originally meant to represent.

'Interviewer bias', on the other hand, refers to the ways interviewers carry out the interview. They may (unconsciously) distort data collection by deviating from the questionnaire, by prompting at the wrong point, or by inadequate recording. If questions are re-phrased, or answers re-written as the interviewer thinks rather than in the words actually said, an unreliable record will be produced (**Interviewing**).

A third kind of bias, and here we edge close to 'lack of objectivity', is where data collection is inherently distorted. If questions are badly phrased or questionnaires poorly constructed (**Questionnaires**), then even good sample design, rigorous fieldwork, and excellent interviewing cannot prevent bias. This is sometimes simply weak procedure, such as asking questions that assume everybody understands technical jargon. Where questions do not cover all aspects of an issue (e.g. asking about what workers *dislike* about their job but not about what they *like*), it is harder to tell whether this is a result of incompetence, or a prior assumption about what is likely to be found (that the workers dislike their work). In some cases, the questions may be more evidently 'loaded': 'Do you agree that your hours of work are too long?'

This kind of 'question bias' opens up survey research to the charge that surveys can be made to produce whatever answers sponsors want. There is some truth in this. Certain symbolic words do influence answers. American popular support for the 2003 war against Iraq was higher in surveys asking about 'American government policy', or 'The President's action', than in those asking simply about the war itself. Correct procedures should prevent abuse of such effects. Not all potential sources of bias are equally transparent, but the visibility of sample designs, questionnaires and archived data (**Secondary Analysis**) helps to support quantitative research's claim to be able to limit bias.

It is less easy for qualitative research to invoke transparency as a defence against accusations of bias. The process of data collection is visible only through 'field notes'. However, the events represented in field notes and transcripts (interviews should always be transcribed, to provide permanent and accessible documents as 'evidence about the evidence') are typically the product of single researchers. Readers are dependent on the researcher's composition of the notes. It is much harder to know how proficiently the fieldwork was conducted. Indeed, the 'rules' of procedure are less clear-cut: one of the strengths of qualitative work is its capacity for flexible response to evolving circumstances as they naturally occur.

The researcher sits between both the events and the readers, and between the technical conduct of the research and the reader. In quantitative work, the research process can in principle be investigated by 'replication' (the study repeated in almost identical fashion – although in practice this very rarely happens). In qualitative work, each setting is treated as unique, and the research process acknowledges the uniqueness of the researcher's own involvement with the informants (**Reflexivity**).

Although there are other factors (**Qualitative Methods**), this is one reason for common criticism that qualitative research is 'biased'. In fact, what is usually meant by 'bias' in this context is 'lack of objectivity' (Hammersley 1998: 58–92). Because we have restricted the label of bias to procedural matters, we would prefer to talk in terms of objectivity, but there is an area of overlap here. To take one example, if participant observers 'go native' (**Participant Observation**), this is both a loss of objectivity (over-identification with one's informants) and bias (an unrepresentative selectivity in data collection and interpretation). A lack of objectivity generates bias.

Key Words

field notes
interviewer bias
prompting
question bias
replication
research setting
sample bias
sample design

Links

Interviewing
Objectivity
Participant Observation
Qualitative Methods
Questionnaires
Reflexivity
Reliability
Sampling: Types
Secondary Analysis
Validity

REFERENCES

General

Hammersley, M. (1998) *Reading Ethnographic Research* (2nd edn). Harlow: Addison Wesley Longman.

Hoinville, G., Jowell, R. and Associates (1982) *Survey Research Practice.* London: Heinemann.

Shipman, M. (1997) *The Limitations of Social Research.* (4th edn). Harlow: Addison Wesley Longman.

Examples

Massey, D. and Denton, N. (1993) *American Apartheid.* Cambridge, MA: Harvard University Press.

Waldinger, R. (1996) *Still the Promised City?* Cambridge, MA: Harvard University Press.

Wilson, W. (1978) *The Declining Significance of Race.* Chicago: University of Chicago Press.

Wilson, W. (1987) *The Truly Disadvantaged.* Chicago: University of Chicago Press.

Wilson, W. (1997) *When Work Disappears.* New York: Vantage Knopf.

Case Study

A case study is a very detailed research enquiry into a single example (of a social process, organisation or collectivity) seen as a social unit in its own right and as a holistic entity.

Section Outline: *Case study of a single distinct social unit. An example, not a sample. Advantages of small-scale research designs. Single case dis-proofs. Intrinsic interest. Generalisability. Critical/unique/revelatory cases. Qualitative case study. The boundaries of a case study.*

A case study is a detailed study of a single social unit. The social unit is usually located in one physical place, the people making up the social unit being differentiated from others who are not part of it. In short, the unit has clear boundaries which make it easy to identify. It might be one school, or one production plant, or a residential home, a community (**Community Studies**), or a street gang, but by definition the case study would not *compare* two or more schools, factories, homes, settlements or gangs. Case studies have been used for many years, and on many topics. Lewis's account of poverty in *The Children of Sanchez* (1961) looked at one family in Mexico. Fifty years later, Stone (2002) used a cultural analysis of a single TV programme to develop reflections on media coverage of the Balkans War (**Documentary Methods**).

The key characteristic of case studies is that the social unit selected is a single example of the many cases that make up the type of unit in question. Researchers do not usually claim that their findings can automatically be generalised. They have studied an *example*, in its own right and for its unique importance, not a *sample* of one. Platt, in Burgess's useful collection (1988), emphasises that case studies serve a rhetorical function (helping to dramatise and persuade by using a powerful example) and a logical function (helping to sort out ideas). Although dealing with only one case, it is not unreasonable that the ideas derived from studying a single unit should be re-considered by other researchers, and treated as a contribution to knowledge. The test of a good case study is how well its data sustain its theoretical statements.

Because case studies focus on single, compact units, they can be carried out on a small-scale, albeit detailed, basis. This is not inevitable: for example, Stacey's study of the town of Banbury used a small team of four researchers for its later stages (Stacey et al. 1975). In practice, however, most case studies are carried out by single researchers without access to substantial research funding, such as postgraduates working for higher degrees or Stacey herself in her initial work, or academics with as yet under-developed ideas that they wish explore and think through. It is the limited scale, and manageability, of the case study that is often the real reason that it is chosen as an approach. By concentrating on one case, it is possible to complete work more quickly, and in much greater depth and detail, than if the researcher were trying to cover several cases. Occasionally, cases can be re-visited over time. 'Middletown' was studied twice by the Lynds (1924–5 and 1935), and a third time by Bahr et al. (1983).

There are other reasons for case studies. While no study can *prove* something, a single case can *disprove* a general statement. Delbridge and Lowe explored 'the role of supervisors/first-line managers within contemporary manufacturing' (1997: 409). Having each carried out a case study, they reviewed current theories of how supervision links with technology, size of firm and regulation, concluding that their case study evidence suggests 'that the "death of the supervisor" has been greatly exaggerated' (ibid.: 423). Their findings cannot establish a new general theory of supervision, but they can challenge the earlier assumptions.

Second, the researcher may be interested in one social unit's particular and unique form. As Macleod acknowledges,

> the choice of Fearnbeg, a cluster of small settlements on a wet and windswept slope of hills in the north-west Highlands of Scotland . . . as a site for sociological investigation may at first seem somewhat esoteric. It is . . . certainly not unrelated to the fact that Fearnbeg (a pseudonym) is where the researcher was born, grew up, and now lives (Macleod 1992: 1).

Although his study adds another account to our stock of knowledge about rural communities, Macleod's prime interest was Fearnbeg, because it was his own community. He was much less interested in community studies in general (**Community Studies**).

The third reason for case study is to begin to develop fresh insights. This should not be confused with a 'pilot study', the step in the research process when methods like questionnaires are 'pre-tested'. By beginning on a small scale, new ways of understanding a specific unit can provide a framework for later research. Stanworth's (1983) stimulating argument that boys receive more of their teachers' attention in the classroom than girls was originally based on the single case of an Advanced Level English class in a College of Further Education. Stanworth herself made no claim that she had discovered a universal law of schooling, applicable to all levels, subjects and school types. Her suggestions were widely discussed: although eventually largely substantiated by further work, her finding was at first mistakenly accepted as generalisable, without further research.

Yin (1991) identifies three types of case study. The 'critical case' challenges a hypothesis or theory: the unit is often chosen deliberately for its likelihood of providing evidence to mount the challenge. The 'unique case' is selected for own intrinsic interest, although in clinical studies the focus on an atypical case is seen as a way of understanding the normal (e.g. studying the brain-damaged to explore the psychology of memory). The 'revelatory case' gives fresh access and generates new ideas. These three types correspond to the case studies by Delbridge and Lowe, Macleod, and Stanworth respectively.

In a strict sense, case study is not a separate research methods technique. It can be conducted as quantitative or qualitative, for example using survey methods or ethnography (**Social Surveys** and **Ethnography**). In practice, however, it is commonly associated with qualitative methods.

This is because the thinking behind **Quantitative Methods** of research is 'deductive': it starts with a theory or a 'hypothesis' and then tests it by collecting data. The intention is that if the data sustain the hypothesis, new statements of general applicability will have been developed. This fits uneasily with the singularity of the case study. However, some studies are less ambitious, but still use quantitative methods, analysing the data in terms of variables, counting frequencies and sampling behaviour *within* the social unit. The study of hospital visiting by Abbott and Payne (1992) is an example of this, being only concerned with solving a problem in two maternity wards, and not hospitals in general. However, this narrow orientation itself open to criticism, as well as being a source of problems when specific cases are in fact treated as the basis for generalisation (Atkinson and Delamont 1985).

Qualitative Methods of research, on the other hand, assume that sociological understanding should be based in the meanings that social actors themselves bring to particular social interactions. Understandings and theories grow 'inductively' out of what is studied. Researchers in this tradition are less concerned with grand theories and generalisability, and so are less likely to be worried about whether the case study example is representative.

Indeed, it can sometimes be difficult to tell if a qualitative study really is a case study (Verschuren (2003) deliberately defines case study in qualitative terms). Case studies using qualitative approaches are likely to use 'observation', 'unstructured interviews', or 'participation' as methods of collecting data. They focus on detail and the natural order of events, seeking to extract meaning and theoretical statements from the data. They are self-contained (studying a single social unit), and not concerned with generalisability. These are all features that case studies share with most qualitative research studies. However, non-case study qualitative research does sometimes treat its site as being sampled ('theoretical sampling': see **Grounded Theory**); does draw on other studies for comparison; and often implicitly handles theoretical conclusions as if they were applicable to other settings. It is probably in Yin's 'critical' and 'unique' cases that the difference can be best seen.

Key Words

case
critical case
deductive
generalisation
inductive
revelatory case
social unit
unique case

Links

Community Studies
Documentary Methods
Ethnography
Grounded Theory
Qualitative Methods
Quantiative Methods
Social Surveys

REFERENCES

General

Atkinson, P. and Delamont, S. (1985) 'Bread and Dreams or Bread and Circuses: a Critique of "Case Study" Research in Education'. In Shipman, M. (ed), *Educational Research: Principles, Policies and Practice.* Lewes: Falmer Press.

Bahr , H., Caplow, T. and Chadwick, B. (1983) 'Middletown 111: Problems of Replication, Longitudinal Measurement and Triangulation'. *Annual Review of Sociology*, 9: 243–64.

Platt, J. (1988) 'What Can Case Studies Do?' In Burgess, R. (ed), *Conducting Qualitative Research (Studies in Qualitative Methodology, Vol. 1)*. Greenwich, CT: JAI Press.

Verschuren, P. (2003) 'Case Study as a Research Strategy'. *International Journal of Social Research Methodology: Theory and Practice*, 6 (2): 121–39.

Yin, R. (1991) *Case Study Research: Design and Methods.* London: Sage.

Examples_

Abbott, P. and Payne, G. (1992) 'Hospital Visiting on Two Wards'. In Abbott, P. and Sapsford, R. (eds), *Research into Practice.* Buckingham: Open University Press.

Delbridge, R. and Lowe, J. (1997) 'Manufacturing Control: Supervisory Systems on the "New" Shopfloor'. *Sociology*, 31 (3): 409–26.

Lewis, O. (1961) *The Children of Sanchez*. New York: Vintage.

Lynd, R. and Lynd, H. (1929) *Middletown: A Study of Contemporary American Culture*. New York: Harcourt, Brace.

Lynd, R. and Lynd, H. (1937) *Middletown in Transition*. New York: Harcourt, Brace.

Macleod, A. (1992) 'Social Identity, Social Change and the Construction of Symbolic Boundaries in a West Highland Settlement'. PhD dissertation, University of Plymouth.

Stacey, M., Batstone, E., Bell, C. and Murcott, A. (1975) *Persistence and Change: a Second Study of Banbury.* London: Routledge & Kegan Paul.

Stanworth, M. (1983) *Gender and Schooling.* London: Hutchinson.

Stone, R. (2002) 'Social Theory, the Civil Imagination and Documentary Film'. *Sociology*, 26 (2): 355–75.

Coding Qualitative Data

Coding organises and conceptualises the detailed components of data into patterns by use of symbols and labels to identify – and in the case of qualitative research, interpret – elements that will feature in the analysis.

Section Outline: *Pre-coding: formats of notes, records and transcriptions. Reviewing the whole text. Making major groupings. Example: domestic diaries. Key words and indexes. Adding content and meaning. Iterative re-coding. Grounded theory. Overlap of coding, data analysis and interpretation.*

Coding is a particular step in analysing data, when the raw materials are converted into a more organised format that is easier for the researcher to inspect and understand. In *quantitative* analysis, this usually involves giving numerical values to answers so that they can be statistically processed on a computer. In qualitative analysis (which needs to be seen in the context of **Qualitative Methods**) the process is more complex and lies at the heart of the research, even when it is planned also to use computer software (Fielding and Lee 1991: 25–53; Gahan and Hannibal 1998; Grbich 1999: 239–57; Richards 1999; Seale 1999: 140–58; Seale 2000).

Data collection, its coding and analysis often go on simultaneously. There are several ways of converting 'fieldwork' into an *interpretation*. The significance of how the researcher brings a personal and professional stamp to the analysis and reporting ('authorship') and the meaning of signs ('semiotics') is demonstrated by Grbich (1999: 218–38). For simplicity, we describe the main features of coding as if this only happened after fieldwork completion. In all cases, the first task in the processing of qualitative data is to get the information into a format suitable for classifying and ordering (Miles and Huberman 1994).

Hand-written field notes, interview notes and diaries (**Fieldwork**) should be computer stored to make them easy to read. If this is not possible, they should at least be made legible. This should be undertaken as soon as possible after the information has been collected. Quickly made notes that appear understandable at the time are often difficult to make sense of afterwards.

Audio tapes have to be transcribed into verbatim written format, not 'cleaned up'. Sometimes transcribers mistakenly want to 'correct the English' or take out the 'mmms'. Transcription takes time and patience; as a rule of thumb, between three and five times as long as the original recording. Rawlings' account (1988) of a therapeutic community shows the importance of careful transcription and its coding for drawing conclusions.

This produces 'texts' that can be stored electronically and manually: in a computer *and* in your filing cabinet – and *always* as more than one copy. These could be organized by text type (interview, notes, diaries) and by any organising principle that initially seems relevant. The texts are now ready for coding.

First, the text of each interview or observation is read (and annotated) as a whole to get an overall impression. This involves summarising the text, making notes in the margin, adding reflexive accounts, and identifying significant words, phrases or passages that might be used in more detailed analysis or for illustrative quotations. The text is also checked for transcription errors and omissions, or irrelevancies, and sorted into broad groups.

These groupings will be determined by the original aims of the research, and should also reflect how and in what format the data will be presented in any subsequent publications (e.g. Solomon et al. 2002). For example, groupings could be by age; gender; occupation; household size; household stage or type; or health status. Each text is then cross-referenced according to the selected groupings. Symbols or colour coding could be used on the front of each text to ease subsequent identification. It is also usual to create an index of text references for each grouping. This is done on index cards or separate computer files. Summaries of this content analysis (**Content Analysis**) are either attached to the main text or, more usually, the text's reference code is indicated on the summary itself.

An example of preliminary analysis is given in Figure 1. In the first box is an informant's diary entry from Townsend's 1950s study of older people, as in his report but with our highlighting and marginal notes. The second box shows our initial interpretation, based on this, and highlighting the routine domestic chores; meal patterns and content; family; neighbours and friends; and leisure. The original instructions given to the research diarists were 'to note the time of day when getting up, having breakfast, calling on relations and friends, etc.'. These have clearly influenced the categories identified in the summary.

(Original text with marginal notes and highlighting added)

Mrs Tucker, 16 Bantam Street, aged sixty, living with infirm husband in terraced cottage

	Monday
order of chores	7.45 a.m. I got up, went down, and put my kettle on the gas – half-way – then I
	raked my fire out and laid it, swept my ashes up, and then cleaned my hearth.
	Then I set light to my fire, then sat down for a while, then I made tea and me and
naming	Dad had a cup.
shopping	9.20 a.m. I went out for the *Daily Mirror* and fags for Dad. About eight people said
people/neighbours	'Good Morning' with a nice smile, then I replied back. Then I went home and
	prepared oats and bread, butter and tea and me and Dad sat for breakfast. When
chores	we finished I cleared away and swept and mopped my kitchen out.
cooking	11.15 a.m. I started to get dinner on, then Mrs Rice, a neighbour, asked me to get
neighbour/	her coals in, and she will take my bag-wash, also get my dog's meat. We had a
reciprocity/chat	nice chat about Mother's Day. I showed her my flowers and card which Alice
[	sent. It was very touching, a box of chocs from John, stockings and card from
family [	Rose, card and 5s. from Bill, as I know they all think dearly of me.
visit from/meal-food	1.0 p.m. My daughter Alice came with baby. We had dinner together.
visit from/drink-snack	2.0 p.m. My daughter Rose and husband came. I made a cup of tea and cake.
leisure	3.15 p.m. Dad and I sat to listen to radio.
meal	5.0 p.m. We both had tea, bread and cheese Dad, bread and jam myself. When
chores	finished I cleared away again.
visit from/check –	7.0 p.m. My son John and his wife called to see if we were all right before they went
concern	home from work.
chores	8.0 p.m. I did a little mending.
	10.0 p.m. We went to bed.

Figure 1 *An example of preliminary data inspection*

Figure 1 *cont.*

Summary:

Female, married, 60. Sick partner.
Routine **domestic chores** – orderly routine on getting up: got up, went down stairs, put kettle on, raked fire out, laid fire, swept ashes, cleaned hearth, lit fire, made tea, shopping, made breakfast, cleared up, cleaned kitchen, prepared dinner, made tea, cleared up after tea, did some mending. Refers to 'my' kettle, 'my' fire, 'my' kitchen, etc.
Division of labour – appears to do everything – husband 'infirm'.
Food/meals – these punctuate the day. Early morning tea, breakfast after paper - ?for spouse to read?, dinner (main meal at mid-day), tea and cakes for p.m. family visitors, their tea (light meal – bread + other – spouse, cheese, she, jam ?cost – man gets the protein?). No mention of any drinks or meal after this.
Family – spouse, 2 daughters, 2 sons, son-in-law, daughter-in-law, grandchild. Refers to husband as 'Dad'. Children referred to by first names, others by relationship to them. Children visited – given meals/tea – Mother's Day, so all offspring visit. Presents and cards. **'they all think dearly of me'**. Son and wife check to see if they're all right – no mention of this checking by other offspring.
Neighbours/Friends – met 8 people she knew while shopping, exchanged pleasantries. Chat with neighbour – called for favour – reciprocity. Talked about MD and family.
Leisure – occasional sit down. Listening to radio. ?dog.

Source: Townsend, 1963: 296–7.

The preliminary analysis here has only been carried out on a single diary entry for one person. Normally it would be undertaken for all diary entries and an overall summary then made. This would be done for each diary. Each respondent's diary is then sorted into groupings and indexed. Some broad themes normally emerge from this preliminary sorting and categorising of the texts.

The next stage is identifying and classifying the categories and concepts to be found in the texts. Going through the texts again, we look for words and phrases describing events, concepts, relationships or categories – devising a coding scheme for the data with the identified words and phrases indicating possible variables. Each word or phrase is part of a potential theme, and is recorded with the text reference number and the page, paragraph and line number within the text.

The first part of the diary text in Figure 1 might result in the following items:

Got up: Respondent number 001/Diary/Day 1/Line 1
Went down: Respondent number 001/Diary/Day 1/Line 1
Kettle on: Respondent number 001/Diary/Day 1/Line 1
Raked fire: Respondent number 001/Diary/Day 1/Line 2
Laid fire: Respondent number 001/Diary/Day 1/Line 2
Swept ashes: Respondent number 001/Diary/Day 1/Line 2
Cleaned hearth: Respondent number 001/Diary/Day 1/Line 2
Lit fire: Respondent number 001/Diary/Day 1/Line 3
Sat down: Respondent number 001/Diary/Day 1/Line 3
Made tea: Respondent number 001/Diary/Day 1/Line 3
Spouse: Respondent number 001/Diary/Day 1/Line 4
Drank tea: Respondent number 001/Diary/Day 1/Line 4.

However, although this categorisation may be accurate, it is most likely that the first two categories would be grouped together as 'getting up'. 'Putting the kettle on' and 'making tea' might be coded as 'preparing a meal/drink', and the processes involved in cleaning out and lighting the fire might be grouped as 'fire chores' or classified with other household chores. Again, the family members could be described in terms of each relationship (husband; daughter; son; son-in-law; daughter-in-law; grandchild) or as broader categories such as partner; offspring; grandchild; or in-laws.

Again, it might be thought important to divide these categories: for example, into positive and negative comments about family and neighbours or, as indicated in the marginal notes in Figure 1, 'visits from' and 'visits to' relatives. The context in which the categories arise is also important. The contextualisation of categories involves noting this down, along with any other categories associated with a particular one. Clearly the level of categorisation or coding is determined by the aims of the research – what *you* want to find out about. You may decide to undertake a partial analysis rather than a full one; identifying categories that refer to your particular view of gender roles, for example. However, even this can be extremely onerous and time-consuming.

When all texts have been processed, the resulting lists are sorted, scrutinised and refined. This involves the inspection of the categories for completeness and redundancy. During this process, ideas and questions arise about the subject matter, and the texts might then be further scrutinised to test out any emerging patterns. The iteration of the qualitative analysis continues until the researcher is satisfied that the data have been fully explored and interpreted. This is particularly important in the grounded theory approach (**Grounded Theory**: see also Flick 1998:

178–98). Interpretation also involves returning to the original texts and summaries to test explanations. Thus 'coding', 'data analysis' and 'interpretation' merge into one another, but depend on the rigorous groundwork of the initial coding.

Key Words

categories
contextualisation
field notes
indexing
iteration
reflexive accounts
text
transcription

Links

Content Analysis
Fieldwork
Grounded Theory
Qualitative Methods

REFERENCES

General

Fielding, N. and Lee, R. (1991) *Using Computers in Qualitative Research*. London: Sage.
Flick, U. (1998) *An Introduction to Qualitative Research*. London: Sage.
Gahan, C. and Hannibal, M. (1998) *Doing Qualitative Research Using QSR NUD*IST.* London: Sage.
Grbich, C. (1999) *Qualitative Research in Health*. London: Sage.
Miles, M. and Huberman, M. (1994) *Qualitative Data Analysis.* London: Sage.
Seale, C. (1999) *The Quality of Qualitative Research*. London: Sage.
Seale, C. (2000) 'Using Computers to Analyse Qualitative Data'. In Silverman, D. (ed), *Doing Qualitative Research*. London: Sage.

Examples

Rawlings, B. (1988) 'Local Knowledge: the Analysis of Transcribed Audio Materials for Organizational Ethnography'. In Burgess, R. (ed), *Conducting Qualitative Research (Studies in Qualitative Methodology, Vol. 1)*. Greenwich, CT: JAI Press.
Richards, L. (1999) 'How to Use QSR NUD*IST for Qualitative Analysis'. In Schutt, R. (ed.), *Investigating the Social World* (2nd edn). Thousand Oaks, CA: Pine Forge Press.
Solomon, Y., Warin, J., Lewis, C. and Langford, W. (2002) 'Intimate Talk between Parents and Their Teenage Children'. *Sociology* 36 (4): 965–83.
Townsend, P. (1963) *The Family Life of Old People.* Harmondsworth: Penguin.

Community Profiles

Community profiles are prepared as an aid to social programming and consist of relatively brief, mainly quantitative descriptions of groups (normally living in one location) and their organisations.

Section Outline: *Wide use of profiling in social and health administration. Types and sources of local data. Departments and internet access. Key informants. Examples of packages: advantages and disadvantages. Rapid appraisal: pyramid. Priority search: scaling local perceptions. Compass: question bank.*

Community profiling covers research procedures to obtain mainly quantitative information to guide public policy or to evaluate policy initiatives, 'community' here meaning a small, locality-based group (**Action Research**; **Evaluation Studies**; **Community Studies**). Although many remain unpublished, community profiles have been undertaken by statutory bodies, pressure groups and communities themselves (Payne 1999). Community profiling is most popular in disciplines such as health, social work and social policy where the research process itself is not the main focus (e.g. Ong and Humphris 1994; Driskell 2002: 177–201). Conversely, the intellectual and political bankruptcy of the British community work movement is largely explained by the ideological indifference in many of its mainstream texts to actual local conditions and its appraisal through research (e.g. Clarke et al. 2002; Jacobs and Popple 1994).

It starts by collecting readily available quantitative data on the locality. The most extensive source of local statistical information is normally the Local Authority, affording information covering population; housing; employment; tourism; environment; transport; education; social services; and crime. The particular department responsible varies between authorities: 'Planning', 'Economic Development', 'Research and Intelligence' or the 'Chief Executive's Office'. 'Housing' and 'Environmental Health' also hold local information for their specific responsibilities.

UK Health Authorities produce annual reports including birth and death rates by cause, cancer registration and other health monitoring information. These rates are for the whole health authority area and are therefore of limited value for small localities. However, health authorities have 'Research and Information' departments which may provide more detailed information for smaller areas.

Local and health authorities often provide information via the internet. However, it is better to make personal contact because you are more likely to obtain more detailed information than is usually found on web pages. Even including face-to-face contact time, a statistical picture of a locality can be rapidly and cheaply constructed, characteristics that account for the method's popularity.

If the project is small-scale, further information, often of a more qualitative kind, can be collected from key informants (**Key Informants**). More comprehensive methods, used particularly in the health field, are:

- *Rapid Appraisal* – an approach suitable for community health needs assessment;
- *Priority Search* – a package used by many Healthy City initiatives; and
- *Compass* – a more general community profiling software package developed from the rural profiling methods of *Village Appraisal*.

A brief description of these will provide an illustration of community profile practice.

Rapid Appraisal adopts a mixed-method approach adapted from community profiling in Third World countries. It uses existing statistical and documentary sources; direct observations in the community; and interviews and group discussions with 'key informants' (**Documentary Methods**; **Key Informants**; **Observation**). The information collected is categorised as an 'information pyramid' with four layers, and nine broad areas, as in Figure 2.

As its name suggests, this is a fairly fast method – one study in Edinburgh took five community professionals, working four hours a day on average, three months – and provides a broad range of information about the community (Murray and Graham 1995). The practical advantages of cost and speed in doing Rapid Appraisal explain its wide usage in Britain by local officials who may be untrained in social research and its complexities, or unconcerned about its 'commonsense' theoretical assumptions about 'communities'.

Its main limitation is reliance for qualitative information on key informants who may not represent the whole range of community attitudes. However, if combined with a wider survey, Rapid Appraisal could contribute to a thorough assessment of a locality-based

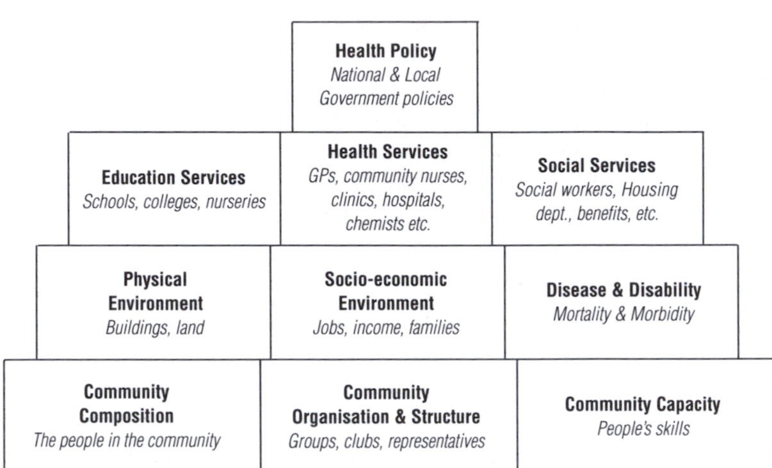

Figure 2 *Example of a Rapid Appraisal information pyramid*

community. The nine broad categories of information provide a sound framework for establishing a project or used as a basis for other methods.

In contrast, *Priority Search* is more clearly a 'package', being a computerised questionnaire developed in the late 1980s by a Sheffield City Council working group. Based on the theory that there are 'underlying consistencies in the way we see, or construct, the world' (Priority Search, 1994: Appendix (v)), it attempts to uncover these. It first identifies a general question to use in focus groups (**Group Discussions/Focus Groups**), e.g. 'What would improve your health, happiness and well-being?' or 'What would make this area a better place to live in?' Responses to the question from focus groups form the basis of a questionnaire.

This repeats the general question, offering alternative responses. Respondents compare each statement with another, using a sliding scale of 50 circles (see Figure 3). Individual statements are included three times; each time being compared with a different statement. This provides for a wide range of alternatives.

The questionnaires are then analysed using 'Principal Component Analysis'. This statistical technique groups all answers and preferences into a smaller number of underlying attitudes: e.g. bullying, racism, safer streets and policing are statements about *security*; more nurseries, play-areas and teenage venues are about *child care*. Although commissioning researchers decide on the general question, with local people involved in interviewing, the Priority Search team have to be employed to undertake

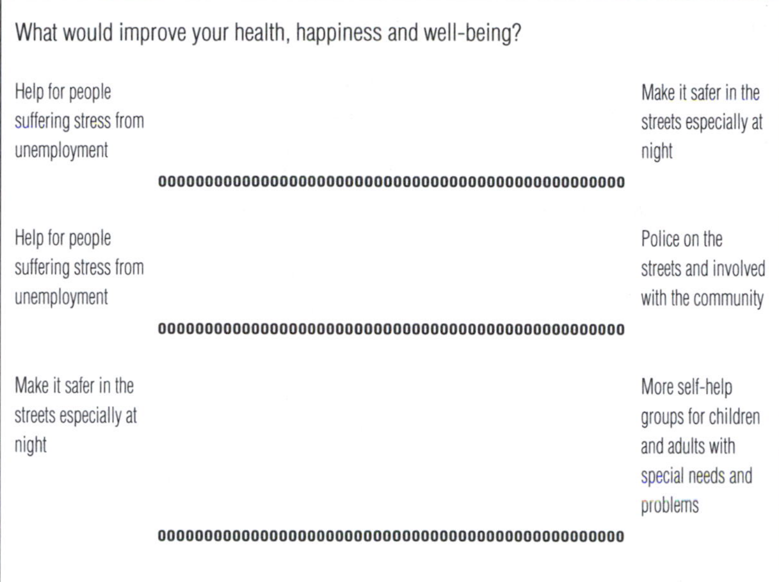

What would improve your health, happiness and well-being?
Help for people suffering stress from unemployment
Make it safer in the streets especially at night
000000000000000000000000000000000000000000000000000
Help for people suffering stress from unemployment
Police on the streets and involved with the community
000000000000000000000000000000000000000000000000000
Make it safer in the streets especially at night
More self-help groups for children and adults with special needs and problems
000000000000000000000000000000000000000000000000000

Figure 3 *An example of a Priority Search comparison scale*

Source: Adapted from Priority Search (1994)

the focus groups, design and analyse the questionnaire, and prepare the final report. Alternatively, an approximation of this method could be done locally at lower cost.

Developed by the Countryside Community Research Unit and the Policy Research Institute, Leeds, *Compass* is also a copyrighted computer package, managing questionnaire design, data processing and analysis. Its over 400 questions cover housing, health, employment, income, education, training, and environment. Users select from this list and/or add their own questions. The selection can be used in self-completion or interview survey formats (**Questionnaires**). The package also generates a data entry form to input responses, and a statistical analysis component to provide tables, charts and graphs: it is well supported by its authors.

The questionnaire's flexibility and its moderate costs make this package a solution for researchers who lack the time or skills to produce their own questionnaire. However, it has not been widely adopted, perhaps because unless a project is completely contracted out, it still requires research inputs, like sampling, interviewing and report writing (see also Hawtin et al. 1994).

Key Words

community
information pyramid
key informant
mixed-methods
principal component analysis

Links

Action Research
Community Studies
Documentary Methods
Evaluation Studies
Group Discussions/Focus Groups
Key Informants
Observation
Questionnaires

REFERENCES

General

Hawtin, M., Hughes, G. and Percy-Smith, J. (1994) *Community Profiling: Auditing Social Needs.* Buckingham: Open University Press.

Ong, B. and Humphris, G. (1994) 'Prioritizing Needs with Communities'. In Popay, J. and Williams, G. (eds), *Researching the People's Health*. London: Routledge.

Payne, J. (1999) *Researching Health Needs.* London: Sage.

Examples

Clarke, S., Byatt, A., Hoban, M. and Powell, D. (eds) (2002) *Community Development in South Wales.* Cardiff: University of Wales Press.

Driskell, D. (2002) *Creating Better Cities with Children and Youth*. London: Earthscan Publications/Paris: UNESCO Publishing.

Jacobs, S. and Popple, K. (eds) (1994) *Community Work in the 1990s.* Nottingham: Spokesman.

Murray, S and Graham, C. (1995) 'Practice-based Health Needs Assessment: Use of Four Methods in a Small Neighbourhood'. *British Medical Journal*, 1443: 8.

Priority Search (1994) *What Would Improve Your Health, Happiness and Well-being?* Swindon: Healthy Thamesdown.

Community Studies

Community studies are typically carried out by researchers living in a settlement in order to investigate local social networks in the residential area, normally through qualitative methods that treat residents as comprising a cohesive social unit.

Section Outline: *Community as a concept. The ethnography of place communities. Three problems of community studies: residence is not community; boundaries; male occupational groups. The survival and development of community studies. Anthropological inputs. Alternatives to ethnography. Living in and studying a community. Selectivity and access. Researchers' illusions about 'belonging'.*

Community studies are an example of research practice associated with a single sociological concept, that of 'community'. Most commonly, community studies have comprised research into 'place communities', i.e. into the social relationships happening in human settlements. The research focus has been the local social systems in the area; these and the people in them being loosely referred to as a 'community'. Almost without exception, such community studies involve the researcher living during part of the duration of the project in the area whose residents are being studied. The methods of research are predominantly qualitative and characteristically ethnographic (**Qualitative Methods**; **Ethnography**).

The concept of community can be used in many subtly different ways (**Indicators and Operationalisations**). Its core ideas are a network of relations between people, a shared sense of identity, a characteristic form of relationships, and – in place communities – a sense of locality. It is also possible to have 'interest communities', where members may not be located physically together but do share a social position in the wider society, and 'communities of attachment', where members share a sense of common identity.

The popularity of the place community study has fluctuated with the changing fortune of the concept of community. In the first half of the twentieth century, American sociology (and British social anthropology) was particularly interested in how human life in the form of social solidarities operated. What held societies together, and what did various social processes contribute to the functional coherence of the wider society? Later, more elaborate frames of reference became important, the discipline split into specialisms, and the idea that the social relationships in a small area could explain wider social patterns lost ground.

There have been three other main objections to community studies. It was argued that living together in a place did not automatically mean the existence of a community (Stacey 1969), and that small settlements had no closed social boundaries, being better understood as part of wider social and cultural systems (see Blaikie et al. forthcoming). Third, studies have typically concentrated narrowly on the lives of males in working-class areas dominated by a single industry (mining, fishing, farming, etc.).

Although many sociologists proclaimed 'the death of community', in fact a considerable number of studies continued. Most of these concentrated on specific topics within the context of community, such as crime, local politics, unemployment, friendships, education, class, race relations, social welfare or housing. They did not necessarily call themselves community studies, even though that is what they were (Payne 1996). From a base in rural settlements – the term 'Celtic fringe' is often applied to British studies of villages in Ireland, Wales and Scotland – these specialist community studies extended to parts of cities. Indeed, this concern with urban communities and estates was a second theme in the tradition, drawing on early work by the Chicago School in the US, and Young and Willmott's work in London. Useful summaries of many community studies can be found in Frankenberg (1966), Bell and Newby (1972) or Crow and Allan (1994).

Community studies started in America, most recognisably in the account of life in the Mid-west by the Lynds, the first stage of which was published as *Middletown* in 1929. This was followed by Warner's *Yankee City*, started in 1930. Warner was influenced by the British social anthropologists, Radcliffe-Brown and Malinowski, and was instrumental in setting up the first 'British' study by Arensberg and Kimball in the early 1930s. The method of living in a Western community suited anthropologists, who subsequently were to find it harder working in the contracting Empire, as well as early qualitative sociologists who wanted to understand social life as a detailed, naturally occurring process, rather than as variables and short-term, de-contextualised analyses.

However, it is not the case that community studies use only ethnographic methods. *Yankee City* drew on sample surveys, for instance for information on household budgets. The original version of *Family and Kinship in East London*, probably the most influential community study in Britain, explained that the card-sorter and (main-frame) computer made possible much of Willmott and Young's research. Brody (1973) uses documentary records like the Census as part of his work on rural Ireland to challenge Arensberg and Kimball's version (1940) which had emphasised stability, coherence and continuity. Foster's account of the re-development of the London *Docklands* (1999) depends as much on her interviews with elite figures outside of the area as on her involvement with the local community. And Bell and Newby suggest that communities can be regarded as samples of a wider culture (1972: 54–81).

None the less, qualitative research methods are better for accessing the senses of identity and locality, and the special kinds of relationship, that are central to place communities. By living and participating (**Participant Observation**) in the community, the researcher can achieve a kind of understanding that other methods cannot provide. First-hand observation of events and unstructured interviews give powerful ways of perceiving social processes and discovering the symbolic meanings that residents use in their everyday lives.

On the other hand, there are three methodological problems that are peculiar to the community study. The first of these is a question of scale. Whereas studying one school or one doctor's practice may be a manageable task, a place community contains a mixture of school, shop, workplace, church, club, bar and home. Even a small team of observers cannot cover everything that goes on, around the clock. What gets covered depends both on the selectivity of the researcher(s) and on serendipity. How can we judge whether the final account is representative of what has happened?

Indeed, it will also depend on how the researcher is socially located in the community. Initial access is usually negotiated through local contacts with one or more key players. Stacey's links with the local Labour Party are an example of how this opened doors in Banbury – but also shut them. Because Stacey and her team were associated with one part of the political scene, this set up counter-reactions among those politically opposed to Labour, and not associated with the Labour Club. Similarly, Macleod's personal links with his home community helped him a great deal, but he felt his public identity made it harder to cope with immigrants, or to access the world of the younger women (**Feminist Research**). This problem of access applies in any field study, but the problem is potentially greater because of the larger size and complexity of place communities (**Fieldwork**).

It may therefore seem surprising that the usual conventional concern about studying communities is that the researcher 'goes native' (a term adopted from colonial administrators whose superiors in London perceived them as siding with those they administered). By identifying too closely with the residents, researchers supposedly lose their freshness and independent vision: the social distance that is said to ensure an analytical view then disappears. However, one of the commonsense things we know about local communities is that incomers always report feelings of being different, and 'not a local' even after decades of living there. How is it that over just a few months, or at best a couple of years, sociologists can go native? It may be that in over-compensating for feelings of isolation, a misconceived belief that the observer has been 'accepted' emerges. But even the most skilled social researcher cannot achieve full community membership or belonging that quickly.

Key Words

'going native'
incomer
place community
sense of identity
social boundaries

Links

Case Study
Ethnography
Feminist Research
Fieldwork
Indicators and Operationalisations
Participant Observation
Qualitative Methods
Quantitative Methods

REFERENCES

General

Arensberg, C. and Kimball, S. (1940) *Family and Community in Ireland*. London: Peter Smith.

Bell, C. and Newby, H. (1972) *Community Studies.* London: Allen & Unwin.

Blaikie, A., Inglis, D. and Payne, G. (in preparation) *Community: Social Solidarities from Local to Global*. Basingstoke: Palgrave.

Payne, G. (1996) 'Imagining the Community'. In Lyon, S. and Busfield, J. (eds), *Methodological Imaginations.* Basingstoke: Macmillan.

Stacey, M. (1969) 'The Myth of Community Studies'. *British Journal of Sociology*, 20 (2): 134–45.

Examples

Brody, H. (1973) *Innishkillane.* London: Allen Lane.

Crow, G. and Allan, G. (1994) *Community Life.* Hemel Hempstead: Harvester Wheatsheaf.

Foster, J. (1999) *Docklands*. London: UCL Press.

Frankenberg, R. (1966) *Communities in Britain*. Harmondsworth: Penguin.

Lynd, R. and Lynd, H. (1929) *Middletown: A Study of Contemporary American Culture*. New York: Harcourt, Brace.

Warner, L. (1963) *Yankee City.* New Haven, CT: Yale University Press.

Willmott, P. and Young, M. (1957) *Family and Kinship in East London*. London: Routledge, Kegan Paul.

Content Analysis

Content analysis seeks to demonstrate the meaning of written or visual sources (like newspapers and advertisements) by systematically allocating their content to pre-determined, detailed categories, and then both quantifying and interpreting the outcomes.

Section Outline: *Content analysis used to analyse written and visual 'texts', including field notes. Counting versus interpreting. Example: conventions in newspaper 'coverage'. Designing content analysis research. Alternative models of the media: audience influence; political bias; commercial operations. Electronic media. Content analysis in undergraduate dissertations. Manifest and latent content.*

Content analysis is one of the more important, and under-rated, research methods. It was originally a quantitative way of evaluating written texts, particularly newspaper 'stories'. This was extended to apply to literature, autobiography and other documents (**Documentary Methods**), and to films, TV, video and still photography (**Visual Methods**), with emphasis shifting to qualitative priorities like interpretation and subjective meaning. Content analysis therefore includes the ways most qualitative researchers codify and analyse their field notes (**Coding Qualitative Data**), although the researchers themselves seldom acknowledge that is what they are doing.

This is partly due to conventions about what methods are called, and partly to early content analysis being seen as 'quantitative'. Content analysis originally concentrated on counting how frequently words or topics were included, how much space or time was devoted to themes, and how much importance was drawn to them. In qualitative research, much of which draws on an anti-quantitative tradition (**Qualitative Methods**), content analysis has to address attitudes, values and motivations. It is the meaning behind the word-symbols that matters: the 'social' is contained in the communication. Qualitative researchers acknowledge that they bring their own cultural meanings to the interpretation of naturally occurring oral texts. There is, however, some reluctance to admit how far this process of 'interpretation' depends on counting of key words or comparison of references in the transcribed 'texts' from the field notes of the first-hand experience they have recorded.

In contrast, the classic form of content analysis investigates how newspapers have reported social phenomena, like crime, election campaigns or women's roles. Samples of editions are searched for references to the topic, which are then examined for quantity and style. Measurements used include: the amount of coverage (usually measured in 'column inches'); location in the paper (front-page news or 'buried inside'); emphasis (headline font size, position on the page, use of photographs); and treatment as factual reporting or comment (a distinction better observed in the US than in Britain). The language is studied to distinguish between neutral vocabulary and words with emotional connotations like nicknames ('Maggie', 'Krauts'), vernacular phrases ('Tories', 'smash'), buzz-words ('muggers', 'terrorists'), and symbolic phrases ('swamping', 'immigrant', 'our boys', 'liberals'). Is the overall tone positive, neutral or negative? How do impressions get built up and then modified through choice of terminology (Jagger 2001)?

These procedures can be used on any text (Holsti 1969). First, the elements to be examined are chosen: words, sentences, paragraphs or 'stories'; images, symbols, characters or themes. What will be regarded as high or low emphasis (e.g. number of mentions or length of coverage) and what will count as positive or negative evaluation? The research topic (e.g. crime) is operationalised into explicit categories that are mutually exclusive, independent and all-inclusive (crime against the person/property crime; crime as reported acts/crime as tried in court; etc.). 'Pilot studies' test the effectiveness of these, and inform sampling decisions and coding protocols, although qualitative studies are less likely to approach this as systematically. Some thought can usefully be given to output: qualitative stances suggest more reporting of detail, verbatim quotation and discussion of interpretation, while quantitative analysis will favour tables, graphs and summaries.

Three features should be highlighted here. First, content analysis can take mundane, taken-for-granted texts and transform them into interesting objects of research. Second, content analysis is essentially systematic and detailed, in both quantitative and qualitative approaches. Third, it is not tied to a single theoretical interpretation: in addition to qualitative and quantitative orientations, as a method it can for instance be used with several different claims about how news media impact on their audiences (Abercrombie and Warde 2000; Harvey and MacDonald 1993: 36–49).

It is also important to recognise variations in the phenomena being studied (Giddens 2001: 364–97). Thus we might take account of the type of newspaper or TV channel being studied. Mass market 'tabloids' give more prominence to popular culture, celebrity gossip and sport. They are written in a simpler language for a readership that has limited literacy skills. 'Quality' or 'broadsheet' papers include more 'serious' news, have longer stories giving more detail, and in Britain, more international news. Produced for a middle-class market, they rely less on pictures and simple words to convey their message. In other words, there is a connection between marketing and content.

Because newspapers are commercial products, researchers also consider who owns and controls their production, the processes of production, and how these are reflected in the output. For example, newspapers tend to back the political party that the owner supports (in Britain, mostly the Conservative Party), but must still be sensitive of what their readership wants. Whether newspapers' political stances – or that to TV – make a substantial difference is debatable (Crewe 1992; Eldridge 1993). Most journalists are not concerned with political outcomes: they face daily struggles with deadlines and editors' instructions, while at the same time building their own careers. Putting out a paper is a process of contestation.

Content analysis helps to explore such issues, as well as throwing light on the connections between coverage and public perceptions, like popular misconceptions about women's roles; rising crime rates; the size of ethnic minorities; or election results. Mass media 'set the agenda' by selecting what they include and prioritise. For instance, Payne (2003) used content analysis of the online *Guardian Archive* to show how exaggerated rates of British adult literacy, even in the 'quality press', generated a sense of social concern.

It is therefore no surprise to find media studies courses addressing the cultural content and significance of soap operas, sports events, advertisements, women's magazines or rock music. The shift from print-based media to electronic forms like TV, video and the internet did not invalidate content analysis (see also **Internet Polling** and **Internet and Other Searches**). Rather, it spawned new forms of codification to handle images and symbolic representations (Glasgow Media Group 1976).

Simple content analysis is a good method for undergraduate dissertations, applied to any written format whether fiction or non-fiction (**Auto/biography and Life Histories**). It avoids imposing on other people for interviews (**Unobtrusive Methods**). Data can be analysed using word-processing packages, or specialist software like 'NUD*IST 4', can produce word counts, key word searches and systematic ordering of the data on a PC. However, the time-consuming preparatory task of data input and coding can be a disincentive to the use of software in small studies.

It is also important to recognise problems of what is available to study. Does the sample of material represent the wider set from which it has been selected? Is the full range of material available (**Documentary Methods**)? Content analysis of electronic sources can be problematic for undergraduate dissertations, because assessment often requires inclusion of material, something more readily done with written texts.

Furthermore, understanding the significance of text is not just word counting. The sequences in which items occur, and the structures of sequences, relate to the original 'author's' ideas, but not in an obvious way. There is a big difference between 'manifest' content (the actual words) and 'latent' content (the implicit messages that can be interpreted: see Holsti 1969). At a more sophisticated level, content analysis becomes more challenging, harder to explain, and its results more difficult to justify. The most common objection to content analysis is researcher bias. The further the method moves from straightforward evidence like word counts, the greater the likelihood of this challenge.

Key Words

agenda setting
broadsheet
column inches
mass media
tabloid
vernacular phrases

Links

Auto/biography and Life Histories
Coding Qualitative Data
Documentary Methods
Internet Polling
Internet and Other Searches
Qualitative Methods
Unobtrusive Methods and Triangulation
Visual Methods

REFERENCES

General

Harvey, L. and MacDonald, M. (1993) *Doing Sociology*. Basingstoke: Macmillan.
Holsti, O. (1969) *Content Analysis in the Social Sciences and Humanities*. Reading, MA: Addison-Wesley.

Examples

Abercrombie, N. and Warde, A. (2000) *Contemporary British Society.* Cambridge: Polity Press.

Crewe, I. (1992) 'Why Did Labour Lose (Yet Again)?' *Politics Review*, September: 10–11.

Eldridge, J. (ed.) (1993) *Getting the Message: News, Truth and Power.* London: Routledge.

Giddens, A. (2001) *Sociology* (4th edn). Cambridge: Polity Press.

Glasgow Media Group (1976) *Bad News*. London: Routledge.

Jagger, E. (2001) 'Marketing Molly and Melville: Dating in a Postmodern, Consumer Society'. *Sociology*, 35 (1): 39–57.

Payne, G. (2003) *Immobility, Inequality and 'Illiteracy': Limits to the Ideal of a Meritocratic Britain*. Paper presented to the 2003 BSA Annual Conference, York.

The Guardian (2003) 'Lexicon of Lies'. Media Guardian supplement. *http://media.guardian.co.uk/mediaguardian/story/o,7558,958622,00.html*

Contingency Tables

A contingency table is a tabulation which shows two (or more) variables, with the distribution of one variable's categories across the rows, and the other's down the columns, so that the interlocking row/column 'cells' give the number (or percentage) of cases in each part of the distributions of the two variables at once.

Section Outline: *Looking at tables of data. Linking two variables. Example without numbers: gender and income. Rows, columns, marginals and cells. Describing cells. Percentages. Example: SPSS format for percentages. Eye-balling and measuring the strength of association. From 2 x 2, to multivariate tables.*

The contingency table (or 'cross-tabulation') is one of the most useful – and simple – techniques in quantitative analysis (**Quantitative Methods**). This is sometimes obscured by the technical names given to the parts of the table, and the more sophisticated statistical routines that can be developed from it. These tables are the data tables in texts that many readers 'bleep over', taking the author's word for what they show, rather than inspecting them. This section does not attempt to cover statistical techniques, because for many less-numerate students the most important step is first to gain confidence in seeing the message and evidence in *tables*.

The basic idea of the table is essentially commonsense: to compare how people (or social organisations) score on two or more variables *together*. For example, do men earn more than women? Is using soft drugs associated with later use of hard drugs? In what ways are people's future jobs linked to their family backgrounds?

In the first example, one variable is *gender*, which has two values, 'men' and 'women'. The second variable is *income* (which could be defined in several ways): in this illustration, we simply group people using three levels, 'high', 'middle' and 'low'. To help readers who are put off by numbers, we start without any numbers at all. Our contingency table of 'gender by income' is shown in Table 1.

Table 1 *An example of a table without numbers. Gender by income: people in paid employment*

Income level	Men	Women	Totals
High	Lots	Few	All high earners
Middle	Some	Some	All middle earners
Low	Few	Lots	All low earners
Totals	All men	All women	All of our sample

The key feature of the contingency table is that it groups people who share a *combination* of its variables. Thus Table 1 tells us that 'lots' of *men* are also *high earners*. You can check this by looking down the men's column, and across the high income row. Where they cross, the 'cell' shows '*lots*'. If you look further across the high income row, the next cell along, in the women's column, shows '*few*'.

Tables consist of 'columns' and 'rows' of data. Here, there is a column for men, and a column for women. There are rows for high, middle, and low income. The size of table is usually referred to by the number of columns and rows: here we have a '2 x 3', gender by income level, cross-tabulation. This leaves out the column and the row showing the totals (or 'marginal totals', often abbreviated to 'marginals'). Sometimes an additional row or column is included for people in the sample where information is incomplete (what the most widely used analysis software – the Statistical Package for Social Sciences, now called the Statistical Package and Service Solutions, or just 'SPSS' – calls 'missing values' unless we specify a 'don't know' or 'not stated' line).

A 2 x 3 table is pretty simple. Tables can go from the simplest, 2 × 2, to any size. However, in practice, the more columns and rows there are, the more difficult it is to 'eye-ball' the table and spot any patterns without resorting to statistical techniques (Bryman 2001; Gilbert et al. 2001). Most social researchers find it hard to interpret anything bigger than a 10 x 10 table (see **Sampling: Questions of Size**).

If our research did show the pattern suggested in Table 1, we might begin to suspect that more men had higher incomes, but we would want to look at the rest of the table before reading a final judgement. We also have to decide which way the variables are related. In this case, it is plausible to argue that being a man or a woman might determine the chances of a good income. It certainly is implausible to suggest that one's gender depends on one's income! With this example, gender is the 'independent variable' that we are presuming determines income, the 'dependent variable'. Which we treat as which will result from our theoretical assumptions, whereas the actual data will be the empirical evidence that are either consistent with our theory, or will disprove it. Tables with two variables ('bivariate tables') conventionally show the independent variable in the columns, and the dependent variable as the rows. (One major exception to this guideline is the 'mobility table', the contingency table for social mobility, which traditionally places family of origin as the rows, and respondents' current occupations or social classes as the columns).

It is rather long-winded to talk about particular columns, rows, and column/row intersections. As a convenient short-hand, each cell of a table can be numbered from the top left-hand corner, with one number for which column it is in, and a second number for the row. This is shown in Table 2.

Now we can conveniently say, for example, that cells 1, 3 and 2, 3 of Table 1 show fewer low-earning men than women.

In practice, tables more often show percentages. The important thing to check is which percentage is shown. There are three main possibilities. We can take the number in a cell, and calculate what percentage it is of all the people in the sample (that total should always be shown in the bottom right-hand corner cell where the two marginals intersect). Second, we can calculate what percentage the cell number is of all the people in

Table 2 *An example of a table with cell identifiers. Gender by income: people in paid employment*

Income level	Men	Women	Totals
High	1, 1	2, 1	All high earners
Middle	1, 2	2, 2	All middle earners
Low	1, 3	2, 3	All low earners
Totals	All men	All women	All of our sample

that row (using the number in the right-hand marginal). Alternatively, we can calculate the percentage of all the people in the column (using the number in the bottom marginal). SPSS prints all three: Table 3 shows the SPSS format for our gender x income example, calculated from real numbers (see also **Levels of Measurement**).

You should actually *look at* these numbers in Table 3: now that the table has been explained, there is no excuse to 'bleep over' them! Better still, in your own project work, you can present your data in a clearer form, possibly mixed with graphs – though preferably not the unfortunately popular 'pie chart', which at first sight seems simple but is actually hard to interpret (Kumar 1999: 226–40; Franfort-Nachmias and Leon-Guerrero 2000: 72–108).

In some cases there are no clear independent and dependent variables, so you might want the row percentages, say, instead of those for the column. It is necessary first to re-calculate the actual *number* for each cell, before re-calculating the new *percentages*. For your own data, this is done automatically by SPSS, which also provides several standardised measures of association (**Association and Causation**), which extend preliminary 'eye-balling' to more systematic interpretations of the table. A number of texts provide a helpful introduction to using SPSS: Bryman 2001; Franfort-Nachmias and Leon-Guerrero 2000; Rose and Sullivan 1993; Schutt 1999.

Tables can also be elaborated by adding extra variables. The association between gender and income might reflect the fact that more women work part-time. We could have *two* columns for men, showing full-timers and part-timers, and *two* for women. This would turn our 2 × 3 table into 4 × 3 one. The length of time in paid employment is likely to be another factor (because of Western cultural traditions of child-rearing): we could

Table 3 *An example of an SPSS table. Gender by income: people in paid employment*

Income level	Men	Women	Totals
HIGH	*90*	*34*	*124*
Row percentage	72.6	27.4	100.0
Column percentage	46.9	17.7	32.3
Total percentage	23.4	8.9	32.3
MIDDLE	*74*	*64*	*138*
Row percentage	53.6	46.4	100.0
Column percentage	38.5	33.3	35.9
Total percentage	19.3	16.7	35.9
Low	*28*	*94*	*122*
Row percentage	23.0	74.0	100.0
Column percentage	14.6	49.0	31.8
Total percentage	7.3	24.5	31.8
COLUMN TOTALS	*192*	*192*	*384*
Row percentage	50.0	50.0	100.0
Column percentage	100.0	100.0	100.0
Total percentage	50.0	50.0	100.0

again subdivide the two genders. Such 'multivariate tables' are a way of bringing in 'intervening variables' (**Association and Causation**) and checking that we are not mistakenly connecting two variables when actually it is some other variable that is more important. An example which argues a case from careful use of ethnicity, gender, industrial sector and time period in various combinations in four tables can be found in Iganski and Payne (1999).

In most situations, while we may concentrate on a pair or trio of variables in a table, the core relationships involve rather more variables. Introducing these into an analysis is called 'elaboration'. A simple introduction to the logic of elaboration can be found in the first chapter of Rose and Sullivan (1993), where this section's framework will be useful. Sapsford (1999: 169–98) gives a more statistical treatment, leading into multivariate analysis. However, multivariate contingency tables are more difficult to read, and there are practical limits to how much information a contingency table can usefully communicate. The main value of contingency tables lies in their simplicity, and as a preliminary way of making sense of one's data.

Key Words

bivariate table
cell
column
row
multivariate table

Links

Association and Causation
Levels of Measurement
Quantitative Methods
Sampling: Questions of Size

REFERENCES

General

Bryman, A. (2001) *Social Research Methods.* Oxford: Oxford University Press.

Franfort-Nachmias, C. and Leon-Guerrero, A. (2000) *Social Statistics for a Diverse Society* (2nd edn). Thousand Oaks, CA: Sage.

Gilbert, N. et al. (2001) *Researching Social Life.* London: Sage.

Kumar, R. (1999) *Research Methodology.* London: Sage.

Rose, D. and Sullivan, O. (1993) *Introducing Data Analysis for Social Scientists.* Buckingham: Open University Press.

Sapsford, R. (1999) *Survey Research.* London: Sage.

Sarantakos, S. (1998) *Social Research* (2nd edn). Basingstoke: Macmillan.

Schutt, R. (1999) *Investigating the Social World.* (2nd edn). Thousand Oaks, CA: Pine Forge Press.

Examples

Iganski, P. and Payne, G. (1999) 'Socio-economic Re-structuring and Employment'. *British Journal of Sociology*, 50 (2): 195–215.

Documentary Methods

Documentary methods are the techniques used to categorise, investigate, interpret and identify the limitations of physical sources, most commonly written documents, whether in the private or public domain (personal papers, commercial records, or state archives, communications or legislation).

Section Outline: *Documents as concrete objects. Three categories: personal; private; public. Restricted access to documents. Secondary analysis, content analysis and documents. Reading between the lines. Beyond the page. Example: Girl Heaven. Four issues: authenticity, credibility; representativeness; meaning. Limitations of documentary methods. Personal, private and public documents and the four issues. Unreliable documentation. Strengths and weaknesses of documentary methods.*

Most social research examines what people do, or say in response to questions. Unlike the physical specimens of physics and chemistry, the people we study are living, thinking and independent entities, who have their own intentions and understandings. However, they do sometimes record their knowledge, ideas and feelings in writing, so creating physical artefacts – documents. Documents are naturally occurring objects (i.e. not deliberately produced for the purpose of social research) with a concrete and semi-permanent existence which tell us indirectly about the social world of the people who created them (**Unobtrusive Methods**). Platt's history of British sociology illustrates the range of archive material that can be combined with other sources (2003: 1–4; 173–6).

To simplify discussion, we start with a narrow definition of documentary methods. Documents fall into three main categories: personal, private and public, depending on *who* wrote them, not the document's ownership or availability to the wider population.

'Personal documents' are individuals' letters, diaries, notes, drafts and files (electronic and hard copy), and even autobiographies (**Auto/biography and Life Histories**). 'Private documents' are produced by and for private organisations like businesses or charities. Some documents are for internal purposes and not normally available to the general public. Examples are committee minutes, personnel records, budgets, training manuals or inter-departmental memos. Other private documents are produced for public consumption: annual reports, media statements and public relations handouts. In the case of the communications industry, much of the product itself – particularly newspapers and TV 'documentaries' – is a ready source of documentary analysis in its right (**Content Analysis**). On-line databases of newspaper articles have been used to show how 'cancer' is represented (Seale 2001) and how 'citizenship' and 'medical authority' may be negotiated (Abraham and Lewis 2002).

Many examples of private documents are also found in 'public documents' produced by local and central governments. Some administrative records (health, education or pensions) can be classified as either, depending on whether the service is provided by the state or purchased commercially. Governmental documents also include Acts, Regulations, and statements of policy and intent, which are very much in the public domain. Much of their internal paperwork is, however, confidential and may even be restricted under codes of national security. While most people accept that access to their government's data on a citizen's taxation, health and criminal conviction should be restricted, a less convincing case can be made for other information being unavailable. The USA has greater freedom of access than in Britain, where the Public Records Office hoards documents considered to be sensitive (e.g. embarrassing to senior politicians, civil servants, powerful citizens or the Royal Family) for several decades before releasing them in partly censored format.

Our narrow definition excludes several allied objects. Although photographs and other visual formats can be treated as 'documents', they have been omitted because they are considered in **Visual Methods**. Second, official statistical sources like the Census, the prior 'research literature' on any topic, and 'research diaries' produced at the request of researchers, are all omitted, because these are intended to be a resource for researchers. A better term for the first two of these is **Secondary Analysis**.

However, if we were studying, say, the beliefs of the statisticians, we might want to look at such documents as evidence. Davies (1980) shows how nineteenth-century ideas about gender and 'productive labour' shaped the definitions used in the USA and UK population censuses, so marginalising women and distorting measures of economic performance. This example also illustrates how we can take documents at face value, for what they explicitly say (how many women are listed in paid employment in a particular industry), but also 'read between the lines' for a deeper interpretation (*why* is 'paid employment' special; *why* are certain industries grouped together; and *who decided*?). It follows that documentary methods can be qualitative or quantitative (**Qualitative Methods**; **Quantitative Methods**; **Content Analysis**).

An emphasis on interpretation of objects is usually part of wider definitions of documentary methods. Those working in cultural studies use the word 'text' not to mean something written, but any product of human existence, not least fiction and film. Russell and Tyler's study of the retail chain *Girl Heaven*, which targets 3–13 year old girls, explores the construction of femininity by use of 'textual analysis and interpretation . . . focussing on representations of femininity in marketing and sales literature, on the company website and in the stores themselves' (2002: 623–4). Their 'text' is the store, not simply the sales literature. There is nothing inherently wrong in this wider definition, except that it broadens discussion and makes it unmanageable here.

Returning to our narrower view, Scott (1990) shows that there four major questions that should be applied to any set of documents. These concern authenticity; credibility; representativeness; and meaning. 'Authenticity' means that the object is what it claims it is: the famous forgery of the 'Hitler Diaries' shows how academic researchers can be misled. 'Credibility' refers to how far the author is to be believed. Was he or she an eye-witness, or learned something at second-hand? Did the author set down an accurate, or mistaken, or deliberately self-serving version of events (**Auto/biography and Life Histories**)?

Documents are almost inevitably a sub-sample. They may be the chance survivors of all their kind (many letters get destroyed, few survive) or a selection from a wider set that we know little about. Researchers often cannot evaluate how *representative* the studied documents are (see **Sampling: Questions of Size**), and therefore whether generalisations can be drawn from them.

The *meaning* of documents is as complex as the 'meaning' of observed social action and language. Interpretation depends on the cultural context both of the authors and the researchers. Meanings understood and shared by the authors and their original intended readers (technical terms, brief neutral references in place of detailed accounts of controversy, opinions of colleagues, personal goals) often have no need to be stated, let alone spelled out. Can the researcher understand documents' meanings, at both face and interpretive levels? (See also **Content Analysis**.)

Documents should be tested against these four criteria. *Private documents*, e.g. letters and diaries, are usually authentic, except where the author's fame has created a market for memorabilia. Their credibility is less assured: we often hide our feelings and try to create positive impressions. Letters are seldom representative: apart from survival factors, letters for all but an elite only became widely used once there was a postal service. Nowadays, e-mail and mobile phones have largely replaced conventional letters (a problem also increasingly true of private and public transactions, which are becoming hard to trace or produce as evidence in general usage, let alone for research). Meanings depend on the legibility of handwriting (and physical condition in older documents), as well as on subject content. Writers of personal letters often share very high levels of mutual understanding with their intended reader, requiring little explicit statement for them, but creating difficulties of comprehension for researchers.

Private documents from commercial organisations are seldom forged. Their credibility, however is more open to doubt. Their formal documents addressing the outside world are designed to create a positive impression. Even when constrained by business law, professional codes of practice and ethics, some firms' public reports have been misleading, as the case of Enron and similar cases of fraudulent accounting show. The internal operations of companies and public services are supposed to follow their manuals and documents giving procedural guidelines. However employees in all such organisations are also motivated by their own priorities, like their career goals, hiding their mistakes, or struggling to get their own way over policies. There is a marked difference between the abstract rules set out in the documents and what in fact takes place 'on the ground'. Where a document like an annual report is in the public domain, it is possible to evaluate its representativeness (is the sampled report typical of other years?). Internal documentation is harder to judge: how can researchers from outside know what documents existed? Did someone in the company pre-select the documents (perhaps via the company archive) released to researchers? Finally, the meaning of documents will depend on understanding their formal business or organisational cultural content, as well as the internal dynamics of the organisation's members.

There have been a few high-profile cases of inauthentic public documents: Chamberlain's 'Peace in Our Time' blank sheet of paper purporting to be a signed agreement with Hitler, and much of the documentary 'evidence' used to justify America and Britain's invasion of oil-rich Iraq in 2003. Most tends to be genuine. However, governance is a field of competition between interest groups, and the ethical standards of politicians are notoriously low. The credibility of public documents is extremely limited, unless the authors believed that nobody outside of their charmed circle would see what they had written. Of course, this lack of credibility can itself be the subject of research. Again, representativeness depends on which documents we are discussing: documents for publication can be assessed as a sample, but internal documents cannot. Sometimes the interest in a document is precisely because it is unique, dealing with what can be regarded as a case study (**Case Study**). The fact that some documents may be inconsistent with others can also be a focus of investigation. By contrast, the meaning of documents, except for some of the complex legal language, is usually fairly clear.

The limitations of documentary methods can be summarised as the failure to meet the four criteria: authenticity, credibility, representativeness and meaning. Such potential failures can only be judged for each document on its own merits. In addition, there can be more general difficulties of access, poor cataloguing, and of current documents of record not being up-to-date. Writing about extensive written documents is also hard to do, due to the confines of space, so that an additional layer of selectivity necessarily occurs.

Against this, documents can give access to the past (indeed they may be the only method available) and are relatively cheap and quick to process. Their physical existence allows other researchers to cross-check findings (although this happens rarely in sociology). Unlike people, documents do not react to being studied. Moreover, in dealing with naturally occurring objects, documentary methods are less open to charges of bias on the part of the researcher. They can be applied to many topics, and a number of well-known studies have made use of them (e.g. Olzaket et al. 1996; Sampson and Laub 1993). When documents do meet the four criteria and are handled sensitively, they are an important social science resource.

Key Words

authenticity
credibility
meaning
personal documents
private documents
public documents
representativeness
text

Links

Auto/biography and Life Histories
Case Study
Content Analysis
Qualitative Methods
Quantitative Methods
Sampling: Questions of Size
Secondary Analysis
Unobtrusive Methods and Triangulation
Visual Methods

REFERENCES

General

Scott, J. (1990) *A Matter of Record*. London: Polity Press.

Examples

Abraham, J. and Lewis, G. (2002) 'Citizenship, Medical Expertise and the Capitalist Regulatory State in Europe'. *Sociology*, 36 (1): 67–88.

Davies, C. (1980) 'Making Sense of the Census in Britain and the USA'. *Sociological Review*, 28 (3): 581–609.
Olzak, S., Shanahan, S. and McEneaney, E. (1996) 'Poverty, Segregation, and Race Riots: 1960 to 1993'. *American Sociological Review*, 61 (4): 590–613.
Platt, J. (2003) *The British Sociological Association: a Sociological History*. Durham: Sociology Press.
Russell, R. and Tyler, M. (2002) 'Thank Heaven for Little Girls'. *Sociology*, 36 (3): 619–37.
Sampson, R. and Laub, J. (1993) 'Structural Variation in Juvenile Court Processing'. *Law and Society Review*, 22 (2): 285–311.
Seale, C. (2001) 'Sporting Cancer: Struggle Language in News Reports of People with Cancer'. *Sociology of Health and Illness*, 23 (3): 308–29.

Ethical Practice

Ethical practice is a moral stance that involves conducting research to achieve not just high professional standards of technical procedures, but also respect and protection for the people actively consenting to be studied.

Section Outline: *Ethical practice as key moral and professional stance. Honesty and confidence in 'scientific' knowledge. Pressure to cut corners. Falsification of evidence. Funding agencies: who controls the findings? Obligations to informants. The BSA Statement of Ethical Practice. Informed consent; anonymity; protection from harm. Consent and covert research. Unobtrusive observation versus collaborative working with informants. Ethics as principles that try to cover practical dilemmas.*

Ethical practice is not an add-on to social research but lies at its very heart. Ethical conduct provides the basis which legitimates the whole enterprise; it permeates research design and project organisation; and extends to minute and momentary decisions, like politeness to informants during fieldwork. Even the decision to do research is based on an ethical judgement that the project is worthwhile and (usually) deserving of public funding (Gorard 2003). The dilemma of what is morally correct, and what is merely expedient is never far away, and is often experienced intensely and uncomfortably by researchers.

Physical and social scientists work on the day-to-day assumption that other scientists behave *honestly*. They are not inventing data, lying about the success of their methods, suppressing findings or selectively reporting only those parts that support their particular theoretical position. Unless this state of affairs prevails, we cannot rely on our discipline's stocks of knowledge – in which case, the collective enterprise of research collapses.

It is hard to convey to those outside of research the horror of discovering scientific dishonesty. The discovery that the psychological work by Burt (central to the shaping the secondary school system in post-war Britain: see Shipman 1997) was unreliable came as much of a shock to other disciplines as to psychologists (see **Bias**). If we cannot trust ourselves, why should the wider public trust our claims to valuable knowledge? Despite what the sociology of science has shown about how researchers actually behave, researchers have to retain faith in good academic practice because the alternative is so unacceptable.

This requirement for proper conduct in the production of knowledge does *not* mean that what is published should be regarded as absolute 'truth'. The rest of this volume demonstrates many ways in which data collection or analysis mistakes can happen. 'Findings' are not self-evident: it is entirely legitimate to debate the strength of evidence (**Validity** and **Reliability**), or its interpretation.

The fact that professional debate depends on a fundamental ethical requirement for honesty in research practice may seem obvious, but it has come under increasing pressure in recent years. Research funders often want not just results on a tight schedule, but findings that support their political or commercial view. Senior university personnel are keen for their staff to produce the good publicity (and royalty earnings) that new discoveries bring. Individual careers depend on publishing research papers. A number of natural science 'discoveries' have been discredited because preliminary findings were publicised before sufficient work had been completed to substantiate them. There are regular cases of academic journals retracting papers because of doubts about authenticity.

Indeed, on the day this section was being written, newspapers reported that Imperial College (one of the leading British higher education institutions) was investigating the withdrawal of a paper by the prestigious *New England Journal of Medicine* because one of the authors had admitted forging the agreement of his joint authors with its findings (*The Guardian* 2003). A couple of weeks earlier, both the US President and the British Prime Minister had backed an intelligence report, parts of which turned out to be plagiarised from a student dissertation. There were even allegations that key phrases had been 'doctored' to provide a justification for the Iraq war. Politicians' credibility is notoriously low, but social science depends on its practitioners telling the truth.

Doing that is not straightforward. Sponsors increasingly control findings, with rights to publish being withheld (e.g. **Evaluation Studies**). Government departments argue that they are entitled to decide the timing of reports and to handle publicity. Politically unwelcome results may be delayed until no longer relevant, or released quietly over holidays, to pass unnoticed by press and opposition politicians. Should researchers accept contracts that restrict publication rights, or not do the research? Should they comply with such contracts if 'unfairly' enforced, or 'leak' their results? Ethical dilemmas surround us. Our judgement of what is right or wrong may even change during our research (Collins 1984; Pring 2000).

Researchers also have obligations to their informants, which are every bit as important as their obligations to their funders. As the British Sociological Association's *Statement of Ethical Practice* notes (drawing on the ethical codes of the American Sociological Association, and several other bodies: ASA 1997; BPS 2000; SRA 2002), advancement of knowledge

> does not, of itself, provide an entitlement to override the rights of others . . . Sociologists have a responsibility to ensure that the physical, social and psychological well-being of research participants is not adversely affected by the research. They should strive to protect the rights of those they study, their interests, sensitivities and privacy (BSA 2002: 2).

This involves three key elements. First, potential informants should, as far as possible, be enabled freely to give their *informed consent* to participate, and advised that they can *terminate their involvement for any reason*, at any time. Informed consent

> implies a responsibility on the sociologists to explain as fully as possible, and in terms meaningful to participants, what the research is about, who is undertaking and financing it, why it is being undertaken, and how it is to be promoted (ibid.: 3).

Second, *informants' identities should be protected* by making them anonymous in published reports. This extends beyond simply changing names, because in some settings, identities could still be recognised from roles played, when events took place, or other contextual clues. Informants should also be assured that any records of their actions or words will remain confidential, seen only by the researchers, and most definitely not reported to other participants in the research setting. Together these make up the third element, that no *harm is done to informants*.

It is one thing to set these outlines, but another to implement them rigorously. Ethical practice applies at all times, and not just in extreme cases of resistant groups or causing physical harm to people (see Bryman 2001: 475–86 for examples). Informants may not fully comprehend what the research entails: one of the authors found 'sociology' was a closed world to certain informants, but they were comfortable with the idea of 'a kind of history of today's happenings'. Explaining about the research takes up time that could be used *doing* the research, time that may be valuable to the informant. Protecting anonymity is challenging when what would otherwise be valuable evidence has to be discarded. Does each person playing a part in a public meeting have to give informed consent, or is their public presence sufficient in itself? Can promises of confidentiality be kept, when research data 'may be liable to subpoena by a court' (ibid.)? Should a student engaged in learning how to do research be turned loose on an unsuspecting public? These are all examples where a balance between principle and expediency must be struck, and re-struck.

Some research can only be done by subterfuge, i.e. 'covert' research into groups who resent being studied, but whose study is in the public interest (e.g. fascists, criminals, religious extremists). Such research involves substantial deception (Festinger et al. 1956). It should only be undertaken after due consideration, and not confused with expediency or morbid curiosity. It clearly breaches the principles of informed consent (Herrera 1999).

This overlaps with some participant observation (**Participant Observation**), where it is normally argued that researchers may legitimately remain unobtrusive by adopting roles that are part of the research setting. Here and in similar cases (**Unobtrusive Methods and Triangulation**), if informed consent has not been obtained beforehand because it would clearly disrupt the behaviour under study, it should be obtained at the end of the fieldwork. However, some advocates of feminist methods (see **Feminist Research**) have criticised this stance as an abuse of power by the researcher. In their view, research should be a collaborative enterprise in which informants are enabled to participate and indeed expand the terms of the project. It follows that anything less than this would be unethical. Their criticisms have also been instrumental in including working relationships with colleagues within the ethics debate. Other areas where special issues of ethical practice arise include **Action Research**; **Ethnography**; **Experiments**; **Internet Polling**; **Interviewing**; **Observation**; **Secondary Analysis**; and **Visual Methods.**

Research studies often brings the sociologist into the domain of other disciplines, where alternative ethical frameworks operate (Spallone et al. 2000). The complexity of ethical practice and the diversity of research styles and settings, explain why universities have 'Ethics' or 'Human Subjects' Committees to vet new research proposals. Most social science departments extend this vetting to undergraduate dissertation research. For the same reasons, the British Sociological Association has a 'Statement' rather than rules, whose strength and binding force 'rest ultimately on active discussion, reflection, and continued use by sociologists'. It is not 'a set of recipes' but of *principles*: 'departures from the principles should be the result of deliberation and not ignorance' (BSA 2002: 1). Student projects can usually obtain ethical clearance by undertaking to abide by the BSA Outline.

Key Words

anonymity
confidentiality
covert
ethics committee
expediency
informed consent

Links

Action Research
Bias
Ethnography
Evaluation Studies
Experiments
Feminist Research
Internet Polling
Interviewing
Observation
Participant Observation
Reliability
Secondary Analysis
Unobtrusive Methods and Triangulation
Validity
Visual Methods

REFERENCES

General

Bryman, A. (2001) *Social Research Methods.* Oxford: Oxford University Press.
Gorard, S. (2003) *The Role of Numbers in Social Science Research*. London: Continuum.
Herrera, C. (1999) 'Two Arguments for "Covert Methods" in Social Research'. *British Journal of Sociology* 50 (2): 331–43.
Pring, R. (200) *Philosophy of Educational Research*. London: Continuum.

Examples

American Sociological Association (ASA) (1997) *Code of Ethics.* www.asanet.org/members/ecointro.html

British Psychological Society (BPS) (2000) *Code of Conduct, Ethical Principles, and Guidelines.* www.bps.org.uk

British Sociological Association (2002) *Statement of Ethical Practice.* www.britsoc.co.uk?index.php?link_id=14&area=item1

Collins, H. (1984) 'Researching Spoonbending'. In Bell, C. and Roberts, H. (eds), *Social Researching.* London: Routledge & Kegan Paul.

Festinger, L., Rieken, H. and Schachter, S. (1956) *When Prophecy Fails.* New York: Harper.

Finch, J. (1984) '"It's Great to Have Someone to Talk to": the Ethics and Politics of Interviewing Women'. In Bell, C. and Roberts, H. (eds) *Social Researching.* London: Routledge & Kegan Paul.

Guardian (2003) 'Research News', *Guardian Education,* 18 Feb. 2003: 11. www.educationguardian.co.uk/higher/research

Shipman, M. (1997) *The Limitations of Social Research.* Harlow: Addison Wesley Longman.

Social Research Association (SRA) (2002) *Ethical Guidelines.* www.the-srs.org/Ethicals.html

Spallone, P., Wilkes, T., Ettorre, E., Haimes, C., Shakespeare, T. and Stacy, M. (2000) 'Putting Sociology on the Bioethics Map'. In Eldridge, J., MacInnes, J., Scott, S., Warhurst, C. and Witz, A. (eds) *For Sociology: Legacies and Practices.* Durham: sociologypress.

Ethnography

Ethnography is the production of highly detailed accounts of how people in a social setting lead their lives, based on systematic and long-term observation of, and conversations with, informants.

Section Outline: *Anthropological origins of ethnography. The Chicago School: direct experience versus book learning. British documentaries. From description to interpretation. Detailed accounts of prolonged, systematic, first-hand encounters. Reflexivity. Natural occurrences, seen in context. Learning participant observation. Gaining access to different groups.*

Ethnography began in the early twentieth century when social anthropology first directly studied societies other than their own. Given the dominance of evolutionary thinking in that period, tribal societies were seen as surviving examples of how humans had lived before advanced technology. Anthropologists documented already disappearing lifestyles, as systems of cultural beliefs, detailed daily practices and artefacts. Every aspect of the lives of peoples living in small-scale, agricultural, largely non-literate, 'simple' societies were fascinating in their own right. However, research could not rely on 'travellers' tales', which treated 'primitive' peoples like exotic plants or animal. It entailed *living among*, and *directly observing over a period of time*, the people in question.

Anthropology was an alternative to archaeology and history, and infinitely better than speculative armchair theorising. Simple societies' small size made them easier to study than vast nations: they could be studied as a whole by one person. They were treated as miniature versions of societies through which debates about basic sociological processes – for example, how is social order maintained – could be investigated. Additionally, these societies presented difficulties for colonial rule because they operated by principles alien to their conquerors. Even racist colonial administrators, and land speculators who despised 'the natives', initially tolerated the anthropologists as possible sources of assistance. Later, anthropologists who 'crossed the colour bar' were less welcome, but this did not subsequently endear them to emerging post-colonial regimes, who saw them as spies.

Although ethnography's 'anthropological heritage' is conventionally traced to Malinowski, Radcliffe-Brown and Boas, there were other sources of inspiration (Payne et al. 1981: 87–115). In America, the world's first Department of Sociology at the University of Chicago was founded in 1892 by Albion Small. His influence created the 'Chicago School', dedicated to the principle that 'the first thing that students of sociology should learn is to observe and record their own observations' (Park and Burgess 1921: v), and which produced ground-breaking studies of slum life: immigrants, gangs, opium-addicts and hoboes. In Britain, early social reformers like Beatrice Webb called for 'deliberate and sustained personal observation' of social institutions (quoted in Payne et al. 1981: 87). The national network of volunteer observers, Mass-Observation, was founded in 1937 by two social scientists, Madge and Harrisson (and the film-maker, Jennings). In the post-war period, the ethnographic tradition was taken up by researchers of local communities (**Community Studies**), factories, and later, deviancy and the position of women (**Feminist Research**). Today, in its various guises within qualitative research, it is strongly represented in the social sciences and is even possibly the dominant method in British sociology.

With such a history, it is not surprising that different traditions have emerged within ethnography. Both the methods of the simpler, highly *descriptive* approach of the early anthropologists, and the name for an account produced by these methods, are referred to as 'ethnography': the scientific study of peoples (i.e. their culture and behaviour). Later work has placed more emphasis on *interpretations* of such descriptive accounts, which is sometimes called *ethnology*. 'Critical ethnology' addresses the unmasking of power structures, seeking to empower and emancipate. Whereas traditionally ethnography recorded life in great detail as a **Case Study** in its own right, contemporary researchers use ethnographic data as evidence in developing theoretical ideas (e.g. Punch 2003).

Despite these orientations, there are strong common threads to ethnographic practice. Unlike the brief encounters of social surveys, it involves a *prolonged*, *systematic*, *first hand* and *direct encounter* with the people concerned, as they act out their lives in a range of interactional contexts (**Qualitative Methods**; **Quantitative Methods**). Because this involves close personal contact and intense experiences, ethnographers must take account of their own reactions, which become part of the research itself. A premium is placed on the researcher's **Reflexivity**. Understanding what is happening across the range of contexts means seeing each specific element of social action as part of a greater unity: i.e. taking a *holistic view*.

The ethnographer accepts the legitimacy of what is encountered, and tries first to understand it on its own terms. This means looking at what happens as it *naturally occurs* in its own setting, and trying to see it through the eyes of the participants. The ethnographer is therefore a learner among the more knowledgeable, and should tackle the research project with the humility appropriate to being in an inferior position to those being researched. The researcher must also convey that new learning in their accounts (Hammersley 1998).

The method of choice for ethnography is **Participant Observation**. Entry into, and involvement in, the chosen social setting is eased by the researcher adopting a role that is naturally part of that setting, facilitating observation. (How open researchers are about their real intentions is an ethical issue; **Ethical Practice**). Ethnographical 'observation' and 'participation' are normally used alongside other methods: asking questions, long interviews and background documentary methods (**Documentary Methods**).

Ethnography's emphasis on taking part, and taking it as it comes, makes it sound fairly easy. It was conventional in the 1980s to claim that ethnography could not be taught: expertise could only be acquired by *doing* it. Certainly many untrained postgraduates had to learn the hard way, a tradition that may be attributed to social anthropology. Evans-Pritchard, recalling the time before he was a leading anthropologist, when the discipline was very male-oriented, reported how he tried 'to get a few tips from experienced fieldworkers':

> I first sought advice from Westermarck. All I got from him was 'don't converse with an informant for more than twenty minutes because if you aren't bored by that time he will be' . . . [Haddon] told me that it was all quite simple: one should always behave like a gentleman. Also very good advice. My teacher Seligman told me to take ten grains of quinine every night and to keep off the women. The famous Egyptologist, Sir Flinders Petrie, just told me not to bother about drinking dirty water as one soon became immune to it. Finally I asked Malinowski and was told not to be a bloody fool (Evans-Pritchard 1973: 1).

However straightforward ethnography may sound, it does present several problems. Gaining initial access is rarely easy (**Fieldwork**; **Key Informants**), while recording what takes place is a constant problem (**Observation**; **Participant Observation**; **Coding Qualitative Data**). It also entails, as we have seen, committing at least implicitly to a fairly sophisticated theoretical orientation about what should be studied, and how (e.g. **Grounded Theory**). Earlier contributors have sometimes played this down: Howard Becker, when asked about theoretical frameworks, replied 'What do you want to worry about that for – You just go out there and do it'. (Payne et al. 1981: 114).

Despite Becker's disparagement, 'doing it' is not that easy. Because the enterprise rides on the quality of interaction between researcher and informants, the personality and social skills of the ethnographer are at a premium. Not all sociologists are naturally suited to this method, although one seldom finds sociologists who seriously ask themselves about their own suitability. Even conversational facility, let alone expertise in slang phraseology, dialect or the local language, are rarely discussed in research reports.

There is also often an over-confidence about the extent to which the researcher has actually been accepted, gained entry to social groups, and understood their cultural meanings (**Community Studies**). The single-handed researcher cannot cover all relevant physical settings at once, at all hours of the day and night. Even if this were possible, some sub-settings will remain closed. Young males are unwelcome among mothers and toddlers (**Feminist Research**); women are 'bad luck on boats'; whites are not in the best position to investigate ethnic minority groups; and middle-class sociologists are not best able to empathise with the lives of either elites or the socially excluded.

Key Words

critical ethnolog
holistic view
naturally occurring
reflexivity
simple societies

Links

Case Study
Coding Qualitative Data
Community Studies
Documentary Methods
Ethnical Practice
Feminist Research
Fieldwork
Grounded Theory
Key Informants
Observation
Participant Observation
Qualitative Methods
Quantitative Methods
Reflexivity

REFERENCES

General

Evans-Pritchard, E. (1973) 'Some Reminiscences and Reflections on Fieldwork'. *Journal of the Anthropological Society of Oxford*, 4 (1): 1–12.

Hammersley, M. (1998) *Reading Ethnographic Research* (2nd edn). Harlow: Addison Wesley Longman.

Park, R. and Burgess, E. (1921) *Introduction to the Science of Sociology*. Chicago: University of Chicago Press.

Payne, G., Dingwall, R., Payne, J. and Carter, M. (1981) *Sociology and Social Research*. London: Routledge & Kegan Paul.

Examples

Allen, C. (2003) 'On the Logic of the "New" Welfare Practice: an Ethnographic Case Study of the "New" Welfare Intermediaries', *Sociological Research Online* 8 (1): www.socresonline.org.uk/socresonline/8/1/allen.html

Punch, S. (2003) 'Childhoods in the Majority World'. *Sociology*, 37 (2): 277–95.

Ethnomethodology and Conversational Analysis

Ethnomethodology and conversational analysis are schools of sociology which focus on the mechanisms by which people use commonsense knowledge in structuring their day-to-day encounters to construct shared meanings and social order from their conversations and interactions.

Section Outline: *Ethnomethodology and ethnography. Interaction: what we bring to it and how we make sense of the world. Origins of ethnomethodology in Husserl and Schutz's phenomenology and collective typifications. Garfinkel: commonsense and making sense of experiences. Reflexivity. Breaching experiments. Conversational analysis. Rigorous analysis of natural talk. Ethnomethodological ethnography: Cicourel. Examples: train drivers; text of talking about ill health.*

We have included ethnomethodology as a key concept, although it is not a research method in itself. However, it is an important sub-field of sociology, with a research style that students sometimes find difficult to distinguish from other qualitative approaches, notably ethnography (**Ethnography**). Despite these genuinely confusing similarities, ethnomethodology does have some of its own particular methods. It also illustrates how social research techniques depend upon theoretical approaches: i.e. how *methods* sit within a framework of *methodology*. What ethnomethodologists study, and how they study it, is integral to their philosophical view of the social world (see Heritage 1984).

The first step in understanding ethnomethodology is recognising that sociologists choose to study different parts of human existence. Some are interested in big public issues like war, class or poverty, which seem to exist outside of individual control. Other sociologists are concerned with such issues only as they impinge on the person through individual experience and sense of identity (e.g. ethnicity, sexuality, disability). Others focus on how people are able to act socially on a day-to-day basis: i.e. on the details of the social interactions through which we communicate with each other. This group includes the ethnomethodologists. Sadly, there is little positive communication between these orientations.

Ethnomethodology and 'conversational analysis' argue that we do not live in a fixed social world which determines exactly how we behave. Rather, each brings a personal set of previous social experiences and cultural knowledge to their interactions with others. Interactions are processes of exploration and negotiation, through which people actively (but often unconsciously) make sense of their experiences. This does not imply that there is absolutely no social order, but rather that individuals deploy their 'personal baggage' of skills to cope with the processes of exploration and understanding without which social life would be impossible. These processes fascinate ethnomethodologists, drawing them towards particular types of social research appropriate to the topics they wish to investigate.

The origin of this view lies in Husserl's philosophical writing. He argued that rather than directly connecting with the world, the human mind first processes the raw data collected by our physical senses, and then builds an interpretation of this information, using prior knowledge (see also **Positivism and Realism**). Without this interpretation process based on concepts about what things are, we cannot comprehend the world. For instance, if you had never encountered a car, how would you know its function? But if you were familiar with horse and carts, it might help: in the early day, cars were called 'horseless carriages'.

Schutz adapted this 'phenomenological' school for sociology, stressing that interpretations are not unique to each person, but dependent on shared, collective categories (called 'typifications'). Different groups do not share exactly the same sets of 'commonsense knowledge'. However, people can only communicate by starting from the assumption that they do share meanings, and then negotiating at least a semblance of agreed mutual comprehension.

During the 1960s and 1970s, this developed into 'ethnomethodology'. Garfinkel (1967) portrays individuals (or 'members') as being themselves social researchers, using their own naturally occurring commonsense knowledge to make sense of a chaotic world. In a similar way, academic social researchers apply more technical and specialist methods of investigation. Hence 'ethnomethodology': from 'ethno' suggesting something pertaining to people (the same root as 'ethnic'), and 'methodology', meaning the process members use in making sense. Ethnomethodology is the *study* of these folk methods, rather than a method per se. Members isolate patterns, try to explain social life through them, and the more this succeeds, the more this reinforces their belief in the validity of those patterns. Garfinkel gives a special meaning to the term 'reflexivity' to describe this.

There are several consequences for ethnomethodological research. Best known are Garfinkel's 'breaching experiments', in which he asked his students to act in unconventional ways in conventional situations. If someone wished them to 'Have a nice day', they queried in what ways 'nice', and was that for 24 hours, or just in daylight? They acted as lodgers in their parental homes. The frustration and quick anger this caused demonstrated the importance of commonsense meanings. A general, if dangerous, implication of this for social researchers is that we can clarify what is 'normal' behaviour by experimentally flouting what we suspect is a convention. Note that 'breaching' involves role-playing and no informed consent by the 'victims' (**Ethical Practice**).

Ethnomethodology focuses on the intricate detail of social life and communication. Sacks promoted one branch of ethnomethodology, 'conversational analysis' (indeed, some sociologists would argue that 'CA' is more important than ethnomethodology: e.g. Seale (1999: 150–3). Here, a small number of texts of naturally occurring talk were transcribed from audio-recordings (and more recently video-recordings) and then analysed in very great detail. The search was for patterns contained in talk, treated as organised sequentially, and in specific situations (e.g. a phone call offering an invitation). The social situation, often limited to the immediately preceding sequence of talk, is very important as it contributes to the particular meanings at work. Although the conversations were 'natural', their treatment was rigorous, technical and capable of replication (**Reliability**; **Validity**). Figure 4 is an example of the coding conventions used, adapted from Silverman (1997: 118).

Influenced by Cicourel (1968) and Winch (1958) a second, less specialised branch achieved a larger following. Drawing on ethnography (**Ethnography**), there is less emphasis on detailed analysis of talk, and more on what is observed and the social context of small-scale interactions. However, commitment is maintained to the view that social order is not pre-ordained. Equally, 'natural' behaviour is treated as patterned, consisting of attempts to make sense and build shared meanings that underpin the social world – meanings which cannot casually be attributed by social researchers. Particularly in more recent 'applied' studies of organisations and professions, it is genuinely difficult to differentiate between ethnomethodology and ethnography.

A good example is a study of drivers on the London Underground:

> Whilst primarily ethnographic, the paper draws on ethnomethodology and conversation analysis and their analytic concern with the occasioned production of normal scenes and appearances, and the methods in and through which such activities are accomplished and rendered intelligible (cf. Garfinkel 1967; Sachs 1972, 1992). In the case in hand, we are particularly interested in the ways in which drivers make sense of the conduct of colleagues and passengers . . . Whilst such assessment and discriminations are thoroughly embedded in the activities in which drivers engaged, or which they will have to undertake, they do provide the sociologist with interesting insights into [the drivers'] practical commonsense and organisational reasoning (Heath et al. 1999: 558–9).

This clearly goes beyond the narrower remit of conversational analysis, but how far cases like this represent a significantly different social research method from ethnography is a moot point.

H: And we were *w*ondering if there's *a*nything we can do to
help
S: [Well 'at's
H: [I mean can we do any shopping for her or something
like that:t?
(0.7)
S: Well that's *most* *k*i:nd Heatherton .hhh At the moment
no:. because we've still got two bo:ys at home

Selected transcription codings

Italics	shows emphasis in the speaker's s talk (sometimes underlining used)
[	left square bracket marks overlapping speaking
:	in a word, the word part before the colon was prolonged
(0.7)	a silence in tenths of a second. 0.7 means seven-tenths of a second
.hhh	in-breath, the more hh the longer (note dot before the hhh)
hhh	out-breath (no dot before the hhh)
.	dot signifies a very small pause of not more than one tenth of a second

Figure 4 *An example of coding conventions in CA. H talks with S, whose wife has a slipped disc*

Key Words

breaching experiments
coding
conversational analysis
phenomenology
reflexivity
typification

Links

Ethical Practice
Ethnography
Positivism and Realism
Reliability
Validity

REFERENCES

General

Cicourel, A. (1968) *Method and Measurement in Sociology*. New York: Free Press.
Garfinkel, H. (1967) *Studies in Ethnomethodology*. Englewood Cliffs, NJ: Prentice-Hall.
Heritage, J. (1984) *Garfinkel and Ethnomethodology*. Cambridge: Polity Press.
Sachs, H. (1992) *Lectures in Conversation: Volumes I and II*. Oxford: Blackwell.
Seale, C. (1999) *The Quality of Qualitative Research*. London: Sage.
Silverman, D. (1997) *Interpreting Qualitative Data*. London: Sage.
Winch, P. (1958) *The Idea of a Social Science and its Relationship to Philosophy*. London: Routledge & Kegan Paul.

Examples

Heath, C., Hindmarsh, J. and Luff, P. (1999) 'Interaction in Isolation'. *Sociology*, 33 (3): 555–75.
Sachs, H. (1972) 'Notes on the Police Assessment of Moral Character'. In Sudnow, D. (ed.), *Studies in Social Interaction*. New York: Free Press.

Evaluation Studies

Evaluation studies assess the processes and consequences of innovations in social policy or organisations.

Section Outline: *Evaluation studies as applied social research. Measuring and explaining social change. Problems with 'external' evaluators. Programme specifications driven by evaluation: 'measurable outcomes'. Focusing on 'process' or 'outcome'? Working with evaluatees. Evaluating programmes: who is involved; how are they involved; did it work? Power and politics in evaluation. Example: the Health Education Authority.*

Evaluative research is undertaken to assess the *worth* or *success* of something: a programme, a policy or a project. Social evaluation is not a method or technique like social surveys or participant observation. It is a particular and increasingly common type of applied social research which might employ any of the other research methods discussed in this book. What distinguishes it is its purpose: its action orientation to support or introduce change (Clarke and Dawson 1999).

Evaluation studies focus on measurements (numeric or descriptive, but usually the former) of social inputs, outputs and processes: it typically studies *change*. At their most basic, evaluations replicate classic scientific experimental methods (**Experiments**). Thus observations of people are made before and after something is done to them, and the two observations are compared. If there are differences in the observations, this is likely to be attributed to what was done. However, human behaviour involves more factors than can easily be controlled in a laboratory experiment. Was it the intervention or some other factor that produced the observed differences? Few evaluations include a 'control group' and this can weaken their credibility.

Evaluation has become a frequent element of large funded projects. This is part of a general trend towards accountability and measurement of performance in social policy, as well as in public and voluntary sector work. Evaluation may be controlled by a national team where there is a series of local projects (the Health Action Zones, for example) or by a locally recruited team. External researchers start with the handicap of little local knowledge, whereas local researchers may have prior loyalties. Either way, evaluators have conventionally remained independent and separate from the main project.

This can lead to two main sorts of difficulty. Evaluation may start too late to see the 'before' situation and be rushed because of the overall schedule. Second, many project leaders resent being assessed by these 'outsiders' who have a different set of values – a 'scientific' frame of reference rather than a sense of identity with the local community, for instance (**Action Research**).

Increasingly, government and charities invite those bidding for funds to specify planned outcomes in terms of concrete results. For example, a programme to 'reduce juvenile crime' might specify that (a) the number of secondary school pupils arrested by the police would be reduced by 25 per cent; and (b) that the annual number of crimes committed in the locality would be halved over two years. Such detailed specifications reduce the room to manoeuvre for those attempting to implement changes, who might legitimately believe that the project's general aims would be better achieved in some other way more suited to their local conditions, or over a different timescale.

Even where no 'measurable outcomes' are pre-specified, there is a strong organisational impetus towards measurable outputs. Suppose that a programme is started to improve educational standards. Teaching staff and administrators may decide to define this in terms of exam success (which is *easy to measure*, say in terms of number of graduates, or pass levels per student), rather than in less tangible terms – quality of class experience, personal development or transferable skills. Effort is then re-directed to achieving performance for the *tests*, regardless of the original aims.

This capacity of evaluation studies to distort local conditions is due to the importance attached to inputs and measurable outputs. Critics of this approach, for instance in community-based evaluations, argue that research should evaluate *processes* rather than, or in addition to, outputs since

> the intervention is not sharply defined, takes different forms in different contexts and cannot be reduced to discrete components. It may not always be possible or relevant to make distinctions between cause and effect. The important questions are rather, what sort of actions, in what sort of circumstances are effective (Curtice 1993: 37).

Thus many of the more recent evaluations of community-based health promotion have concentrated on the processes involved in instituting change; seeing evaluation as an on-going practice. For example, the initial evaluation of the Drumchapel health project in Glasgow began during the first year of the project. This evaluation focused on specific areas of the project and investigated paid staff, volunteers and residents. Thus, the Drumchapel evaluator negotiated about what and how to investigate with members of the project (McGhee and McEwen 1993).

In this approach evaluators play an active and collaborative role with the sponsors and main players (stakeholders). Evaluators should

> neither assume that stakeholders should act as 'respondents' providing answers to the predetermined questions of the researcher, nor assume that their task is the 'faithful' reproduction of the privileged views of the stakeholder . . . The research act thus involves 'learning' the stakeholders' theories, formalizing them, 'teaching' them back to the informant, who is then in a position to comment upon, clarify and further refine key ideas (Pawson and Tilley 1997: 218).

Equipped with these sociological insights, closer collaboration at the start of a project need not result in the evaluators losing their sense of perspective. House and Howe (1999: xxi) argued that evaluators 'must be savvy negotiators, willing to engage in compromise, but they must place limits on how far compromise can go'. What they take as 'fact', as distinct from 'value', depends on strict adherence to methodological convention.

Effective evaluation is thus concerned with social perspective and action, not just output. It should ask about

- *Numbers:* How much has been done? How many people are involved?
- *Processes:* What is the nature of the activities? How have people been involved?
- *Outcomes:* Has it worked? (after Laughlin and Black 1995: 142)

These questions can then be elaborated into a topic list, as for other types of research, and an appropriate method or group of methods selected.

Such processual, collaborative evaluations raise questions about information provision. In traditional evaluations, outside researchers were usually commissioned to undertake investigations and report to sponsors. The project and those working on it – and those being 'acted' upon – were the subjects of the evaluation. They had no influence on the report or subsequent actions. Collaborative evaluation, on the other hand, seeks to involve all participants equally; with sponsors, project workers and the public having access to the resulting information. This approach is better **Ethical Practice**, but can lead to problems, particularly in relation to control by sponsors.

Evaluations may even be halted and reports suppressed by sponsors. One Open University team was commissioned by the Health Education Authority to undertake an evaluation of community development as a method in health promotion. However, the areas investigated, staff involvement and the proposed dissemination of the report seem to have gone beyond what the sponsors originally envisaged:

> The HEA . . . did not seem to regard the participation of its staff, procedures, culture and policies as relevant topics of research . . . [T]he intention was always that the review outcomes should be fed back to all the people that participated . . . [T]o date the document . . . remains unpublished (Smithies and Adams 1993: 66–8).

The above example of things going wrong in evaluative research is not unique. Policy-related research, by definition, has a political dimension and is often, therefore, problematic. This does not apply solely to work related to governmental agencies (**Official Statistics**) or national studies: locally recruited researchers are more exposed to local political pressures because of their place in competing power networks. Even universities have to live in peace with their home towns. One of the present authors was angrily berated by their Vice-Chancellor for studying local unemployment, because 'there is no problem – everybody *I* talk to locally says it's only lazy people who don't have jobs!' In evaluative research, such problems are compounded by the number of interest groups involved (evaluated) and disagreements about ownership of the resulting knowledge.

Key Words

collaborative evaluation
measurable outcomes
processual evaluation
social inputs and outputs
stakeholders

Links

Action Research
Ethical Practice
Experiments
Official Statistics

REFERENCES

General

Clarke, A. and Dawson, R. (1999) *Evaluation Research*. London: Sage.
House, E. and Howe, K. (1999) *Values in Evaluation and Social Research*. London: Sage.
Pawson, R. and Tilley, N. (1997) *Realistic Evaluation*. London: Sage.

Examples

Curtice, L. (1993) 'The WHO Healthy Cities Project in Europe'. In Davies, J. and Kelly, M. (eds), *Healthy Cities: Research and Practice*. London: Routledge.
Laughlin, S. and Black, D. (eds) (1995) *Poverty and Health: Tools for Change*. Birmingham: Public Health Alliance.
McGhee, J. and McEwen, J. (1993) 'Evaluating the Healthy Cities Project in Drumchapel, Glasgow'. In Davies, J. and Kelly, M. (eds), *Healthy Cities: Research and Practice*. London: Routledge.
Smithies, J. and Adams, L. (1993) 'Walking the Tightrope: Issues in Evaluation and Community Participation for Health for All'. In Davies, J. and Kelly, M. (eds), *Healthy Cities: Research and Practice*. London: Routledge.

Experiments

Experiments are ways of assessing causal relationships, by randomly allocating 'subjects' to two groups and then comparing one (the 'control group') in which no changes are made, with the other (the 'test group') who are subjected to some manipulation or stimulus.

Section Outline: *Laboratory experiments. OXO. Randomised controlled trials. Experiment and control groups; matched pairs; closure. Social life not reducible to laboratory conditions. Extraneous social factors. Informed consent and prior approval create Hawthorne Effect. Quasi-experimental designs: comparison and post hoc matching. Cross-sectional designs and social change. Quantitative tradition.*

Anybody who has done secondary school science will be familiar with laboratory experiments. Physical substances are subjected to some kind of stimulus (chemicals are heated or mixed with other chemicals; electrical currents are applied to wires; plants are given varying amounts of water or light, etc.). A change is predicted and (usually) found, the change being interpreted as caused by the stimulus.

This is a simplification of the classic scientific experimental method or 'OXO'. Units are observed ('O') before, and after, something ('X') is done to them, and the observed measurements are compared and evaluated. It is fairly easy, in the laboratory setting, to make sure that factors other than 'X' are not introduced between the two observation points. However, when dealing with people and social activities, we cannot control the variables in the same way, and therefore different approaches are needed. We can demonstrate this by looking first at conventional experimentation.

The clinical research method of 'randomised controlled trials' (Shepperd et al. 1997) was developed to minimise the influence of extraneous factors. This approach matches people on certain characteristics (age, gender, education, occupation etc.) into 'matched pairs', which should be representative of the general population. These are then *randomly allocated* (**Sampling: Questions of Size**), one of each pair to an 'experimental group' and one to a 'control group'. This is intended to make the two groups as similar as possible by removing any differences between the groups that might 'bias' or distort the outcome of the experiment. There has been 'closure' around the experiment, achieved by 'controlling for' variations between its subjects and excluding extraneous effects.

Tests ('O') are then undertaken on both groups; treatment ('X') is given only to the experimental group, and further tests ('O') of both groups are carried out. The results are then analysed and an evaluation of the treatment is made. If there are after-treatment differences between the two groups, it is assumed that the treatment is the cause, because the control group did not receive it. The control group are taken to show what the experimental group would have been like had the treatment not been given (e.g. Gordon's (1992) study of depression in women).

This approach, however, has limited application for sociological studies. The kinds of things that sociologists wish to study often cannot be manipulated in the same way as in a laboratory experiment. It would be impractical, at the very least, to transfer children between families to test how upbringing is connected with educational performance or occupational achievement. On a smaller scale, such as couples' domestic division of labour, or neighbours' mutual perceptions, or the performance of newscasters, how could one actually persuade the participants to make the experimental changes happen? Not only would it be impractical, but it would show a scant regard for one's fellow human beings and their lives. This is not to say that sociological experiment is impossible, but rather, it operates within constraints so that it has conventionally not been seen as a mainstream method (Oakley 2000).

For example, what does 'matching' really mean when we are dealing with complex entities like human beings? Even if we can agree on which factors should be matched – and this could be a long list – there are great practical difficulties in finding people to match into pairs (or even into groups with an average match) and in implementing matching consistently (**Sampling: Types**). These difficulties usually result in small experimental and control groups, where the benefits of random allocation are less convincingly demonstrated.

Second, even if we have achieved matching pairs, the closure of the experiment is not complete. Whereas in laboratory conditions other extraneous factors can be reduced, social research typically takes place outside of the laboratory (**Association and Causation**). People have complete lives (and previous life histories) that exist outside of the limited part that is being studied. They are living beings who continue social interactions and independent actions outside of experimental control. In sociology, the problems of the most famous 'experiment' in the Hawthorne factory have become immortalised as the **Hawthorne Effect**.

The independence of experimental subjects is crucial, and not just in such sociological 'field experiments'. British social psychologists, despite the advantages of working in the laboratory, have long lamented that their experimental subjects – usually British students – do not show the same high levels of conformism and co-operation as their American counterparts (American students), so making clear experimental results harder to achieve!

This bring us to ethical issues in experiments. If 'subjects' are told in advance the nature of the experiment, so that they can give 'informed consent' (**Ethical Practice**), this is likely to bias the outcome. For that reason, ethical statements in psychology stress *post*-experiment disclosure to the subject, whereas sociological ethical statements require *prior approval*. The very term 'subject', widely used in psychology, is abhorrent to many sociologists, who prefer a collaborative style of research which places a value on the humanity of all those involved. For some, this extends to demonstrating actual *benefits* for those studied, and not just the absence of harm. In medicine, where new treatments can have a direct effect on patient health, experiments are sometimes abandoned before completion, because of significant interim indications. This need not be seen as sinister: in 2002, a major international trial of statins, then a new cholesterol drug, was terminated when the treatment benefits came through so early and strongly that not offering statins to the control group was regarded as unethical.

Thus experiments as a social research method offer the attractions of control and confidence about conclusions, but in practice are very difficult to implement.

A simpler form of experiment is that of 'comparison' and 'post-hoc matching'. This approach was adopted by many early evaluations in social care (see Goldberg and Connelly 1981). Further, this may be the only model to use if the need to evaluate arises only after the changes have been undertaken. Here, you would attempt to match the 'group' that had been subject to change with another 'group' with similar characteristics. For example, an evaluation of the Triage community care package in Connecticut was commissioned after the package was introduced, and a comparison group had to be drawn from a different area (Caro 1981: **Evaluation Studies**). While not as rigorous as a proper control group, the addition of any comparison group considerably strengthens research designs.

There is a wide range of research designs like these, that meet some but not all of the classic requirements of an experiment. Such 'quasi-experiments' cannot claim the experiment's rigorous logical conditions and internal consistency (**Evaluation Studies**), but they are more practical to mount. The series of British General Election Studies, for example, uses the 'naturally occurring' events of the elections to monitor changes in political attitude.

By including a change process in the design, the researchers improve on the 'bog-standard' design of a cross-sectional study. This uses a sample of people investigated at any one time, so that the only comparison can be between members of that sample. While this is not strictly an experimental design (and should be thought of as a separate method), there are parallels when survey data are analysed by examining the different effects of several variables in turn (see **Contingency Tables**). This approach is the basis for distinguishing between main and hidden relationships between variables (**Association and Causation**), and also most 'multivariate statistical analysis'.

Studies that operate by investigating unplanned changes in their own setting can claim that the researchers have remained more true to that setting than the artifice of a formal experiment, even if there was no control group. This is true whether the research style in the experiment or quasi-experiment is quantitative or qualitative. However, the experiment's emphasis on measurement and objectivity means that it appeals more to researchers working in a philosophical context that is quantitative, than to most qualitative researchers (**Positivism and Realism**).

Key Words

control group
controlling for
experimental group
field experiment
matched pair
OXO
quasi-experiment
random allocation

Links

Action Research
Association and Causation
Contingency Tables
Ethical Practice
Evaluation Studies
Hawthorne Effect
Positivism and Realism
Sampling: Questions of Size
Sampling: Types

REFERENCES

General

Goldberg, E.M. and Connelly, N. (1981) *Evaluative Research and Social Care*. London: Heinemann for PSI.

Oakley, A. (2000) *Experiments in Knowing: Gender and Method in the Social Sciences.* Cambridge: Polity.

Shepperd, S., Doll, H. and Jenkinson, C. (1997) 'Randomised Controlled Trials'. In Jenkinson, C. (ed.), *Assessment and Evaluation of Health and Medical Care*. Buckingham: Open University Press.

Examples

Caro, F. (1981) 'Demonstrating Community-based Long-term Care in the United States: an Evaluative Research Perspective'. In Goldberg, E.M. and Connelly, N. (eds), *Evaluative Research and Social Care*. London: Heinemann for PSI.

Gordon, V. (1992) 'Treatment of Depressed Women by Nurses'. In Abbott, P. and Sapsford, R. (eds), *Research into Practice*. Buckingham: Open University Press.

Feminist Research

Feminist research is an approach to social research which uses a specific sub-set of methods, and/or makes a particular selection of topics, with the goal of challenging methodologies developed by men, and enhancing the position of women in society.

Section Outline: *Feminist research: new methods or new perspectives? Types of feminist research. The feminist project and feminist research. Challenging masculine research: public versus private topics; gender blindness; hierarchy versus collaboration. Are quantitative and qualitative methods gendered? Feminist standpoint theory. Recent shifts to feminist* topics, *away from feminist* research methods.

There has been extensive debate over whether feminist research represents new research methods or a new perspective using a sub-set of pre-existing methods (Hammersley 1992; Reinharz 1992). This is not our major preoccupation here: we have included **Ethnomethodology** and **Community Studies** as key concepts even though they are not strictly research methods. They do, however, represent a style of research and are part of social research activities. Feminist research at the very least also justifies inclusion because of the scale of its output.

Just as there are several forms of feminism, so too are there several forms of feminist research. Earlier feminists tended to believe that all ideas and practices not originated by women were by definition masculine, and therefore necessarily inimical to women. Later contributors evolved a more sophisticated view, differentiating procedures, like a method of research, from the purpose to which it is put, and the way in which it is implemented. The complexity of feminist practice needs to be kept in mind.

The key to understanding feminist research is the revolutionary nature of academic feminism, which from around 1970 began to challenge what had hitherto been male-dominated, social science disciplines. Female academics engaged on a political campaign to improve the lot of women in general. They also worked to replace their male 'colleagues' with a new breed of female academics, and to supplant 'malestream' intellectual conventions with a rival conceptualisation of the social world. This required the energy and single-mindedness that only ideological purity can provide.

Thus one definition of feminist research argued that only research done by women, published in feminist journals, funded by feminist bodies, antagonistic to all non-feminist ideas, and expressly seeking to change the world in a feminist way, could count as feminist research. Unless these criteria were satisfied, other features – grounding in feminist theory or a concern with the relationship between researcher and those researched – were insufficient (Reinharz 1992). Women who met only these last two criteria could not do feminist research; nor indeed could men sympathetic to the feminist cause.

In seeking to break the mode of masculine domination, feminists argued that the conventional intellectual frameworks previously developed by men must necessarily be inadequate. There were three main elements to this critique. First, and most obviously, most sociological research had studied men, not women. By concentrating on the public sphere of work and civic life, they had excluded the private sphere to which many women were restricted. Worse, social scientists wrote as if what applied to men was not specifically masculine, but 'universal': 'people' actually meant 'men', because data on women had simply not been collected. Social regularities were assumed to be gender blind, applying to men and women alike (e.g. the social mobility studies of the 1970s talk for the most part about 'social mobility' rather than 'male social mobility': see Payne and Abbott 1990). Feminist research called not only for fresh study of women's lives, but for a dismantling of prior knowledge that failed to take account of gender differences.

A second theme in feminist research stresses equality and sisterhood. In the realm of research, this was taken to mean that the 'subjects' of research should not be treated as external objects, which can be examined and then excluded after relevant information had been extracted from them to suit the needs of the researcher (Oakley 1981). Rather than the researcher dominating the agenda and the data collection event, there should be a move towards a collaborative, non-hierarchical and inclusive relationship, entailing an equality of standing between researcher and researched (**Ethical Practice**).

(Female) 'subjects' should be given more information about the research both before and after data collection. The researcher should attempt to build a personal relationship – a rapport – with the people being studied.

Furthermore, the research should take full account of their view of the matters being studied. This 'account' includes feelings, other interests and even unconscious beliefs, these being the third dimension of feminist work.

This is a very different model from that of classic survey research (**Social Surveys**). Here questions are pre-set; they concentrate on material that can be easily intellectualised (statements of 'fact' and 'attitudes' which can be quantified); answers are constrained by pre-coded closed questions; interviewers instructed not to engage in information exchange or social conversation because it might bias the data collected; and no contact with those interviewed is established outside of the unique interview situation. Objectivity and control over the research process (**Bias**; **Objectivity**) are valued above interpersonal relationships with those from whom data are extracted. Stanley and Wise reject this as being 'a power relationship every bit as obscene as the power relationship that leads women to be sexually assaulted, murdered' (1983: 169).

As is often the case in academic debates, this view of 'classic' survey research is something of an exaggeration (**Positivism and Realism**). However, that did not prevent a rejection of quantitative analysis and the theoretical frameworks that supported them, in favour of **Qualitative Methods**. Attempts were made to move away from the researcher controlling all aspects (away from 'hierarchy', particularly in the interview: **Interviewing**), and towards a broadening of topics to include emotion and felt experience. Female researchers, having experienced male oppression, were in a unique position to empathise with other women, and so were able to analyse how this was experienced (**Reflexivity**).

This sensitivity towards the position of those being researched has had a wider influence outside of feminist research. The politics (with a small 'p') of research in areas like race, disability and social exclusion have changed, with growing emphasis on putting control into the hands of those who experience, rather than those who research. Equally, much of the work in these areas has become Political (with a capital 'P'): the purpose and format of the research being consciously geared to argue for political change from a particular 'standpoint' (**Ethical Practice**; **Objectivity**: Seale 1999: 9–13; Phillimore and Moffatt 1994).

The rejection of more established **Quantitative Methods** opened the way for the introduction of alternatives. Partly to accommodate women working in cultural studies and the humanities, feminist research began to use personal histories, diaries (including shared 'group diaries'), self-recorded monologues, autobiography and network mapping, non-directive group discussions, role-play and drama, and expression through art works. There was a new emphasis on naturally occurring dialogue (rather than questions seeking answers) about what women *felt* about what they believed had happened to them.

In practice, feminist research was more marked by a swing towards *existing* **Qualitative Methods** than to these new formats. However, critics of the new approaches argued that, in practice, data collection did not proceed in an egalitarian manner, but was dependent on the differing personalities of the participants. Some people had more say than others. How were feminist researchers to handle the responses of non-feminist women (Millen 1997)?

Further, the argument about objectivity and validity of observations was turned back on the feminists. In interpreting sociological data, let alone more open-ended or artistic constructions, the researcher does not operate from a neutral position which can be agreed to by others. There is no 'value-free' research, so that feminist researchers were selecting and interpreting their data in ways that simply confirmed their prior conceptions. These were familiar objections to pre-existing qualitative research techniques (Silverman 1993).

Partly in response, two new versions of feminist research gained ground. Oakley's later work (1998; 2000) observes how

> Feminism holds on to qualitative methodology because this has become part of its normal intellectual repertoire . . . Feminism needed a research method, a different methodology, in order to occupy a distinctive place in the academy and acquire social status and moral legitimacy. Opposition to 'traditional' research methods as much as innovation of alternative ones thus provided an organising platform . . . The case against quantitative ways of knowing is based on a rejection of reason and science as masculine and an embracing of experience as feminine; but this is essentialist thinking which buys into the very paradox that it protests about (1998: 716, 725).

An alternative view was advocated by Stanley and Wise (1983), placing an emphasis on the particular capacity of female researchers to understand other women. This 'feminist standpoint theory' puts women in a unique position to determine what is relevant knowledge about the social world, and how it should be studied (Ramazanoglu 2002). Work in this school, such as that of the Women's Workshop on Qualitative Family/Household Research, shows declining interest in research methods per se (Ribbens and Edwards 1998: 15–16). Indeed, most current feminist research publication follows a conventional, qualitative path (Payne et al in press), being more concerned with the topic of gender than with how the research was conducted.

Key Words

empathy
essentialism
feminism
feminist standpoint theory
hierarchy
rapport

Links

Bias
Community Studies
Ethical Practice
Ethnomethodology and Conversational Analysis
Interviewing
Objectivity
Positivism and Realism
Qualitative Methods
Quantitative Methods
Reflexivity
Social Surveys
Validity

REFERENCES

General

Hammersley, M. (1992) 'On Feminist Methodology'. *Sociology.* 26 (2): 187–206.

Oakley, A. (1981) 'Interviewing Women: a Contradiction in Terms'. In Roberts, H. (ed.), *Doing Feminist Research*. London: Routledge & Kegan Paul.

Oakley, A. (1998) 'Gender, Methodology and People's Ways of Knowing'. *Sociology*, 32 (4): 707–31.

Oakley, A. (2000) *Experiments in Knowing: Gender and Method in the Social Sciences.* Cambridge: Polity.

Ramazanoglu, C. (2002) *Feminist Methodology.* London: Sage.

Reinharz, S. (1992) *Feminist Methods in Social Research*. New York: Oxford University Press.

Silverman, D. (1993) *Interpreting Qualitative Data.* London: Sage.

Stanley, L. and Wise, S. (1983) *Breaking Out: Feminist Consciousness and Feminist Research*. London: Routledge & Kegan Paul.

Examples

Millen, D. (1997) 'Some Methodological and Epistemological Issues Raised by Doing Feminist Research on Non-Feminist Women'. *Sociological Research Online.* Vol. 2: www.socresonline.org.uk/socresonline/2/3/3.html

Payne, G. and Abbott, P. (eds) (1990) *The Social Mobility of Women*. London: Falmer Press.

Payne, G., Williams, M. and Chamberlain, S. (in press) 'Methodological Pluralism in British Sociology'. *Sociology* 38 (1): in press.

Phillimore, P. and Moffatt, S. 'Discounted Knowledge: Local Experience, Environmental Pollution and Health'. In Popay, J. and Williams, G. (eds) *Researching the People's Health*. London: Routledge.

Ribbens, J. and Edwards, R. (eds) 1998) *Feminist Dilemmas in Qualitative Research.* London: Sage.

Seale, C. (1999) *The Quality of Qualitative Research*. London: Sage.

Fieldwork

Fieldwork can mean the data collection stage of a project (particularly in the qualitative tradition); or how researchers go about collecting data; or more narrowly, data collection in a social setting that tries to reflect the naturally occurring order of events and subjective meanings of those being studied.

Section Outline: *Fieldwork as qualitative research. The natural setting. Anthropological inheritance: 'going into the field'. The drama of fieldwork. Making records of events as they happen. Preparations for fieldwork. Fieldwork as an exploratory stage. Planning inductive research. Access; gatekeepers; rules of engagement. Reactions to the fieldworker. 'Acceptance' and moral obligations.*

'Fieldwork' is used in two distinct ways in social research. It can be a general term for several kinds of **Qualitative Methods**:

> a style of investigation that is also referred to as . . . 'qualitative method', 'interpretative research', 'case study method' and 'ethnography' (Burgess 1982: 1).

More specifically, it can refer to that part of the qualitative research process where data are collected in a naturally occurring setting, i.e. what researchers actually *do* when they are 'in the field' – in, say, a village, school, bar, factory, club, hospital, church, care home or gang. As qualitative research has become more specialist and widespread, the word has become slightly less fashionable in its first sense. However, including 'fieldwork' here, with our links, allows us to reflect how extensive such methods have become (Payne et al. in press) and in particular, we can draw attention to the practicalities of doing fieldwork.

Our model of fieldwork comes from social anthropology, where anthropologists left the comfort and familiarity of their homes and colleges to travel to distant places, to camp out with people they did not know, and live in non-industrial cultures very different from their own

(**Ethnography**; **Community Studies**). Although sociologists today may travel only a short way for their research (say, to the local school or a business), returning home and to the university each day, there still remains a sense of adventure and uncertainty even about this enterprise. Much of the excitement comes from the researchers not being in control of the place where they are collecting data, and the people from whom they are collecting them. The researcher must perform in an unfamiliar setting, responding ad lib to events, making sense of the detailed doings of other people's lives – people who owe the researcher no favours (the Zuni people even demanded payment from Pandey in return for being studied! (Srinivas et al. 1979)). Researchers' performances, and reactions to them, must be constantly reviewed, self-interogated and re-interpreted (**Reflexivity**).

The intensity of fieldwork experience can be gauged from the many retrospective accounts published by sociologists (e.g. Burgess 1982; Srinivas et al. 1979; see also references in McKeganey and Cunningham-Burley 1987). They may subsequently write about their experiences, but researchers are notoriously defensive of 'their' fieldwork patches, discouraging others from 'intruding'. This is one reason why very few follow-ups or replications are carried out in the original settings.

Of course, not all fieldwork involves the drama of hanging out with motor-cycle gangs, soccer hooligans, Ulster Protestant terrorists, the inmates of mental hospitals, naturists, undertakers, homeless men, sex industry workers, religious cultists, jazz musicians or drug dealers. Fieldwork also includes visiting a school while pupils complete a questionnaire under teacher supervision, or analysing what happened at an academic conference one has attended. Indeed, almost any data collection trip out of the office, using whatever research methods, can be referred to as fieldwork. However, the term is more typically reserved for qualitative research, over a period of time, in some specific setting. The most popular data collection methods are currently in-depth **Interviewing** and **Participant Observation**.

As an enterprise, fieldwork is primarily undertaken to encounter life *as it happens* in the place or organisation where it usually occurs; to identify its patterns; and to produce an *understanding* of these (Grills 1998). Two things follow from this. First, there are practical problems around what data are recorded and how they are recorded for later analysis: this is further discussed in **Coding Qualitative Data** (see also Grbich 1999: 121–38; 158–92). Second, it is not simply that mainstream fieldwork takes place 'in the field': it is part of a specific theoretical position. There is a prior commitment to a theoretical orientation that assumes there is a world external to the researcher which is best interpreted in its own context; as coherent units of action; through direct interaction with, and interpretation by, the researcher.

While this implies understanding things on their own terms, that does not mean fieldwork can be blithely entered into without preparation. Good fieldwork is based on systematic thinking *before* it starts, with literature review, discussion, reflection, and at least outline formulation of propositions about what may be encountered and its meaning. Even

> in [**Grounded Theory**] development, the literature review provides theoretical constructs, categories, and their properties that can be used to organize the data and discover new connections between theory and real-world phenomena (Marshall and Rossman 1999: 52; added emphasis)

There are, however, two variations to this guideline. Fieldwork is sometimes undertaken as a brief, *preliminary exploration* precisely in order to develop ideas and hypotheses; the natural setting stimulating questions and hypotheses to be addressed in subsequent research through quantitative methods. Second, some researchers would argue that, because the setting is not under control, and needs to be understood on its own terms, research must necessarily proceed in a relatively unplanned and open-minded way. Rather than imposing our preconceptions on the data, our concepts and theories should emerge from the data in an inductive way. It is certainly true that if we knew all the answers in advance, there would be no point in doing research. Serendipity does play a part in determining the path that some projects follow. None the less, nothing is more likely to expose a project to the criticisms of being sloppy, subjective, superficial and 'soft' in the worst sense – criticisms often levelled against qualitative methods – than inadequate prior conceptualisation of the 'problem' to be researched.

Preparation for fieldwork is not just intellectual. One of the major problems is *access*, the selection of a research site and the negotiation necessary to gain entry to it. Sometimes there is little alternative but to take whatever site is available. Physical location (distance to be travelled), type of site, and how restricted the entry, can all constrain choice. Often access follows from a personal contact. A researcher's colleagues, supervisor, friends, family or prior paid or voluntary work may open a door that would otherwise remain closed. Limitations on access mean that researchers often have to make do with what they can get, whether or not it best suits their topics of interest.

Central to gaining access is the question of who can give permission –

or, as it is usually put, who are the 'gatekeepers'? Gatekeepers may be the senior managers in organisations who give formal approval, trade union officials who expect to be consulted, or unofficial 'leaders' who by personality or experience can influence their colleagues. The latter are less obvious during the preliminary stage.

Any requests for access, however initiated, should be followed by face-to-face negotiation, to establish 'rules of engagement'. It is important that the project is clearly, fully and honestly explained (**Ethical Practice**). The price of access may well be a compromise on schedules, goals or personnel. An offer of feedback may facilitate access, but it is crucial to be clear about who 'owns' the results and right to publish.

Even with 'permission', or the support of a 'sponsor' who can vouch for the researcher, co-operation from every member of an organisation cannot be guaranteed. Any given sponsor will represent only one faction. Once into a setting, continuing access depends on researchers' social and research skills in maintaining acceptance of their roles and tolerance of their presence. Researchers can expect to be 'tested' by confrontations or involvement in activities that should be reported as rule breaches. Is the researcher really just a management spy? Can he/she be trusted to keep secrets? Is he/she what is being claimed?

Continued acceptance can best be achieved by consistency of role-playing (most fieldwork involves some kind of role-adoption). Indeed, consistency is generally important: if a position has been adopted, with the gatekeepers or others, it must be kept up. If undertakings about confidentiality have been given, or offers of feedback made, then these must be delivered, both on moral grounds and the expediency of ensuring further access. The project is not accomplished until all its aspects have been completed.

Key Words

access
gatekeeper
inductive
role-playing
rules of engagement
sponsor

Links

Coding Qualitative Data
Community Studies
Ethical Practice
Ethnography
Grounded Theory
Interviewing
Participant Observation
Qualitative Methods
Reflexivity

REFERENCES

General

Grbich, C. (1999) *Qualitative Research in Health*. London: Sage.
Grills, S. (ed.) (1998) *Doing Ethnographic Research*. London: Sage.
Marshall, C. and Rossman, G. (1999) *Designing Qualitative Research* (3rd edn). London: Sage.
Payne, G., Williams, M. and Chamberlain, S. (in press) 'Methodological Pluralism in British Sociology'. *Sociology*, 38 (1): (in press).

Examples

Burgess, R. (ed.) (1982) *Field Research: a Sourcebook and Field Manual*. London: Allen & Unwin.
McKeganey, N. and Cunningham-Burley, S. (eds) (1987) *Enter the Sociologist*. Aldershot: Avebury.
Punch, S. (2003) 'Childhoods in the Majority World'. *Sociology*, 37 (2): 277–95.
Srinivas, M., Shah, A. and Ramaswamy, E. (eds) (1979) *The Fieldworker and the Field*. Delhi: Oxford University Press.

Grounded Theory

Grounded theory seeks to build systematic theoretical statements inductively from coding and analysing observational data, by developing and refining conceptual categories which are then tested and re-tested in further data collection.

Section Outline: *Correct use of 'grounded theory' as a rigorous method. Combining induction with deduction. Elaborating pre-existing understandings. Testing emerging concepts. Stages in grounded theory. Open sampling and coding. Axial coding. Relational and variational sampling. Testing and re-testing concepts. Selective and discriminate sampling. Theoretical saturation.*

Grounded theory is one of the more widely used, and abused, current research methods. It involves a precise and systematic set of methods, but inexperienced researchers frequently invoke it when what they really mean is that they believe (quite sensibly) that theoretical knowledge should be based on the social phenomena described, and that they wish to take an inductive stance. Miscalling this 'grounded theory' is no substitute for rigorous fieldwork (**Fieldwork**). Any study that does not embrace its full set of procedures cannot, and should not, be properly called 'grounded theory'.

Grounded theory works within both an *inductive* and a *deductive* framework (**Qualitative Methods**; **Positivism and Realism**). In induction, the researcher explores data, allowing them to suggest meanings and explanations that may cumulate into a theoretical model. Induction claims to start with fewer preconceptions, and to be 'truer' to the data (and indeed, may be slow to identify what is and what is not data). Most qualitative methods operate within this framework. In deduction, the researcher starts with theories and hypotheses, then collects data to test them. This is the basis of most quantitative methods (e.g. Allen 2003).

Grounded theory starts by approaching fieldwork and data collection from an inductive perspective.

> The researcher begins with an area of study and allows the theory to emerge from the data. Theory derived from data is more likely to resemble the 'reality' than is theory derived from putting together a series of concepts based on experience or solely through speculation (how one thinks things ought to work). Grounded theories, because they are drawn from data, are likely to offer insight, enhance understanding, and provide a meaningful guide to action (Strauss and Corbin 1998: 12).

However, this emphasis on *building* rather than testing preconceived theories does not mean that researchers start with no ideas at all. Strauss and Corbin recognise that researchers bring a considerable background knowledge to their projects, including concepts that they will use in confronting their data (ibid.: 48–9). They approve of researchers whose 'purpose is to elaborate and extend existing theory' (ibid.: 12). Even where researchers are trying to maximise their open-mindedness, they must give prior thought to what question the research addresses and where best it might be researched (ibid.: 53, 215).

As the project progresses, the approach shifts from induction to deduction. The initial ideas derived from the data are tested back against new data. This process clarifies and elaborates the concepts (or 'categories'). 'Validation' is repeated until the researcher feels confident that a theoretical statement can be made which rigorously accounts for the phenomena being studied (Huberman and Miles 2002: section three).

This approach's origin was a collaboration between Glaser and Strauss, whose evolving methods of researching the sociology of dying led to the publication of *The Discovery of Grounded Theory* (1967) and several further books, most notably Strauss's *Qualitative Analysis for Social Scientists* (1987). Glaser had originally come from a **Quantitative Methods** background, from which he brought an emphasis on using empirical data to develop theories. He identified internal comparison of one's data as the key source of specifying concepts and connections between them. Strauss was a product of the Chicago School (**Ethnography**). Influenced by social interactionism, he recognised the importance of people as actors bringing complex meanings to the negotiation of everyday activities (**Ethnomethodology**).

The results of their collaboration can be understood as two parallel processes, *sampling* and *coding*, each with three main stages:

1. Open Sampling
2. Relational and Variational Sampling
3. Discriminate Sampling

1. Open Coding
2. Axial Coding
3. Selective Coding

At the outset, people and events are 'sampled' as they conveniently occur. This *open sampling* might simply follow informants who happen to be available, or picking up the sorts of situations in which the topic of interest seems likely to present itself. If an opportunity to collect data comes along, the researcher goes with the flow. This is very different from the idea of 'random sampling' (**Sampling: Questions of Size** and **Sampling: Estimates and Size**). Its purpose is not to represent a 'population', but to keep the data collection as unconstrained as possible.

During this phase, researchers begin to process their data, applying *open coding* (see also **Coding Qualitative Data**; **Levels of Measurement**). This lists the information (typically statements, answers and comments by informants) in sequence, reviewing it in sections, and writing 'code notes' to record initial interpretations of the information. Data might be examined line by line (which emphasises micro-analysis of words and phrases); sentence – or paragraph – by sentence; or starting with a whole episode and trying to grasp its significance in a holistic way. Whatever the level, the researcher highlights those items that seem to be important, without attempting to group or compare the items very much at all. It is important to keep the coding 'open' and not quickly to organise data into categories. This allows the researcher to remain receptive to new experiences and 'hear the voice' of informants. However, open coding progressively moves into identifying concepts.

Comparison and grouping become more intensive in the next stage, *axial coding*. The researcher begins organising and re-labelling data under collective headings, which in turn build towards concepts (or 'categories'). For instance, informants' talk about 'football', 'hockey' and 'athletics' could be grouped under 'sport', whereas 'sport', 'concerts', 'films' and 'parties' might be grouped under 'leisure'. Alternatively, the grouping might be organised around *who* took part in such activities, or as examples of *age-specific peer grouping*, or of *consumption patterns*. These are processes of data reduction and preliminary theory building.

What is happening here is that real-world phenomena are labelled so that they can be identified. The label is an abstract idea or name, or 'category'. In grounded theory, an important category is used as a central point around which to explore associated concepts, or 'sub-categories'. Typically these sub-categories ask: who, when, where, how, why, what follows from, the main category. The main category is the axis along which this exploration and elaboration takes place, by comparing items highlighted in case notes.

Axial coding is therefore not just a technical task but an intellectual process. It identifies the properties and dimensions of an axial category: what variant forms does it take; under what conditions? Axial coding goes with *relational* and *variational sampling*, by which the researcher seeks out those cases or events that help to demonstrate properties and dimensions, and the connections between concepts. This is a purposive sampling technique, designed to show the maximum similarities and maximum differences in cases of the concepts.

Axial coding, based on relational and variational sampling, is a process of testing and re-testing. It is here that grounded theory shifts from its initial emphasis on induction, to *deduction*, as ideas originally developed by induction from the initial data are re-explored in the light of further empirical data. This procedure of re-testing evolving ideas, to validate or negate them, is the most distinctive feature of the whole approach (compare this with **Hypothesis** and **Validity**).

The third stage of *selective coding* is the final integration and refining of the central or 'core' category, the theme that predominates in the project. The final category should be shown as compatible with the data, with its links to sub-categories and variations in its form explained. It should be logically consistent and 'theoretically dense', i.e. its full range of variability explored, and any gaps in this identified. This 'refining' is supported by *discriminate sampling*, a very careful selection of items designed to fill gaps and make final internal comparative tests of the core category.

The procedure is completed when *theoretical saturation* is achieved. New data no longer add to conceptual density. The core category has been fully refined and could be re-used in other research. This does not imply that all possible situations have been covered, nor that generalisation to other situations is possible on the basis of some statistical process. The sampling has been entirely subordinate to the emergent nature of the core category: hence its general name, *theoretical sampling* (Devine and Heath 1999: 56–60). The key issue is that a rigorous conceptual understanding has been built from data, and validated against further data.

Key Words

axial coding
category
deduction
discriminate sampling
induction
open coding
open sampling
relational sampling
selective coding
theoretical sampling
validation
variational sampling

Links

Coding Qualitative Data
Ethnography
Ethnomethodology and Conversational Analysis
Fieldwork
Hypothesis
Levels of Measurement
Positivism and Realism
Qualitative Methods
Quantitative Methods
Sampling: Estimates and Size
Sampling: Questions of Size
Validity

REFERENCES

General

Glaser, B. and Strauss, A. (1967) *The Discovery of Grounded Theory*. Chicago: Aldine.
Strauss, A. (1987) *Qualitative Analysis for Social Scientists*. Cambridge: Cambridge University Press.
Strauss, A. and Corbin, J. (1998) *Basics of Qualitative Research* (2nd edn). London: Sage.

Examples

Allen, C. (2003) 'On the Logic of the "New" Welfare Practice: an Ethnographic Case Study of the "New" Welfare Intermediaries'. *Sociological Research Online*, 8 (1): www.socresonline.org.uk/socresonline/8/1/allen.html
Devine, F. and Heath, S. (1999) *Sociological Research Methods in Context*. Basingstoke: Macmillan.
Huberman, M. and Miles, M. (2002) (eds) *The Qualitative Researcher's Companion*. London: Sage.

Group Discussions/Focus Groups

Group discussion is a means of collecting data in one go from several people (who usually share common experiences) and which concentrates on their shared meanings, whereas a focus group is a special type of group discussion with a narrowly focused topic discussed by group members of equal status who do not know one another.

Section Outline: *Tapping into collective opinions and feelings. Public meetings: who really participates? Smaller informal groups. Expressed and underlying attitudes. Group discussions are cheap, quick and non-individualist. Social dynamics in group discussions. Focus groups as a special case. Size and procedures for focus groups. Selection of participants. Arrangements for meeting. The roles of 'facilitator' and 'scribe'. Focus groups: cheap and dirty substitute for research.*

Our opinions, feelings and attitudes are formed through our contacts with others. Unlike research methods based on questionnaires or even less-structured interviews, group discussions attempt to reflect this by obtaining information from people in groups. These range from large public meetings, through small get-togethers of about eight to ten invited informants, to highly specialised focus groups. A focus group is a special kind of group discussion.

Researchers sometimes arrange public meetings to take soundings. This typically happens early in the research project, to explore possible lines of enquiry and to inform people about what is being planned. Those who work with or represent communities or organisations might be thought to have a good idea of what 'the community at large' may feel. This is not necessarily the case. These people's views are likely to be influenced by their particular function in the community. Community representatives usually only meet a sub-section of the population. Local politicians tend to have knowledge only of constituents who consult them.

It is also impossible for everyone to have an equal share of speaking in a large meeting. The opinions most strongly expressed are those of community leaders, 'experts', and those who regularly attend meetings. This form of group discussion is a collective version of conducting individual interviews with **Key Informants**. It is useful in the early stages of a project, as a means of getting a feel of some of the issues and topics to explore. However, if used as a main method of investigation, the opinions of the vocally or politically dominant, rather than the whole range of views, will be over-represented.

A better use of group discussions is on a smaller scale, with groups consisting of the kinds of people with whom the participants normally mix. However, because the group has usually been specially created by the researcher, the participants are in an artificial situation. The researcher is therefore interested not only in the ideas, opinions, etc. as they are communicated in that specific and artificially created group, but also the *underlying* opinions, feelings, etc. that members already have, and which are expressed, amplified and possibly modified through the collective interaction in the group. The presence of other members may also suggest ways in which individuals adapt when faced with alternative views.

The value of group discussion as a method lies in its speed and cheapness. In the time that a couple of one-to-one interviews might take, it is possible to obtain responses from eight or ten people. Less detail or depth is achieved for each informant, but we also see how the individual's comments are received by other people. In this sense, it is a *social* rather than an *individualistic* research tool. Its sympathy for social settings of the informants has established it in **Feminist Research**. In a wider context, during the exploratory stage of a project, group discussion is an effective tool to test preliminary ideas and discover the expressed concerns of potential informants.

The success of this depends on how well group discussions are managed, and the data analysed. Discussion groups, like all new groups, have their own dynamic which depends on who is taking part. Initially, even with the researcher's guidance, there are few 'rules' governing participants' behaviour, and it takes a while before informants negotiate their own roles and contributions. As informants begin to co-operate with each other, a productive period follows in which many new topics will be raised. Gradually, a structure and consensus emerge, which constrain themes for further discussion. Although the set-up of such groups is less formalised than in focus groups, the researcher's tasks are much the same.

Focus groups are a special type of group discussion, first used by Merton (Merton et al. 1956). The techniques for conducting them have since been developed by market research companies. They are now widely used in the public sector and by political parties as a method of assessing public opinion. *The media attention this has received has encouraged inexperienced researchers incorrectly to call any form of group discussion a focus group.* Focus groups are one, specific, more formal type of group discussion (see Krueger 1994; Krueger and King 1998; Morgan 1997, 1998; Morgan and Krueger 1997–8).

As implied by the name, focus groups *focus* on particular issues that are introduced in a predetermined order as carefully worded, open-ended questions or topics. These groups should normally consist of between six and ten people; more than 12 has been found to inhibit discussion. The group members are chosen because they have similar education, social status, occupation and income, etc. (Brannen and Nilsen 2002). How closely similar is a matter for judgement: does a discussion of disabilities require participants to be disabled, or to have the same disability (Edwards and Imrie 2003)? Participants should not know each other. Those invited to attend will cover various sections of the community. For example, a series of discussions could be held with particular interest groups – community leaders, teenagers, women, the elderly – as in the Glasgow study of the health needs of black and ethnic minority women (Avan 1995).

Two methods of selection for focus groups are normally used. Existing groups can be approached and discussions held with the members who agree to participate. Alternatively, random sampling followed by allocation to groups could be used, as in a study for Somerset Health Authority (Richardson and Bowie 1995). This helps to ensure that a wider range of opinion is represented rather than being dominated by 'professional volunteers'.

When organising focus groups, it is important to arrange a convenient time and a suitable location, accessible for all attendees. The venue should be comfortable, so that people will feel free to talk and share their experiences and opinions. People may have problems in attending meetings because of family or employment commitments. Transport and crèche facilities may even be provided, and it is usual to supply light refreshments. To encourage attendance, financial inducements or small gifts are sometimes given to those attending (the Somerset study paid each person £10).

The interviewer, often called the *facilitator*, needs different skills and techniques than in the one-to-one interview (**Interviewing**). He/she must be very well informed and prepared. An additional expert may also attend to provide specialist information. The methods of question construction and interviewer probing will be the same, but with the added problems of group control. The interviewer must ensure that only one person speaks at a time; that everyone is encouraged to speak in turn; and that no-one dominates. In this last case, the interviewer needs to be able to say 'shut up' without sounding threatening or inhibiting the others. Seating arrangements can be changed (perhaps after refreshments or a comfort break) to influence participation. The more reticent members should be re-seated opposite the facilitator so that eye contact can be used to encourage them to join in. In contrast, the vociferous should be moved to a position that makes it difficult for them to catch the facilitator's eye.

It is also common to use a second interviewer (or *scribe*) to operate the tape recorder and to act as note-taker. Usually name-badges or place-names are used to aid later transcription. Facilitators should not be members of the community or at least not identified with any particular faction, and not be known to members of the group.

As Grbich has shown, focus groups, like other discussion groups, are useful for finding out about underlying issues and opinions, provided they are properly conducted (1999: 108–15). Comments by members can trigger a whole range of views from others in the group. Because they give quick results, and are relatively cheap and easy to set up, discussion groups are widely used as an aid to policy planning and prioritising, and evaluation of programmes (**Community Profiles**). Without other inputs, however, focus groups are a 'cheap and dirty' substitute for real research. It is all too easy to be tempted into making wild and unjustified generalisations based on what, after all, are a few people talking about a handful of selected issues. The isolation of the leadership of 'New Labour' from the core membership of the British Labour Party during its first two terms of government is a stark reminder of the damage that can be done by an over-reliance on fashionable focus groups.

Key Words

consensus
facilitator
group dynamics
key informant
scribe

Links

Community Profiles
Feminist Research
Interviewing
Key Informants

REFERENCES

General

Grbich, C. (1999) *Qualitative Research in Health*. London: Sage.

Krueger, R. (1994) *Focus Groups: a Practical Guide for Applied Research*. (2nd edn). Thousand Oaks, CA: Sage.

Krueger, R. and King, J. (1998) *Involving Community Members in Focus Groups*. (Focus Group Kit, 5) Thousand Oaks, CA: Sage.

Merton, R., Fiske, M. and Kendall, P. (1956) *The Focused Interview*. Glencoe, IL: Free Press.

Morgan, D. (1997) *Focus Groups in Qualitative Research* (2nd edn) (*Qualitative Research Methods, Vol. 16*). London: Sage.

Morgan, D. (1998) *The Focus Group Guide Book*. Thousand Oaks, CA: Sage.

Morgan, D. and Krueger, R. (1997–8) *The Focus Group Kit* (6 vols). Thousand Oaks, CA: Sage.

Examples

Avan, G. (1995) *Perceived Health Needs of Black and Ethnic Minority Women: An Exploratory Study*. Glasgow: Community Support Unit, Healthy Glasgow.

Brannen, J. and Nilsen, A. (2002) 'Young People's Time Perspectives: from Youth to Adulthood'. *Sociology*, 36 (3): 513–37.

Edwards, C. and Imrie, R. (2003) 'Disability and Bodies as Bearers of Value'. *Sociology*, 37 (2): 239–56.

Richardson, A. and Bowie, C. (1995) 'Public Opinion'. *Health Service Journal*, 11 (May): 25–6.

The Hawthorne Effect

The Hawthorne Effect is the tendency, particularly in social experiments, for people to modify their behaviour because they know they are being studied, and so to distort (usually unwittingly) the research findings.

Section Outline: *How people respond to being studied. The original experiments at the Hawthorne plant. Responses to real and imagined changes in lighting. Manipulating working conditions. The move from psychology to ethnography. Unofficial worker practices. Being studied versus engagement with the researcher. Hawthorne as poor experimental design. Extraneous influences: the Depression.*

When people know that they are being studied, they change the way they behave. The researcher's difficulty is to know *how* things have changed. Informants may disguise their actions and feelings, because they do not want to share them with somebody outside of their everyday lives. Alternatively, they may feel flattered that somebody has chosen them for study. They may even adapt their behaviour to fit what they believe the researcher wants. These reactions are often referred to by the shorthand phrase, the 'Hawthorne Effect'.

The phrase takes its name from one of the most influential projects in sociology and management studies, a study of workers in the Western Electric Company's Hawthorne Works in Chicago, mainly between 1927 and 1933. This used two main, detailed experiments with small groups, continuing in various forms for several years, and an extensive interviewing programme (less relevant here). The experiments introduced variations in working conditions, to see how these affected output. We describe these experiments fairly fully, to show the Hawthorne Effect, and also illustrate some problems of doing this kind of long-term applied research. The Hawthorne Effect is one form of 'experimenter effect' or 'reactivity': the fact that it is not regularly referred to in recent research literature paradoxically illustrates a certain unwillingness by many researchers to face up to problems of their own practice.

The first phase of 'lighting experiments' at the Hawthorne plant investigated whether levels of illumination had an effect on output. Lighting levels were changed in three departments, without clear results. Then two groups of workers, matched for previous output performance, were moved to separate buildings. Lighting for the experimental group (**Experiments**) was varied. Output *increased* with each change, whether brighter or dimmer, or real change or pretended change, even when the workers could hardly see what they were doing. Output also increased in the control group! The only conclusion reached was that *some other variable must be intervening* between lighting and output (**Association and Causation**).

The second phase consisted of four experiments: the First Relay Assembly Group; the Second Relay Assembly Group; the Mica Splitting Group; and the Bank Wiring Observation Room. The first group, of six women making telephone components called relays, was housed separately with an observer (**Observation**), and their work conditions (permutations of pay rates, rest times and shorter hours) experimentally improved over two years. The observer reported how the work group increased in friendliness, including to him. He became an unofficial supervisor, protecting them from the official supervisors. Output, as compared with secret pre-experiment measurements, increased in 12 out of 13 trials (even in the one test when improvements were revoked). However, as anxieties about unemployment came to dominate in the summer of 1929, group cohesion and output fell away.

The Second Relay Assembly Group was essentially a re-run of the First, started before the latter had been completed. This group remained in the main department, only payment methods being manipulated. The investigators appear at this point to be concluding that output was not directly influenced by payments, fatigue or work method, but they wanted a further check. However, the different payment scheme caused such bad feeling between the group and other workers that the experiment was stopped.

The five women in the Mica Splitting Group were therefore housed separately, but its temperamentally and socially dissimilar members did not get on well together. Output initially increased during five improvements to work conditions (but no changes in pay rates). Output fell in the second year as business declined, until there was insufficient work to continue the experiment.

The fourth group consisted of 14 men wiring banks of telephone switchgear, separately located with an observer. It was felt that they rapidly grew used to the observer, and a series of key observations were made during what was more a descriptive ethnographic study than an experiment (**Ethnography**). Workers were found to share a sense of how much work should be done, bringing group pressure onto 'rate-busters' who produced too much and 'chisellers' who did too little. They under-reported output if they got ahead of their own output norm. This experiment in particular was seen as demonstrating how unofficial or 'informal' workers' practices co-exist with the 'formal structure' and organisation of production in a company (three different assessments of the contribution of these experiments to industrial sociology can be found in Brown (1992), Grint (1991), and Rose (1988)).

Although the 'Hawthorne Effect' is usually invoked in a general sense to indicate informants changing their behaviour due to being researched, it is possible to distinguish two main effects. The lighting experiments show a simple 'I am being studied' effect (compare this with **Unobtrusive Methods**). Being in repetitive and highly controlled work conditions, the research interest was a welcome change. While it involved little connection with the researchers, the *awareness that they were being studied* was sufficient for the workers to feel that they were *special*. Knowing that output level was important, they increased it, as that seemed to be what was expected.

In the First Relay Assembly Group, this effect was amplified by the friendly interaction with the observer. This might be called a second, 'I'm on good terms with a researcher who fixes thing for me' effect. The workers could see a *tangible benefit* from co-operation: it continued their advantageous position in respect of supervision. This effect was stronger, because of their closer inter-personal identification with the researcher.

Parsons (1974) identifies a third Hawthorne Effect. Workers *knew* that increased output was rewarded by higher payments. The reward reinforced their new performance, so that it became implanted as a new, normal behaviour, a process called 'operant conditioning'. This widely recognised effect received less attention within the Hawthorne Studies because the investigators' main frame of reference was showing how a wider range of work condition factors can all affect production.

These 'effects' undermine the credibility of the Hawthorne experiments, serving as a warning to later researchers. Nor were these the only technical limitations, even allowing for when the work was done. The lighting experiments did not have rigorous matching and control groups (**Experiments**). Worse, no proper control groups were used in the later experiments, and changes to working conditions were not systematically implemented. Informants were selected for their co-operation The observer's participant role (**Participant Observation**) in the groups was not adequately understood.

Because the researchers wished to demonstrate that pay rates alone did not explain output, they failed to see the strength of economic factors, including events outside of the experiment like the Depression and threat of job losses. Nor did their reports consider the role of Western Electric Company as an anti-union employer. Two of the key researchers, Dickson and Pennock, were employees, supported by Roethlisberger (and to a lesser extent, Mayo) from the Harvard Business School. The company, although more open to new ideas than many, and influenced by their own employees Dickson and Pennock, did not support the project for altruistic reasons. It wanted to increase productivity for market advantage, and intervened to delay initial publication of the findings. The researchers also comment adversely in places on the performance of management and supervision, but could hardly attribute production problems to the senior power-players in the company.

Remarkably high levels of resources were invested into their lengthy research programme, which turned out to be less of a help than might be expected. *Methods* and *perspectives* shifted from psychological experiment to ethnographic observation and on to structured and depth interviews. As the main report shows, the researchers were overwhelmed by the complexity and quantity of the data they amassed (Roethlisberger and Dickson 1939). Their influence on Human Relations management was through Mayo's contribution of simplifying and publicising their results (Mayo 1933). It was not until 30 years later that a systematic interpretation appeared (Landsberger 1958). Paradoxically, the experiments are best remembered in sociology for their limitations as a key example of informant reactivity (Du Boulay and Williams 1987; Parry 1987), rather than for their innovatory research developments.

Key Words

experiment
formal structure
informal structure
operant conditioning
output level

Links

Association and Causation
Ethnography
Experiments
Observation
Participant Observation
Unobtrusive Measures and Triangulation

REFERENCES

General

Brown, R. (1992) *Understanding Industrial Organisations.* London: Routledge.
Grint, K. (1991) *The Sociology of Work*. Oxford: Polity Press.
Mayo, E. (1933) *Human Problems of an Industrial Civilization.* New York: Macmillan.
Parsons, H. (1974) 'What Happened at Hawthorne?' *Science*, 183: 922–32.
Roethlisberger, F. and Dickson, W. (1939) *Management and the Worker.* New York: Wiley.
Rose, M. (1988) *Industrial Behaviour* (2nd edn). Harmondsworth: Penguin.

Examples

Du Boulay, J. and Williams, R. (1987) 'To See Ourselves: Images of the Fieldworker in Scotland and Greece, with Some Reflections upon the Fieldwork'. In McKeganey, N. and Cunningham-Burley, S. (eds), *Enter the Sociologist*. Aldershot: Avebury.
Landsberger, H. (1958) *Hawthorne Revisited*. Ithaca, NY: Cornell University Press.
Parry, O. (1987) 'Uncovering the Ethnographer'. In McKeganey, N. and Cunningham-Burley, S. (eds), *Enter the Sociologist.* Aldershot: Avebury.

Hypothesis

A hypothesis is a reasoned but provisional supposition about the relationship between two or more social phenomena, stated in terms that can be empirically tested and which forms the focus for research, particularly in quantitative studies.

Section Outline: *Preliminaries to research, and 'anticipations'. Working hypotheses as a starting point. Example: student phone ownership. Evolving descriptive and relational hypotheses. Direction of relationship and theoretical models. Example: social mobility. Format of hypotheses in quantitative methods: statement; about single relationship or phenomenon; clearly expressed; empirically testable. Format of hypotheses in qualitative methods: less specific 'propositions'; discovered from data; limited applicability. Confirmation, proof and disproof. The 'null hypothesis'. 'Rejecting' the null hypothesis.*

In research, we work from 'knowing less' towards 'knowing more'. We do not collect data without prior information or reflection. We decide what we want to know about; how much is already known about it; the varieties of form it might present; where it can be studied; how we might best collect information about it; and how we intend to analyse data once they have been collected. While researchers do not exclusively seek those findings that support their prior ideas, they have at least implicit anticipations about what they might find. It is in this area of 'anticipation' that we encounter the hypothesis.

A hypothesis is a tentative suggestion about what we might find. At its simplest, it takes the form that 'something is happening'. For example, from general observation on campus, we might guess that 'a lot of students own mobile phones'. Our research task following from such a general hypothesis would be to collect trustworthy information so that we could confidently report phone ownership rates.

What we have here is a 'working hypothesis', a statement that is imprecise, but which expresses the research's main direction. Its usefulness is providing a starting point from which more precise hypotheses can be developed, and to help in designing the research. It narrows the topic (student phone ownership is *about phones*, and *students*, not about, or say, TV and elderly people). It may suggest extra ideas, like whether male and female students have the same level of ownership, or use them for the same purposes, and is best understood as a stage in the research process (Kumar 1999: 64–70).

Working hypotheses differ from the more conventional use of the term, particularly in quantitative research, to mean a more precise statement about descriptive or relational phenomena. By '*descriptive hypotheses*', we mean statements about events, i.e. that something is happening, or happening at a certain rate. In our example, 'a lot of students' could be made more precise by rephrasing it as '85 per cent of undergraduates'. Our fact-gathering exercise would become more focused.

'*Relational hypotheses*', on the other hand, express the anticipation that two or more items in the research will be related to one another in a particular way. The hypothesis that 'female ownership rates are higher than male ones' relates the variable 'gender' to the variable 'phone ownership'. It relates the variables in two specific ways. First it plausibly assumes gender behaviour determines phone usage, rather than the reverse. The relationship has a direction. Second, it posits that female gender behaviour leads to greater ownership, not less. Whereas a descriptive hypothesis leads to simple exploration, or fact-gathering, a relational hypothesis points towards investigating a more complex set of things, their interconnection, and a *theoretical model* that explains why there is that interconnection.

The student phone example was drawn from casual observation, but most relational hypotheses are derived from findings or theoretical models from previous studies. For example, a social mobility study might hypothesise from Marx's class *theory* that 'sons are likely to become members of the same class as their fathers'. This because under Marx's idea of capitalism, the upper class have more material assets to assist their children than do the working class. Equally, the same hypothesis could draw on the previous findings of Glass's 1949 pioneering British mobility study, that about two-thirds of 'service class' men had fathers from that class (Rose 1982; Schutt 1999: 38–42).

Thus in quantitative research, a hypothesis has four main characteristics:

1 It is expressed as a statement, not a question (though it may answer an implicit question): '85 per cent of students own mobile phones', not 'Do 85 per cent of students own mobile phones?'.

2 It addresses a single phenomenon, or a single relation between phenomena.
3 It is stated clearly and is logically consistent.
4 And most important of all it is empirically testable ('God is Great' is not a hypothesis).

In qualitative research (**Qualitative Methods**), hypotheses are rarely stated at the outset. This is because most qualitative researchers believe social behaviour is complex and transitory, and does not consist of constant regularities. Human actions therefore do not follow 'laws'. They see relational hypotheses as falsely implying that we can discover law-like patterns that predetermine action. Furthermore, adopting a hypothesis at an early stage can restrict the scope of enquiry, and not reflect the realities of the research setting. Because relational hypotheses connect 'variables', this arbitrarily isolates one part of people's lives from their context, doing violence to the 'true' nature of context-specific events and human experience.

This does not mean that qualitative researchers never use hypotheses. They too start with theories and findings, operationalise their concepts, and have anticipations. However, they favour looser, descriptive hypotheses; using the term 'hypothesis' less, and sometimes preferring the word 'proposition' (Strauss and Corbin 1998: 102). They restrict any hypothesis or proposition to a specific social situation, and avoid statistical techniques for evaluating their interpretations. Perhaps most important of all, they engage with their data in order to discover their preliminary hypotheses, and refine them by further data collection (**Grounded Theory**). *The hypothesis emerges progressively from the data, rather than the hypothesis determining from the outset what data are collected*.

In quantitative research, the operational measurements we make cannot logically *prove* that a relationship exists as hypothesised (**Positivism and Realism**). Our limited empirical activities can never establish that a relation holds true for all situations at all times, although we can find supporting evidence that helps to *confirm* it. In practice, we work the other way around, seeing if something is *untrue*. If we find a single case that goes contrary to our hypothesis, that is a sufficient disproof: we would have to modify or abandon our hypothesis.

For this reason, statistical analysis often works with a special kind of hypothesis. Up to this point we have talked about hypotheses as general theoretical statements about relationships between factors. In statistical work, the term 'hypothesis' is more precise, indicating a numerically measurable association which can be 'tested', and normally referred to as 'the null hypothesis'.

This takes the form of stating the *reverse* of the more theoretical one with which we started. So 'female ownership rates are higher than male ones' yields the null hypothesis that 'there is no difference between male and female phone ownership rates'. If we do then find a difference, we can 'reject the null hypothesis' (an introduction to the statistical treatment of this process can be found in most statistics textbooks: a particularly clear one is to be found in Rose and Sullivan 1993).

In rejecting the null hypothesis, we will have established a *disproof* of it (which as we noted before, we can legitimately do, whereas we could not logically prove something). If we disprove the null hypothesis, that leaves us with our original hypothesis: we do not unquestioningly 'accept' it, but we have increased the chances that it is right. In our phone ownership example, we might have shown that ownership rates differ, but not that they differ in the anticipated way, or that outside of our study, ownership rates always differ in the way we seem to have found. Of course, we cannot prove that absolutely.

If our hypothesis takes the general form of 'A is greater than B' ('female ownership rates are higher than male ones'), then the null hypothesis usually takes the form of 'There is no difference between A and B' ('there is no difference between male and female phone ownership rates'). In fact, we might find that what disproves our null hypothesis is evidence that not only shows a difference, but a difference showing male rates are actually *higher* than female rates. This would also be a disproof of our hypothesis.

We must set our empirical tests carefully. If we are too generous, we might confirm our original hypothesis when it is actually wrong (we would be accepting evidence to disprove the null hypothesis when it is insufficient). If we are too rigorous, we might mistakenly reject a basically valid hypothesis (we would in fact find enough support for the null hypothesis not to reject it). The mathematical methods for balancing these problems are covered in all introductory statistics texts.

Key Words

descriptive hypothesis
disproof
empirical test
null hypothesis
relational hypothesis
working hypothesis

Links

Grounded Theory
Positivism and Realism
Qualitative Methods

REFERENCES

General

Kumar, R. (1999) *Research Methodology*. London: Sage.
Rose, D. and Sullivan, O. (1993) *Introducing Data Analysis for Social Scientists*. Buckingham: Open University Press.
Strauss, A. and Corbin, J. (1998) *Basics of Qualitative Research* (2nd edn). London: Sage.

Examples

Rose, G. (1982) *Decyphering Sociological Research*. London: Macmillan.
Schutt, R. (1999) *Investigating the Social World* (2nd edn). Thousand Oaks, CA: Pine Forge Press.

Indicators and Operationalisations

Indicators, often combined into indices, are indirect empirical representations used to define or refer to concepts when no direct measurement is possible, whereas operationalisations (which include indicators) are the precise definitions of any social phenomena in empirical terms ready for data collection.

Section Outline: *Can concepts be directly 'measured'? Examples of concepts needing operationalisation. Sets of indicators. Examples of simple operationalisations. Selecting indicators: reflecting the concept; covering all its aspects; excluding other concepts; generating appropriate data. Indicators based on availability rather than precision. Examples: social deprivation; class. Theory, concept, indicator, measurement. Qualitative methods' objections to indicator research.*

Sociology studies many topics that, by their nature, cannot be *directly* accessed in research. They can only be researched by means of first establishing some way of representing them in a measurable form. General and often abstract 'concepts' have to be converted into separate, clearly specified components that can be studied empirically.

To take the topics covered in just one issue of a recent journal, 'refugee'; 'forced migration'; 'community'; 'social integration'; 'gypsy'; 'inner city schooling' and 'governance' are all social phenomena requiring operationalisation. We cannot tell whether the 'thing' is present or absent, how often it occurs, in what circumstances and what importance it has, without intermediate constructions. To take one example from our list, one cannot measure 'community' (the acid test is to ask 'where would you go to buy half a pound of it?', i.e. how would you know what to look for?). We could however decide that one essential feature was 'a sense of shared identity' (**Community Studies**), and then devise questions to discover with whom and in what ways people identified (Payne 2000).

Shared identity is not in itself a full characterisation of community. It is an indicator of one part of the total concept, to be combined with other indicators such as sense of locality, or density of social networks, etc. to provide a full picture. The original idea, community, has to be *operationally defined* into these indicators which enable us to study it. Thus 'indicators' and 'operational definitions' are very similar and often interchangeable terms.

Some operational definitions are very simple, and come close to being the original idea itself. In western societies, age is easy to research: it is conventionally measured in *years*, and almost everybody knows their date of birth (but in other societies and times, 'age' was a very approximate thing). Gender may be a complex social construct, but most people are content to describe themselves as either *male*, or *female*. Most forms of 'housing occupation' are covered by *ownership, mortgaged ownership, or rental (private or social)*. The indicators – years; biological sex; ownership/rental – are straightforward, lending themselves to quantified measurements. If they are part of a cluster of variables in an explanation (**Validity**), they would normally suffice as measures, although if one were the central focus of a study or the dependent variable, minor caveats might become substantial objections. Thus the cut-off points of age-bands, or gender identification, or tied housing and household dependency, might each become issues, depending on the research focus.

This process of operationalisation is central to research design. It may seem obvious that indicators should correspond to the concept being researched. However, challenges to research findings are often based on disputes over whether the indicators adequately characterise the core concept. The debate over secularisation is as much about what counts as evidence, as about its meaning, causes and significance. Bruce (1995) tends to operationalise secularisation in terms of low church attendance rates, whereas Davie (1994) pays more attention to statements of belief in God and membership of new social movements. Because the two versions of indicators characterise the key concept in slightly different ways, the protagonists argue past one another.

Indicators should therefore achieve four goals.

1 They must properly reflect the essential nature of the core concept.
2 They must cover the whole of the concept (it is usual to have more than one indicator for each concept).
3 They must not pick up some other concept.
4 They must produce evidence in a form appropriate to the level of study, either as a quantified form of measurement (**Levels of Measurement**) or contributing to a plausible narrative of meanings and interpretations (see below and **Qualitative Methods**).

Operational definitions can be drawn from several sources. Some ('years of life' to measure 'age') are just commonsense. Others follow logically from reflecting about the nature of the concept: sense of identity measurements derive from our model of community. Exploratory studies are a good way of discovering and clarifying the components and variations in the empirical manifestations of a concept.

In some cases, indicators are chosen because they are effective rather than exact. Miners used to take canaries down the pits: when the canary collapsed, it was time to escape, because the air was bad. The bird was more susceptible to carbon monoxide than were the men. The miners did not measure the gas, they 'measured' the indicator, the canary's health.

In sociology, concepts like poverty and social exclusion have been measured by sets of variables that are similarly known to be associated with the key concept (**Association and Causation**). Local areas of social deprivation have been identified using a combination of scores for, among others: unemployment rates; over-crowding; lack of housing amenities; renting; residential turnover; car ownership; occupational profile; single parent and pensioner household structures; young children; qualification levels; and illness – together with death rates; derelict land; benefit recipients; and contents insurance premium levels (Payne et al. 1996). The first set of a dozen variables are conveniently available from the Census (albeit likely to be out of date because the Census is only taken once a decade), while the remainder are obtained from other official statistics. They may not be the best possible indicators, but they have been chosen because the data are readily to hand, in some cases for local authority areas, and in others down to ward or enumeration district.

No single indicator would be sufficient on its own, nor do scores precisely measure the underlying concept (Carley 1981). Alternative indices of deprivation (the 'Carstairs Index', the 'Jarman Index', etc.) have chosen different combinations to meet particular needs: health resources allocation or determining local government grants. Social indices of disadvantage can be seen as an alternative to dependence on social class; some, like Townsend et al. (1992), seeking to expand class's explanatory powers, while others, like Carr-Hill (1990), wishing to escape class altogether. Indicators may be about measurement, but they are embedded in *theoretical perspectives*.

However, indicators may change independently of the original concept. Social class is about social groupings developing from ownership and control of production. Traditionally, this has been empirically represented by *occupation*. That worked tolerably well while most workers were men in full-time paid employment, in an unchanging labour market consisting of large blocks of similar occupations. However, the rise of female employment, part-time working, self-employment, second jobs, early retirement, high levels of unemployment, training-delayed entry into the labour market, and new types of occupation have all complicated the scene. Nor is lifestyle or social identity as neatly associated with occupation as they once were. It is impossible to tell if social class per se has changed, independent of the changes in the indicator. If we measure something indirectly, this must always be a risk (**Social Surveys**).

This tendency for operational definitions to freeze concepts in a fixed way is one of the main reasons why qualitative researchers reject prior operationalisation, preferring to retain flexibility of response to field encounters (**Qualitative Methods**). Pre-conceptualisation cannot cover the full complexity of a concept, and dependence on commonsense is likely to result in the researcher's own ideas being imposed at the expense of the informants' subjective meanings. Being less concerned with measurement per se, and oriented to inductive procedures (**Positivism and Realism**), qualitative methods by-pass the rigour of operationalisation, substituting detailed accounts as the basis for **Validity** and **Reliability** claims.

Key Words

dependent variable
empirical
operational definition
secularisation
social class

Links

Association and Causality
Community Studies
Levels of Measurement
Positivism and Realism
Qualitative Methods
Reliabilty
Social Surveys
Validity

REFERENCES

General

Carley, M. (1981) *Social Measurement and Social Indicators.* London: Allen & Unwin.
Carr-Hill, R. (1990) 'The Measurement of Inequalities in Health'. *Social Science and Medicine.* 31 (3): 393–404.

Examples

Bruce, S. (1995) *Religion in the Modern World.* Oxford: Oxford University Press.
Davie, G. (1994) *Religion in Britain since 1945.* Oxford: Blackwell.
Payne, G. (ed.) (2000) *Social Divisions.* Basingstoke: Palgrave.
Payne, J., Payne, G. and Hyde, M. (1996) 'The Refuse of all Classes', *Sociological Research OnLine,* 1 (1).
Townsend, P., Davidson, N. and Whitehead, M. (1992) *Inequalities in Health: the Black Report and the Health Divide* (revised edn). Harmondsworth: Penguin.

Internet and Other Searches

Internet searches are the planned and strategic use of networked computing to track down reliable data, reference materials and other relevant sources for use in research, differing only in scale and technical procedures from other searches such as literature reviews, library catalogues and archives.

Section Outline: *Growing importance of the internet for background literature, data-sets and polling. Problems of reliability of sources on the net, and time wasted in inefficient searches/surfing. Keyword searches. Example: health. CD-ROM catalogues. Sources listing other sources. Using search engines efficiently. Accessing agencies and statistical information.*

Around the start of this millennium, British social science students made a marked shift in sourcing their assessment assignments. Their bibliographies became less library book-based, instead consisting increasingly of websites. Undergraduates need little explanation of this: the internet is open when you want to work, and its vast contents are always available, unlike the University Library. Thus a literature review may start in the library, but soon expands into the virtual library of the web (Fink 1988: 15–38; Schutt 1999: 498–513).

Researchers use the internet in several ways. Like students, they search for previous literature on their topics. They can also download data in their original detail from earlier studies, and re-analyse them (**Secondary Analysis**). Data about other users can be collected by placing questionnaires on-line, or from more open-ended bulletin boards or chat rooms (**Internet Polling**; **Questionnaires**; **Social Surveys**). People's use of the internet can itself be the subject of study (e.g. Hine 2000). The web is, as the author of *The Hitchhiker's Guide to the Galaxy* said, 'a huge all-singing, all-dancing, hopping, beeping, flash-ridden brochure' (Adams 2003: 92). Even writing about it seems dull, archaic and unreliable, as the speed of its changes outpaces print-production.

However, that speed of change is itself a difficulty, because we need to evolve new rules about good practice. Many undergraduates lack discrimination in using websites. The fact that something is present on the web seems to give it sufficient and equal credibility.

> The Internet is a way of transmitting bits of information from one computer to another . . . The meaning of the bits comes from the patterns which they make and of course from the users who send and receive them (Hine 2000: 2).

It is easy to forget to ask who has put them up, what expertise do the authors have, what special interests do the authors serve and can they be trusted to abide by the conventions of social research practice and method? When is a source academically respectable, and when is it just a weblog?

The internet needs to be used systematically, because being such a large resource, it can absorb so much time (and in some cases expense). A useful starting model for internet searching is the more limited search of a library's computerised catalogue, based on *key words*. After all, the internet is only another tool: the purpose of literature searches (Hart 1998: 26–72) has not changed because of the new *technology*. You must first work out the particular categories or areas that interest you: e.g. 'health statistics' (this section draws heavily on Payne 1999: 37–52). When you select the keyword option of the 'catalogue search' facility, you enter these two words separated by a space. The computer software package then searches database references that match both words, separately and combined. You can view the references for each separate category ('statistics', 'health') or for the combined category ('statistics' and 'health' together). An example of an on-line catalogue search is given in Figure 5.

If you use broad categories like 'statistics' and 'health', it is best to choose the combined option. You might otherwise be presented with too many references to handle. Alternatively, you might want to refine your search categories by adding a further category such as 'mortality', or a particular geographical location or time period. The challenge if you cannot find what you seek is to think laterally to find other key words to try. The more fully you can think out what you are intending to achieve, the easier this is (**Indicators and Operationalisations**).

Your library will have other information sources on either CD-ROM catalogues or via the internet. Your data librarian can help you with this information. CD-ROM catalogues are used in the same way as other computer CD-ROM disks. Each one will have its own query facilities, but are fairly easy to use. You can also consult the International Bibliography of the Social Sciences (IBSS) at *www.bids.ac.uk*, but this requires a username and password (see your librarian or computer advisor). Another possible source is the Social Science Citation Index, useful once you have a publication or author as a starting point *www.isinet.com/isi/products/citation/ssci*.

When you log on to the internet (strictly, the 'world wide web' or www), you will need to use a search engine like 'Google'. However, you can spend a considerable amount of time and effort using these as direct search tools. Instead, you could use them to access the websites of central and local government departments, health authorities and organisations, universities and other on-line gateways and indexes. These often open up specialist resources like databases (Fink 1998: 15–38). Many national statistics are also available on CD-ROM computer disks or via on-line

SEARCH THE ON-LINE CATALOGUE

1. Enquiry using AUTHOR with TITLE
2. KEYWORD enquiry
3. TITLE enquiry
4. NAME enquiry
5. JOURNAL title or keyword enquiry
6. Other

Enter code: **2**

Enter brief description: **health statistics**

'health'	4000+ items found
'statistics'	1000+ items found

---

178 items match your search

1. Display records
2. Go back
3. Amend or edit this search

Enter code: **3**

Enter brief description: health statistics **mortality**

'health'	4000+ items found
'statistics'	1000+ items found
'mortality'	85 items found

---

29 items match your search

1. Display records
2. Go back
3. Amend or edit this search

Enter code: **3**

Enter brief description: health statistics mortality **smoking**

'health'	4000+ items found
'statistics'	1000+ items found
'mortality'	85 items found
'smoking'	80 items found

---

1 items match your search

1. Display records
2. Go back
3. Amend or edit this search

Enter code: **1**

---

1. Mortality from smoking in developed countries, 1950-2000: indirect estimates from national vital statistics/ Richard Peto . . . . . . [et al] 1994

FULL, LOCATION, BACK

Enter code:

Figure 5 *An example of using an on-line library catalogue*

Note: Each box represents an interactive screen on a computer. Words in **bold** are user responses enquiries. At the time of writing, the main British suppliers are the Office of National Statistics (ONS) via StatBase; and the Economic and Social Data Service (ESDS) Data Archive. The latter is a recent collaboration between the International Data Service and Cathie Marsh Centre for Census and Survey Research (MIMAS) at Manchester University, together with the UK Data Archive (the Qualitative Data Service, the Data Archiving and Dissemination Service, and the Longitudinal Data Service) at Essex University. A convenient starting point is *www.data-archive.ac.uk*. SOSIG, the Social Science Information Gateway gives access to wider social science sources at *www.sosig.ac.uk*. Information from these websites is much more likely to be reliable than general trawls through the web.

A good starting point for on-line enquiries about government statistical information is the government information service at *www.open.gov.uk*. Some of these sites only provide data to bona fide researchers. For these, you may need to complete a licence application form and possibly purchase the data sets (**Secondary Analysis**).

Key Words

academic respectability
ESDS
IBSS
key words
SOSIG
StatBase

Links

Indicators and Operationalisations
Internet Polling
Questionnaires
Secondary Analysis
Social Surveys

REFERENCES

General

Adams, D. (2003) *The Salmon of Doubt*. London: Pan Macmillan.
Hine, C. (2000) *Virtual Ethnography*. London: Sage.

Examples

Fink, A. (1998) *Conducting Research Literature Reviews*. London: Sage.
Hart, C. (1998) *Doing a Literature Review*. London: Sage.
Payne, J. (1999) *Researching Health Needs*. London: Sage.
Schutt, R. (1999) *Investigating the Social World* (2nd edn). Thousand Oaks, CA: Pine Forge Press.

Internet Polling

Internet polling is a relatively new, growing, but still untested means of carrying out social surveys and opinion polls by use of either direct e-mailing to potentially interested groups via message boards, or a website accessible only to a previously recruited panel.

Section Outline: *Internet polling for dissertations: cheap, safe, comfortable. Web users as a subject to be studied: user demographics; user ethnography. Polling: responding at convenient times. Otherwise much like postal questionnaires; same design requirements. Hardware and software incompatibilities. Software for coding. Limitations: scheduling for problems; confidentiality and anonymity; Netiquette. Cost savings versus sample bias.*

For university students, the ready availability of computing facilities offers the prospect of using the internet, not just as a way to search for published sources of information (**Internet and Other Searches**; **Secondary Analysis**), but also for collecting raw data. This is particularly useful for undergraduate dissertations, because internet 'fieldwork' is cheaper, quicker, safer and more comfortable (it can be done from home or the campus library).

There are three main types of internet social research. The most direct focuses on computer usage and the web itself as *topics of research*. For example, such work tells us about the 'demographics' of computer/internet users, i.e. respondents are 'more likely to be white, male, first world residents, relatively affluent and relatively well educated' (Coomber 1997: 5.1). The main pitfall in this field of research is depending for ideas on misleading non-sociological publications that make sweeping assertions about 'global villages', 'personal empowerment', 'the computerised society', etc.

A special case of treating internet use as a topic is the still relatively undeveloped field of ethnographic analysis (**Ethnography**). Here the key issues are: How do users understand the internet as a system of communication? How are its social relationships different from 'real life', and what does it mean for self-identity? Hine (2000) has used a 'media event' (the Louise Woodward case) to explore many of the issues in this kind of work, which concentrates on exchanges within newsgroups (Fisher et al. 1996).

The third kind of internet-based research is primarily concerned with using it to contact respondents. These may be samples intended to represent the general population, as in voting intention polling, or sub-groups which are otherwise difficult to contact (e.g. self-harmers: Fox et al. 2003). The technology is only important in so far as it affects the findings (by producing different results from other methods), or the conduct of the research (offering practical advantages in procedures).

While there have been some comparisons between internet surveys' findings and findings from other methods, at this stage there has been little direct research on how people go about the process of *responding* to internet questionnaires. Hine's (2000) research does not report observational studies of user practice, for example. It is believed that recipients tackle electronic questionnaires in essentially the same way as reacting to postal questionnaires. This includes putting off completion from the moment of receipt to a more convenient time, notably at the weekend.

It follows that most of the issues in questionnaire design applying to postal surveys (**Social Surveys**; **Questionnaires**) – phrasing questions, putting them in the right sequence, and providing clear instructions – also apply to internet polling. With no face-to-face interviewers, people are more likely to complete the questionnaire if it is clear, unambiguous and easy to fill in. Equally, questionnaires should be introduced with explanations of researchers' identities and intentions, giving honest information about anonymity (see below) and confidentiality (**Ethical Practice**).

One difference is that whereas self-completion surveys operate on the simple system of either handing in, or using pre-paid return envelopes through the postal service, internet surveys have to rely on the compatibility of two main hardware platforms (MACs and PCs). Each of these can run different internet software (e.g. Netscape and Microsoft Explorer), connected to one of several service providers. It is important that interconnections between these are compatible.

This is less of a problem where the target respondents are known (for instance, a sample from the student e-mail directory within a university) and the contact method is an e-mail containing the questionnaire as an attachment. Where there is no comprehensive list ('sampling frame':

Sampling: Types) the usual method is to make contact via message boards or newsgroups, 'advertising' the survey as available at one's website. This increases the chances of technological incompatibility.

If data collection is set up through a website, more sophisticated tools can be brought into play. The questionnaire itself can contain software-based instructions (selective, real-time 'prompts'; offers of support through FAQs; or 'eye-candy' encouragements). In more sophisticated (and expensive) projects, incoming data can be handled by additional software at the server to pre-sort responses for speed of analysis (and to remove clerical error in coding: Fox et al. 2003). Commercial packages are already available (e.g. 'SphinxSurvey' 2003). Whatever the level of software, all data-collection tools should be pre-tested on a range of technologies, not just the researcher's own hardware and software.

Even with technical pre-testing, it is sensible to allow for down-time due to potential server crashes. 'Murphy's Law' (if it can happen, it will) works well in computing – internet polling is not the method of last resort when time for other methods seems to be running out! Research schedules should also cover possible need for e-mail correspondence with would-be respondents, about the questionnaire or ethical issues like confidentiality.

Promises of anonymity are less credible when e-mail replies will contain names and electronic addresses. Confidentiality is easier to deliver: although the emerging data-set will obviously be at risk to hackers, it is not significantly more vulnerable than other data-sets held on computers. The greater visibility of the original 'advertisement' might attract more hacking, but prompt data transfer via portable disks is one useful step to inhibit tracking. The technology should not distract researchers from their fundamental ethical obligations to be honest and to protect informants.

Indeed, the internet introduces new ethical issues. 'Netiquette' conventions, not least about 'spamming', have to be observed. 'Advertising' on bulletin boards or to newsgroups makes the survey less intrusive (nobody is obliged to respond, or deal with it at an inconvenient time). 'Difficult' topics can be tackled without the presence of an interviewer (although of course most qualitative researchers would not regard this as a benefit: **Ethnography**). Conversely, researchers are exposed to other people's bad internet practices, including speculative hacking, multiple replying to bias the results (checks can constrain this), deliberate false reporting, or other sabotage attempts where the topic has a political or moral dimension.

The technological limitation of internet polling, and the considerable but often unanticipated time expended in preparation, can be balanced against more obvious advantages, like the absence of paper, printing and postage costs. As the data are in electronic form, there is much less need to transcribe prior to processing for analysis (**Quantitative Methods**; **Coding Qualitative Data**; **Content Analysis**). Data return quickly: Fox et al. (2003) suggest that replies from interest groups tail off within two weeks. 'Follow-ups' (**Social Surveys**) are as easy as with any other method, and take less of researchers' time.

The big remaining question is sampling. There is normally no sampling frame from which to select a representative sub-set of respondents (**Sampling: Types**). We noted above that internet users differ in their demographics from non-users. We therefore cannot be confident in generalising our findings beyond these types of people. For research about a general population, such as in opinion polling (e.g. *YouGov* 2003: Fisher et al. 1996), collecting extensive demographic data (including country of residence: the internet is international) from each respondent, and then weighting the data is one way to handle this (see **Telephone and Computer-assisted Polling**).

However, even if we match demographics, it is still impossible to tell how the people who self-select to respond are different from non-responders in other ways. The best that can be claimed is that, for specific difficult groups (e.g. drug-dealers, self harmers: see Coomber 1997; Fox et al. 2003), internet sampling may achieve larger samples than other methods equally dependent on defective samples. As with other methods, the choice is often about the 'least worst' solution rather than achieving perfection.

Key Words

anonymity
confidentiality
defective samples
demographics
'difficult' topics
media event
newsgroup
technological compatibility

Links

Coding Qualitative Data
Content Analysis
Ethical Practice
Ethnography
Internet and Other Searches
Quantiative Methods
Questionnaires
Sampling: Types
Secondary Analysis
Social Surveys
Telephone and Computer-assisted Polling

REFERENCES

General

Coomber, R. (1997) 'Using the Internet for Survey Research', *Sociological Research Online*, 2 (2), www.socresonline.org.uk/socresonline/2/2/2.html

Fisher, B., Margolis, M. and Resnik, D. (1996) 'Surveying the Internet: Democratic Theory and Civic Life in Cyberspace', *Southeastern Political Review*, 24 (3).

Fox, J., Craig, M. and Warm. A. (2003) 'Conducting Research Using Web-based Questionnaires', *International Journal of Social Research Methodology*, 6 (2): 167–80.

Examples

Hine, C. (2000) *Virtual Ethnography*. London: Sage.

SphinxSurvey (2003) www.scolari.co.uk/sphinx/shinx.html.

YouGov (2003) www.YouGov.co.uk

Interviewing

Interviewing is data collection in face-to-face settings, using an oral question-and-answer format which either employs the same questions in a systematic and structured way for all respondents, or allows respondents to talk about issues in less directed but discursive manner.

Section Outline: *Many varieties of interviewing. Face-to-face interviewing in social surveys. Interviewer instructions, training and briefing. 'Neutrality'. Refusals. Interviewer bias. Qualitative interviewing: depth interviews and bias. Semi-structured and unstructured interviews. Recording answers. Limitations of interviews: cost; less anonymous; field-force hard to set up and manage. Benefits over other methods: high response rates; contacting the right people; handling more complex material; elaboration on answers.*

The most extensive social research method, namely interviewing, covers a range of styles (Sarantakos 1998 lists nearly 30 sub-types). Here, we concentrate on the face-to-face encounter of one interviewer with one person being interviewed – the 'informant' or 'respondent' (**Group Discussions/Focus Groups**; **Telephone and Computer-assisted Polling**; **Social Surveys**). This kind of encounter takes two main forms: those in surveys using standardised questionnaires, and those done in qualitative research where the questioning is less structured. In both cases, the quality of the data depends on the quality of the interviewing (Polgar and Thomas 1991).

In survey interviewing, information from large numbers of people is obtained via the same questions put in a standardised way, so that no differences, or **Bias**, is introduced by the person asking the questions (McFarlane Smith 1972). Interviewers are trained to follow instructions closely. This includes who is interviewed (**Sampling: Questions of Size**: **Sampling**; **Types**) and how they are approached (McCrossan 1991). Respondents are usually given a letter explaining the nature of the interview, and interviewers are briefed to show their identity cards and to make a standard introductory statement. A basic level of informed consent (**Ethical Practice**) is obtained, the emphasis being on interviewers completing the interview as quickly, and as accurately recorded, as possible.

Interviewers are instructed to follow the questionnaire exactly in order, and not to change the question wording (**Questionnaires**). They may 'prompt' for more information ('What else is there? What else?') or 'probe' to clarify ('What exactly do you mean when you say . . . ?). However, these interventions are usually at points marked in the questionnaire. Other deviations or paraphrasings are forbidden, because they could introduce additional extraneous factors into the data collection and so distort findings. Thus any temptation for interviewers to establish a social relationship or personal rapport by chatting, or the giving of opinions, is strongly discouraged, both as time-wasting and a source of biasing what respondents might say. Interviewers are instructed to be polite and positive in general attitude, but neutral on opinions and not demanding.

Interviewers are briefed to handle any problems that might arise. Only a very few people refuse to be interviewed if the survey is being carried out correctly. In this case interviewers should attempt to find out the reason for the refusal. It might be because they called at an inconvenient time, in which case a more suitable time should be arranged. Other reasons include fear, worry about views becoming known, being 'not interested', or informants feeling they know too little about the topic. The interviewer should attempt to reassure them. The interviewer's 'neutrality' (plus the matching where possible of interviewers and informants for gender, ethnicity, age, etc.) is designed to be non-threatening. In the case of people not being in, the interviewer is instructed to call back twice more, at different times of the day, before a non-contact is recorded.

The potential for 'interviewer bias' is a major issue, because researchers cannot directly control every member of the interviewer field-force. Less able interviewers may contact the wrong respondents, deviate from the questionnaire or misrecord answers. Personal appearance, facial expression, tone of voice, in addition to comments, may misdirect the informant. Dishonest interviewers may fabricate interview results. This makes interviewer selection and training, backed up by good administration, skilled fieldwork supervisors, and checking of returns, all essential.

Some of these problems are less pressing in interviewing for qualitative research, because conventionally the numbers of people interviewed, and therefore the number of interviewers needed, are much smaller. It is common for the researcher to do all of the interviewing. While qualitative interviewing relies on the inter-personal skills and knowledge of the interviewer as an initiator of topics rather than on a carefully worded questionnaire, interviewers must still take care to avoid expressing their own opinions or suggesting answers. As the name suggests, the aim of this type of *depth interview* is to obtain an in-depth account of particular topics, but that account has to be the informant's and not simply a projection of the researcher's preconceptions.

Interviewer bias is a frequent accusation made against depth interviewing. Qualitative research regards the social world as too complex to be represented by fixed questions, so that establishing a rapport is needed to access the informant's 'world'. Feminists have also argued that male researchers exploit their position of power over their informants, ignoring both ethical obligations and differences in gender experience (**Feminist Research**; also Finch 1984; Tang 2002). The conduct of interviews depends on who is being interviewed, what the interview is about, and which type of interview technique is being used. Children and 'sensitive' topics raise particular issues (Harden et al. 2000). Depth interviewing's distinctive theoretical frame of reference makes it a very different activity from survey interviewing.

There are two main types of depth interview, now one of the most popular sociological research methods. *Semi-structured (or 'focused') interviews* are based on a small number of open-ended questions, the answers to which are actively and freely probed by the interviewer for elaboration. Often a sub-set of topics is listed, to help the interviewer concentrate on these issues. The questions or topics have to be put in the order that they appear on the question sheet ('interview schedule'). The respondent can then be led from a general first question to more specific ones.

The *unstructured (or 'non-directive') interview* is the least structured form of interview. No pre-defined questions are given and there is no ordering of topics. Instead, topics are simply listed as an *aide mémoire*. The interview enables respondents to give their accounts of their experiences, opinions and feelings in their own way. The interviewer's task is to probe for further details and ask for clarification when necessary. Thus, the questions the interviewer asks are determined by the direction taken in each interview. This type of interview often requires interviewers to have detailed knowledge of the issues so that suitable probing and supplementary questions can be asked.

Obviously these interviews cannot be recorded on a standard form, and copious note-taking might inhibit the flow of the interview. Instead, audio or video recorders are normally used if the respondent is agreeable. This is much better than relying on note-taking. The recorder should be placed as unobtrusively as possible and the interviewer should change tapes in a way that avoids too much interruption to the flow of the interview. Some basic notes should, however, also be made in case of mechanical failure. The recording should be checked for any problems as soon as possible afterwards. Good data collection is the basis both for team working and for the quotations to be selected later for inclusion in publications (e.g. Thomson et al. 2002).

The transcription of recordings is probably the most tedious and time-consuming aspect of these interviewing methods. It is usual for the recordings to be transcribed verbatim into readable text. This can then be manually processed or input into a text-coding computer program, like 'NUD*IST 4' (**Coding Qualitative Data**).

Things can go wrong, however well prepared the interviewer may be. For example, after completing an unstructured interview for a study of childless couples, one of the authors found that the audio tape had snarled up. Parking the car around the corner, she wrote down as much of the interview as possible. On later rescuing most of the tape, the hastily written notes proved to be accurate, but not comprehensive. Had she waited for the tape to be transcribed, much of the detail would have been forgotten (Payne 1978). Good memory is an asset.

Compared with other methods, the main disadvantages of interviewing are their cost (in money and time terms) and the potential for interviewer bias. They seem less anonymous, and may be inferior to self-written accounts on sensitive issues. Despite the semblance of the interviewer being in control, fieldwork is hard to organise and both researchers and their readers cannot know everything that goes on.

The main benefits are high response rates from appropriate informants. Respondents need no special skills, and a longer session of more complex questions is possible without misunderstandings, because the interviewer is physically present. This also permits recording of non-verbal signals and spontaneous reactions. Survey interviewing produces greater *consistency of data*, while qualitative interviewing provides *flexibility and elaboration* of answers. The capacity for instant responsiveness by the interviewer differentiates interviewing techniques from less direct methods (**Documentary Methods**; **Auto/biographies and Life Histories**; **Unobtrusive Methods**).

Key Words

bias
depth interview
probe
prompt
semi-structured
transcription
unstructured

Links

Auto/biographies and Life Histories
Bias
Coding Qualitative Data
Documentary Methods
Ethical Practice
Feminist Research
Group Discussion/Focus Groups
Questionnaires
Sampling: Questions of Size
Sampling: Types
Social Surveys
Telephone and Computer-assisted Polling
Unobtrusive Methods

REFERENCES

General

Harden, J., Scott, S., Beckett-Milburn, K. and Jackson, S. (2000) '"Can't Talk, Won't Talk": Methodological Issues in Researching Children'. *Sociological Research Online* 5 (2). www.socresonline.org.uk/socresonline/5/2/harden.html

McCrossan, L. (1991) *A Handbook for Interviewers* (2nd edn). London: HMSO (for OPCS).

MacFarlane Smith, J. (1972) *Interviewing in Market and Social Research*. London: Routledge & Kegan Paul.

Polgar, S. and Thomas, S. (1991) *Introduction to Research in Health Sciences* (2nd edn). Harlow: Churchill Livingston.

Sarantakos, S. (1998) *Social Research*. Basingstoke: Macmillan.

Examples

Finch, J. (1984) '"It's great to Have Someone to Talk to": the Ethics and Politics of Interviewing Women'. In Bell, C. and Roberts, H. (eds) *Social Researching.* London: Routledge & Kegan Paul.

Payne, J. (1978) 'Talking about Children: an Examination of Accounts about Reproduction and Family Life'. *Journal of Biosocial Science*, 10 (4): 367–74.

Powney, J. and Watts, M. (eds) (1987) *Interviewing in Educational Research*. London: Routledge & Kegan Paul.

Tang, N. (2002) 'Interviewer and Interviewee Relationships between Women'. *Sociology*, 36 (3): 703–21.

Thomson, R., Bell, R., Holland, J., Henderson, S., McGrellis, S. and Sharpe, S. (2002) 'Critical Moments: Choice, Chance and Opportunity in Young People's Narrative of Transition'. *Sociology* 36 (2): 335–54.

Key Informants

Key informants are those whose social positions in a research setting give them specialist knowledge about other people, processes or happenings that is more extensive, detailed or privileged than ordinary people, and who are therefore particularly valuable sources of information to a researcher, not least in the early stages of a project.

Section Outline: *Key informants and student dissertations. 'Leading players' in the community or organisation who have more information than most 'ordinary people'. Identifying potential key informants. Counter-culture key informants? Key informants speak from their own perspective, although are quickly accessed and may be the only sources. Example: 'tribal elders' misled anthropologists. Key informants as power-brokers: gatekeepers and speaking 'off the record'. Unique specialist knowledge versus unreliable witnesses.*

While research methods textbooks discuss key informants, very few say much about them as a method. This is a pity, because the key informant method is uniquely suitable for undergraduate dissertations and projects.

One can quickly glean a lot of rich information from relatively small numbers of interviewees, which is a great benefit when time and resources are short. The way these data are conceptualised, particularly when the degree of critical appraisal it receives is high, can produce an analysis of considerable depth and insight. In the account that follows, we have tried to show the complexity of the method, but this is not intended as a discouragement from doing key informant research.

Key informants (or 'expert witnesses') are different from 'ordinary' informants to the extent that they have *more information to impart*, and are more *visible*. The usual reason for their visibility is that they occupy formal positions of authority. If we look at local communities, we can quickly identify the ward councillor, the police inspector, the doctor, the bank manager and the church ministers. With only a little more effort, we can find social workers, teachers, health professionals, committee members of voluntary associations, council officials, works managers, journalists, small businessmen, shopkeepers, bar and club-owners.

> A key informant is simply someone who, by virtue of his [sic] particular position in the society, knows a great deal about the subject of the research. It may be that his expertise is to know who knows, so that he refers the research worker to others more knowledgeable than himself (Stacey 1969: 47).

Stacey used key informants to identify 'who knew whom' in a small town.

> We listed all voluntary associations. We then interviewed the secretary or other officer of each . . . The key informants were defined by their office in a voluntary organisation (ibid.: 103).

Alternatively, we might be interested in a single organisation, like a school, factory or club. Again, the role-players suggest themselves: teachers, caretaker, secretary, governors; managers, directors, supervisors, trade union officials; chair, secretary, treasurer, past committee members. However, these latter lists may suggest other types of key informants who do not occupy such formal roles: the school bully or sports hero; the old hand on the production line; the club member who has seen it all before – indeed the former member who has resigned.

Such people may sound like representatives of a counter-culture, but they may have that extra knowledge that we seek, by virtue of their personalities or place in the *informal system*, rather than their official positions. They may be less immediately visible, but their variant accounts help to round out data collection. They offer different views from the first set, because they represent different interest groups. Nobody speaks for 'the community' or 'the organisation'; only for the sub-set that they know and to which they belong. There is no consensus: part of the research will consist of making sense out of the competing views collected.

Foster, contrasting local residents' views with those of her 'official' key informants, observes:

> All of the councillors, Development Corporation executives, Board members and employers, affluent residents, business people and developers I interviewed had legitimacy if they were considered within the frame of reference of the individual's experience or the interest group from which they originated (Foster 1999: 1).

In quickly completed projects, researchers often have no time to go beyond the first group of more visible key informants. Such people are likely to dominate any meetings called (**Group Discussions/Focus Groups**). It is also inevitable that they will feature in **Community Profiles**. One of the authors investigated what health-related research voluntary bodies were conducting. The only method was to contact the secretaries of those groups in the local directory, and to take the responses of these people at face value. In the same way, when research 'consultants' do short-term contracts, a first step is contacting key informants to learn something basic about the locality.

Researchers in this situation are rather like early social anthropologists who studied small, isolated tribal societies. Their **Ethnography** was largely based on listening to those in authority: typically the tribal elders. These aging *men*, like their counterparts elsewhere, tended to talk about how things *should* be. The social descriptions they gave the anthropologists were simplified ones, stressing the cultural norms of societies, rather than what was actually happening. That they were men meant that they gave a narrowly masculine view of how their society worked. If researchers do not go beyond key informants' accounts, they run the risk of accepting a biased version of the social processes under study.

Gaining access to closed social systems (i.e. almost any organisation like a school or factory) means negotiating powerful figures who can permit or deny access: the 'gatekeepers' (**Fieldwork**). Once entry has been gained, the gatekeeper may become a key informant, not just as an individual, but by providing other key informants. This is useful, but it can trap researchers inside a particular interest group associated with the gatekeeper. One team gained access to a major company by using

> the status and authority of the chairman to obtain the compliance of other actors. . . . [but] it meant that effective control over the negotiation was taken out of the hands of the researchers (Brannen 1987: 168).

This indicates the powerful people's capacity to shape one's research.

> For those in positions of power, interviews in a variety of forms go with the job . . . These encounters left me with a very different set of questions and emotions to ponder – had they told me the truth? Were their emotions spontaneous or engineered? How much had they revealed . . . ? In some cases individuals moved between talking 'on' and 'off' the record, a sure sign that they were consciously constructing and controlling their accounts. Some of the best data were inevitably 'off the record' and I have not used this material (Foster 1999: 3).

Even 'informal' key informants, or those who want to be helpful, can limit and focus data collection. In *Street Corner Society*, Whyte's well-meaning key informant on gang life, 'Doc' tells him 'When you want some information, I'll ask for it and you listen' and also warns Whyte off from pushing too many questions (Whyte 1955: 292, 303).

This illustrates how key informant research is limited by whom we contact, what they know, and how able they are to open up further channels of information. Key informant information must be used with caution. It is better used as a starting point, when informants' partiality can be balanced by further research. Even so, some critics have objected to the way powerful gatekeepers reveal information, or commit others to co-operation in research, without asking their permission. This breaches the principle of obtaining 'informed consent' from all informants. It also sits uneasily with notions of collaboration and equality of participants in the research process, as advocated by many feminists (**Ethical Practice**; **Feminist Research**).

The main attractions of using key informants as a method are its quickness and easy application. Second, key informants *do* know more than other people: Raab's 16 key former educational administrators

> were able to reflect upon their experiences for research purposes. They were able to augment the public record of events by bringing additional information to bear upon it: in particular, information about motives, understandings and outlooks which helps to explain actions and constraints. They were able to provide insights into the way educational and governmental assumptions were, or were not, intertwined in [their] minds (Raab 1987: 118).

We intentionally select such key informants because of their atypical potential knowledge, a good example of 'purposive sampling' being in this case better than representative random sampling.

Key Words

counter-culture
gatekeeper
informal system
interest group
purposive sampling

Links

Community Profiles
Ethical Practice
Ethnography
Fieldwork
Feminist Research
Group Discussions/Focus Groups

REFERENCES

General

Stacey, M. (1969) *Methods of Social Research*. Oxford: Pergamon Press.

Examples

Brannen, P. (1987) 'Working on Directors: Some Methodological Issues'. In Moyser, G. and Wagstaffe, M. (eds), *Research Methods for Elite Studies.* London: Allen & Unwin.
Foster, J. (1999) *Docklands*. London: UCL Press.
Raab, C. (1987) 'Oral History as an Instrument of Research into Scottish Educational Policy-making'. In Moyser, G. and Wagstaffe, M. (eds) *Research Methods for Elite Studies.* London: Allen & Unwin.
Shaw, A. (1999) 'What Are "They" Doing with Our Food?' *Sociological Research Online*, 4 (3). www.socresonline.org.uk/socresonline/4/3/shaw.html
Whyte, W. F. (1955) *Street Corner Society* (2nd edn). Chicago: Chicago University Press.

Levels of Measurement

Depending upon their nature, social phenomena can be measured with one of four distinctive levels of measurement precision, which range from very simple (doing no more than giving a label or an approximate comparative size like 'more than' or 'less than') to numerically sophisticated (on which arithmetic calculations can be made).

> ***Section Outline:*** *All research entails measurement. Quantitative measurement describes in brief precise ways, which can be mathematically manipulated. Nominal level: labels. Ordinal levels: rankings. Interval level: uniform differences. Ratio level: zero-based numbers. Attributing numbers to sociological concepts.*

All social research – indeed work in all disciplines (Rose and Sullivan 1993; Polgar and Thomas 1991) – involves measurement. Even qualitative researchers (**Qualitative Methods**) who are often reluctant to admit it, use measurement (albeit low precision level measurements) to analyse data and report findings. The judgement that some observation is important, whereas another one is not, says that one is *more* important than the other, or that there is a presence or absence of importance. Coding field notes (**Grounded Theory**) involves classifying (deciding how much one thing resembles another), discovering if some things come up frequently or rarely, or are expressed with greater intensity. Reports, particularly by inexperienced qualitative researchers, often talk about 'many' or 'most' informants behaving in some way, sometimes expressing this in proportions (e.g. 'two-thirds') or even percentages.

However, although we all think in quantities, explicitly quantitative research (**Quantitative Methods**) makes greater use of more elaborate measurements (e.g. Sampson et al. 1997). The popularity of such techniques varies over time and between national traditions. Most American sociology journals show current dominance of statistical analysis techniques, whereas in the leading British journals, barely 5 per cent of articles now depend on quantitative analysis (Payne et al. in press).

'Measurement' then extends from simple (absent/present; more/less; frequent/rare) to a complexity of statistical modelling requiring assistance from professional statisticians. The three attractions of measurement are:

1 its capacity to yield very short and specific descriptions, i.e. by counting;
2 its capacity to define and differentiate between things very precisely (counting goes beyond 'more' or 'less' by saying *how much* more); and
3 its capacity to manipulate numbers directly (by statistical techniques) in a way not possible with actual people.

There are four distinctive levels of measurement. The extent to which these benefits are attained depends on the *level* of measurement.

The lowest level is *nominal measurement*. Here we identify things by *name*, putting them into a set of categories. Sociological phenomena can be identified by a name but that in itself does not give mathematical properties. Thus 'male' and 'female' are two categories of gender. We usually call the connecting element (here, gender) a 'variable' because it can take more than one form. 'Male' and 'female' are two forms or 'values' that the variable gender can take. To be 'measured' as male (grouped together with other males) means that one is not measured as female. We might allocate people to the religious categories of Christian, Muslim, Hindu, Buddhist, Jewish or Atheist, or to ethnic groups called Afro-Caribbean, European, Indian, Pakistani/Bangladeshi or Chinese. For some purposes a crude grouping will suffice (Christian/non-Christian; black/white), whereas in others we need much more detail (denominations of Christianity; regional and cultural origins). But until we count the people in each category, the categories have no numerical value.

A set of nominal categories (sometimes called a 'nominal scale') must consist of units that are distinct and mutually exclusive: one cannot be Christian and Buddhist at the same time. The scale should also be exhaustive, including all possible versions of the phenomenon (hence we included non-believers in a scale of religious affiliation). Although the members of one category – women; Christians; Europeans – may sometimes regard themselves as superior to others – men; Hindu; Indians – there is no measurement implication that one nominal category is better or larger than another.

The nominal categories in our scale *identify*, but they cannot be divided or multiplied together like mathematical numbers (we cannot do useful sums with them). The best we can achieve is to show what proportion of the total sample fall into each category. But if we combine categories, this creates a new category, at a different level of abstraction. For instance, you cannot add 'Christians' to 'Buddhists' and make something that has much sociological sense: even combining all 'believers', as distinct from 'non-believers', does not make for very insightful analysis of belief systems.

In some cases we can select categories that are organised in relation to each other, and put in order according to some criteria. This second level of measurement is called *ordinal level measurement*, and expresses a sense of magnitude. Social classes may be referred to as upper, middle or lower classes, or categorised into a more detailed hierarchy (Payne and Roberts 2002: Rose and O'Reilly 1998). People might be grouped by age into elderly; middle-aged; youths; and children (Vincent 2000). Thus we not only name the categories, but identify a sequence that they take according to some principle. Thus we can distinguish between using smaller, more precise categories (e.g. more specific classes) and using a measuring system that places each category in relation to the others.

However, we are only ranking the groups: we are not saying anything about the size of differences between any two pairs. The elderly are older than the middle-aged, but not, say, twice as old as them. The difference between being a youth and middle-aged is not the same as the difference between being middle-aged and elderly. Our ordinal scale adds something to the nominal level (at each level of measurement, the lower-level characteristics like mutually exclusivity of categories are retained), by showing an order of magnitude, i.e. having more or less of something. However, we still cannot do sums with ordinal categories.

We can start addition and subtraction once we define our categories so that the difference between them is the same. IQ tests illustrate the third level of measurement – the *interval level of measurement*. IQ tests are designed to show precise differences, and to have the same distance between scores wherever they occur along the IQ scale. Suppose we take three people, with IQ scores of 90, 100 and 110. If IQ were just nominal, it would tell us these three were different. If IQ were merely ordinal, we would know that the third person scored higher. As an interval scale, we can say that the first pair of scores differ to the same degree as the second pair of scores: 100 – 90 = 10, and 110 – 100 = 10. The person scoring 110 has twice as much difference in score from the first person (90) as does the second person (100): 110 – 90 = 20, whereas 110 – 100 = 10.

However, mathematics as a logical system needs to include a zero point before we can multiply or divide. Interval scales do not have a zero, whereas ratio level scales do. *Ratio level measurement* is the fourth level of measurement. Age, income, family size, number of employees and assessment marks are examples of ratio measurement: all can take a value of zero. We can correctly talk about someone being half the age of another, or one group's pay being five times higher than another's.

Although attitude scales are strictly speaking not ratio level measurements, it is permissible to treat them as if they were. If we score one extreme (e.g. 'disagree strongly') as zero, and the other responses as each one step higher (disagree = 1, neutral = 2, agree = 3 and strongly agree = 4), we can handle the data as ratio scales. Similarly we could assign the value of 0 to neutral responses, and score agreements 1 or 2, and disagreements –1 or –2. The higher the level of measurement, the more mathematical they become, and the more sophisticated the statistical operations that can be carried out on the data (Schutt 1999: 92–102: **Contingency Tables**). However, many sociologists using

Quantitative Methods do use lower levels of measurement, which in turn influences attitudes to, and reporting on, sampling procedures (**Sampling: Estimates and Size**).

Attitude scales illustrate how in practice, many social science phenomena do not really meet the requirements of interval or ratio measurement levels. **Attitude Scales** do not really start at 0 and range to 5 – we have merely attributed numerical values to the statements given by informants. The rules are often bent, scales treated 'as if' they were actually at a higher level of measurement. Social mobility treats movement between *any two* classes (normally out of 7 or 8 classes) as the same kind of mobility, despite the classes being only ordinal level categories. By artificially raising the level of measurement, researchers can use more sophisticated statistical techniques. This blurs the distinction between our four levels. Some of qualitative researchers' objections to quantification stem from these sleights of hand. More generally, as such treatments become more abstract, they move further away from the natural form of the original phenomenon.

In the quantitative tradition, researchers need to define their concepts and think about their intended analysis before measurement is possible (Bryman 2001: 214–26). The translation of an abstract theoretical concept into something that can be empirically measured is called *operationalisation*. We operationalised 'religion' in a previous example by naming five religions, leaving out Taoism and Confucianism which are followed by millions of people. This might be acceptable for some Western countries, but would be nonsense for a study of China. Operationalisation is central to the research process, not least because it must produce both a measurement that 'validly' represents the phenomenon, and also 'reliably' indicates it in successive measurements over time and by other researchers (**Indicators and Operationalisations**; **Validity**; **Reliability**).

Key Words

exhaustive
interval
mutually exclusive
nominal
operationalisation
ordinal
ratio
variable

Links

Attitude Scales
Contingency Tables
Grounded Theory
Indicators and Operationalisations
Qualitative Methods
Quantitative Methods
Reliability
Sampling: Estimates and Size
Validity

REFERENCES

General

Bryman, A. (2001) *Social Research Methods*. Oxford: Oxford University Press.

Payne, G., Williams, M. and Chamberlain, S. (in press) 'Methodological Pluralism in British Sociology'. *Sociology* 38 (1).

Polgar, S. and Thomas, S. (1991) *Introduction to Research in the Health Sciences* (2nd edn). Harlow: Churchill Livingstone.

Rose, D. and Sullivan, O. (1993) *Introducing Data Analysis for Social Scientists*. Buckingham: Open University Press.

Schutt, R. (1999) *Investigating the Social World* (2nd edn). Thousand Oaks, CA: Pine Forge Press.

Examples

Payne, G. and Roberts, J. (2002) 'Opening and Closing the Gates: Recent Developments in British Male Social Mobility'. *Sociological Research OnLine*, 6/6/4/payne.html.

Rose, D. and O'Reilly, K. (1998) *The ESRC Review of Government Social Classifications*. Swindon: ESRC/ONS.

Sampson, R., Raudenbush, S., and Earls, F. (1997) 'Neighborhoods and Violent Crime'. *Science*, 277: 918–24.

Vincent, J. (2000) 'Age and Old Age'. In Payne, G. (ed.) *Social Divisions*. Basingstoke: Palgrave.

Longitudinal and Cross-sectional Studies

Longitudinal studies collect data from the same sample (a 'panel') of people on more than one occasion (usually using the same methods) over a period of time, so that unlike cross-sectional studies that collect data only once and in one short period, sequences of action and social change over time can be analysed.

Section Outline: *Social phenomena have 'histories', which single cross-sectional research studies cannot directly access. We could however compare two or more independent cross-sectional studies, from different times and samples, if available. However, comparing older and younger respondents in a single study is a very unreliable guide to social change. Example; social mobility. Cross-sections cannot show direction of associations; are subject to extraneous factor and 'omitted outcomes'. But longitudinal studies also have problems: waiting years for data; higher cost of data collection (though can do secondary analysis of some major longitudinal studies). Attrition; Hawthorne Effects; original may no longer be topical.*

Social phenomena do not just exist for a fraction of a second, they are part of processes happening over a period of time. Things that have already happened – people's previous *experiences* – lead into the events we study. We cannot directly research these backgrounds except through memories and documents, which are always incomplete, socially constructed, and of course themselves produced by previous interactions (**Auto/biography and Life Histories**).

Normally, there is no practical solution to this problem. Researchers resign themselves to the fact that their studies are just snapshots; a still photo rather than a video. We have to hope that the time point of our study is not atypical. If we think of a process as a plank of wood, whose whole length we cannot examine, we might still cut across it at one point to see a single 'cross-section'. It would be better to study the whole plank (things over time), but such 'longitudinal studies' are seldom possible.

Some topics address issues where time, or rather social change over time, is crucial. We now understand the roots of poor health better from longitudinal studies (e.g. the 'Whitehall Studies' of British civil servants at all levels). These also show us that poor work conditions are not just social inequalities, but through their association with heart disease, are also physiological conditions (Marmot and Wilkinson 1999; Payne and Payne 2000: 208–15). Again, in social mobility, we want to see the effect of earlier experiences, like family background, on later outcomes like occupational achievement. In an ideal world, we could follow our informants throughout their lives, collecting data as we went.

Although we cannot normally do this, researchers have used two main techniques to get around the problem. If two or more studies are done at different times, the results can be compared. The individuals studied will not be the same, so some of any differences found might be attributable to the fact that we have looked at different people. However, the informants will have been chosen to represent categories of person, so we claim a reasonable approximation of how the categories have changed. Serial studies, like the British General Election Studies, the British Social Attitudes Surveys, or the major official statistical series (Census, General Household Survey, Labour Force Survey, etc.) take this line. Payne and Roberts (2002) used this method to show how social mobility rates of men have increased over 30 years.

The second method is far less reliable. If a sample were divided into younger and older groups (or 'cohorts'), differences between them might be caused by social change. Innovation would have more impact on the younger informants, whereas the older would be more subject to earlier conditions. Goldthorpe's (1980/1987) hugely influential work wrongly claimed that social fluidity rates were not increasing (and therefore social class was still important and unchanging), because there was little difference between older and younger men. His 'cohort analysis' in fact confused age effects (how far advanced through their careers men are at certain ages) with cohort effects (the unique historical experience that each age group has by virtue of their birth in a particular era). Increasing mobility among younger men was hidden by the greater career progress of the older men.

Davies (1987: 2–14) identifies three other limitations of cross-sectional studies. If two factors are associated (**Association and Causation**), we cannot tell from cross-sectional analysis which one is causing the other. Unemployed people have poorer health than those in paid work: is this because unemployment (through poverty and stress) causes ill health, or are unhealthy people more prone to be unemployed? Which comes first? Nor can we be sure about the effects of *unobserved factors* on our association. Growing up in poor ghetto housing might predispose adults to ill health, but in addition their physical location may make it harder for them to find work.

The third problem is whether we have collected all relevant previous data on prior experiences that may be influencing current outcomes. Being unemployed means having to start a new job. But security in the new job is less assured: redundancies often displace the more recently hired workers (the 'First In, Last Out' philosophy). Having once been unemployed, the probability of being unemployed later is increased. Such omitted outcomes make other associations (e.g. between health and unemployment) seem stronger than they actually are.

Although longitudinal studies would help avoid such problems, they bring their own difficulties. The most significant of these are time and money. Researchers do not want to wait for 30 years, following the same group of informants, before they get results. Nor can they afford the higher costs of doing several data collections, or the extra cost of keeping track of respondents between interviews. There have been few longitudinal studies in social science, and several of these started in the better-financed medical field (e.g. the National Child Development Study, the 'Whitehall' studies, British Cohort Study and the ONS Longitudinal Study).

Obviously, no undergraduate project is going to set up a longitudinal study, but recent re-organisation of the British studies makes their data more available for **Secondary Analysis**. A consortium has been established linking the ESRC UK Longitudinal Studies Centre (www.iser.essex.ac.uk), which provides advice on the British Household Panel Study (BHPS), with the Centre for Longitudinal Studies (www.cls.ioe.ac.uk) which houses the National Child Development Study (NCDS), the British Cohort Study (BCS), and the new Millennium Cohort Study (MCS). Data can be obtained from the Economic and Social Data Service at www.esds.ac.uk. The Centre for Longitudinal Study and User Support (CeLSIUS) now enables access to the Office of National Statistics' Longitudinal Study, the 'LS' (www.celsius.Ishtm.ac.uk).

These major studies are based either on an all-ages 'panel' drawn by a probability sample (BHPS), or a 'birth cohort' of same-age people born on certain days (NCDS, 17,000 children born 3–9 March 1958: BCS, 14,000 children born 5–11 April 1970). The MCS and LS sit between the two. The MCS has drawn a sample of 15,000 children from all those born in 2000–01. The LS started with 500,000 people of all ages in the 1971 Census, born on four dates, to which were added new births and immigrants born on those dates from the Censuses in 1981, 1991 and 2001 (the latter available from 2004). It currently numbers 800,000 cases, and links to births, deaths and other medical records. Information about other American and European longitudinal studies can be found in Ruspini (2002).

Despite the advantages of these studies in providing data on social change, there are several drawbacks. We have already mentioned cost and delay. The time scale also makes it hard to maintain contact with respondents. Great effort goes into seeking to retain informants, with regular letters, birthday cards and newsletters being sent out, but 'attrition' is inevitable. The BHPS lost nearly half of its original sample by its tenth annual re-interview. Naturally, some of the losses are deaths or emigrations, but the value of the surviving sample depends on it being representative.

This problem applies from the outset. Researchers have to persuade prospective respondents – or their parents – that there is value (to them and/or society) in a commitment to be re-studied over a period of years. Even when this is forthcoming, follow-up problems arise in maintaining contact, motivation and co-operation. Longitudinal studies with successive 'waves' of interviews can also suffer the **Hawthorne Effect**; respondents may become conditioned to being studied as part of a 'panel' and so behave in ways they think researchers want.

A further problem is that data relevant at the study's start may become obsolete, while data now currently important may not have been collected, or properly coded. Hence, longitudinal studies risk becoming costly 'white elephants'; providing decreasing research benefits. Related to this is the problem of staff continuity. Although good documentation, briefing and training reduce problems caused by staff turnover, researchers' interests, and fashions in topics and research style, change over time.

To take one example, data from the National Child Development Study have been used to address many topics, including making a major (if somewhat misleading) contribution to national policies to promote literacy (Bynner and Parsons 1997; Payne 2003). Similarly, until the recent secondary analysis of the British General Election Studies, the NCDS was the major – if somewhat inconclusive – source of evidence in debates about whether Britain had become a meritocratic society (e.g. Breen and Goldthorpe 1999; Saunders 1996). However, over nearly half a century, the study has been run by three different organisations and has used six different data collection agencies (www.essex.ac.uk/keeptrack/). It has 'lost' its original Northern Ireland coverage, and after successive 'sweeps' in 1965, 1969, 1974, 1981, 1985, 1996 and 1999–2000, it retains contact with 11,419 of its original 17,414 respondents (66 per cent). Its next sweep is due in 2004–05. It started as a medical project, branching out into education when its cohort were in primary school, and later into employment as the sample entered their thirties. Thus although it has proved to be a useful, indeed often the only, source of data, its contribution has been constrained by inevitable technical limitations.

Key Words

age effect
attrition
cohort
cohort effect
omitted outcome
panel
unobserved factor

Links

Association and Causation
Auto/biography and Life Histories
Hawthorne Effect
Secondary Analysis

REFERENCES

General

Davies, R. (1987) 'The Limitations of Cross Sectional Analysis'. In Crouchley, R. (ed.), *Longitudinal Data Analysis.* Aldershot: Avebury.

Ruspini, E. (2002) *An Introduction to Longitudinal Research*. London: Routledge.

Examples

Breen, R. and Goldthorpe, J. (1999) 'Class Inequality and Social Mobility'. *British Journal of Sociology* 50 (1): 1–27.

Bynner, J. and Parsons, S. (1997) *It Doesn't Get Any Better.* London: Basic Skills Agency.

Goldthorpe, J. (1980/1987) *Social Mobility and Class Structure in Modern Britain.* Oxford: Clarendon Press.

Marmot, M. and Wilkinson, R. (1999) *Social Determinants of Health*. Oxford: Oxford University Press.

Payne, G. (2003) *Immobility, Inequality and 'Illiteracy'*. Paper presented to the Annual Conference of British Sociological Association, York.

Payne, J. and Payne, G. (2000) 'Health'. In Payne, G. (ed.), *Social Divisions.* Basingstoke: Palgrave.

Payne, G. and Roberts, J. (2002) 'Opening and Closing the Gates: Recent Developments in British Male Social Mobility'. *Sociological Research OnLine,* 6/6/4/payne.html..

Saunders, P. (1996) *Unequal but Fair?* London: Institute for Economic Affairs.

Methods and Methodologies

Methods are the specific techniques used in social research whereas, although strictly meaning studies of methods, the term, 'methodologies' is usually employed to indicate the sets of conceptual and philosophical assumptions that justify the use of particular methods.

Section Outline: *Methods as 'tools': correct selection and use. Methodological pluralism. Explaining the use of methods. Methods and their conceptual baggage: assumptions about the nature of the social world. Methodologies as the study of methods. Incorrect use to mean just 'methods' or to signal philosophical stance. Topics often dictate methods choice. Example: social mobility rates. But what determines choice of topic? Interests; fashion; collective and individualist orientations.*

Methods of social research are the *technical practices* used to identify research questions, collect and analyse data, and present findings. We can think about methods at three levels. At their simplest, they are a tool, in the same way that we use a hammer to drive in nails. Provided we hit the nails without bending them, there should be no problems – although we do need to be sure that a nail is the right fixing, the right size, and that the wood won't split. Note, we do not use a hammer to drive in a screw, or a screwdriver to put in a nail. In other words, our simple view of the tool actually hides the fact that, at a second level, its use is governed by limitations: it has to be used correctly, and it has to be the correct tool for the job.

This approach, *methodological pluralism*, treats all methods as equal, assessing the merits of any given method in terms of how appropriately it tackles the research task on hand. The method(s) chosen should depend on what we want to discover, i.e. the nature of the research question. Methodological pluralism was advocated in the 1970s, when violent disagreements broke out between British qualitative and quantitative researchers (**Qualitative Methods**; **Quantitative Methods**: Bell and Newby 1977; Payne et al. 1981: 42–61). In practice, few sociologists use both kinds of method. 'Pluralism' refers to overall output, not to an individual's plurality of methods (Payne et al. in press), nor to the use of several methods in one study – a 'multi-methods' approach. (Interestingly, general methods textbooks (as distinct from specialist works) tend to be written by sociologists who have personally used quantitative methods, not by sociologists who have only practised qualitative methods.)

Methodological pluralism means that readers need to know both *how well* we used our research tool, and why we believe it was the right method to select. Even short articles in journals discuss their methods, to help readers evaluate what researchers did and how this influenced the claimed research findings. In a survey, did we complete interviews with 80 per cent of our sample, or only 40 per cent? And if our 'response rate' was low, can we nevertheless show that those who were interviewed resembled the population they are meant to represent (**Sampling: Questions of Size**)?

Continuing with our example, the selection of a survey as the method involves decisions at our second level (the correct tool for the job) and at another level altogether. Surveys work on the assumption that an interviewer asking highly specific, pre-determined questions, in a short period of time, can elicit answers that tell the researcher something valuable about social life (**Social Surveys**). Not all social scientists share that assumption.

Many point to the complexity of human existence compared with the simplifications of a questionnaire; the importance of seeing the informant's life as a whole, rather than as isolated answers; and the capacity of humans to think, attribute meanings and act.

> Giving reasons, justifications, explanations, making descriptions, are themselves profoundly social activities and, consequently, make social life what it is . . . compared to the natural (world), human life is essentially different . . . this difference requires another methodology to that required by a positivistic conception (Hughes and Sharrock 1997: 114–15).

Our point here is not that the survey is a *bad* method, but that it brings with it a particular set of intellectual baggage, or theoretical assumptions (**Positivism and Realism**). If you buy into a survey, you are normally also buying into the conceptual baggage. The same general point applies equally well to every other research method, even though the specific assumptions and objections will differ.

That is why social research methods modules (and sections of this book) move between descriptions of fairly specific, concrete, technical actions, and reflections about conceptual and philosophical issues. We move from directions for drawing a sample, phrasing a question, or gaining access to a research site, to asking how we might know that there is a world external to the observer, what are other people's intentions and motivations, and is human action structured or negotiated? The tools make little sense without such ideas.

The term 'methodology' in a literal sense means the science or study of *methods*. Thus social research methods modules, or this book, could be called methodological in approach. Methodology deals with the characteristics of methods, the principles on which methods operate, and the standards governing their selection and application. Unfortunately, sociologists have appropriated the word 'methodology' to mean at least two other things.

One is as a synonym for 'method', often used in the context of describing a researcher's own work: 'The methodology used in this study entailed . . .' This owes something to language: 'methodology' sounds more impressive than 'method'. It rolls off the tongue or page more mellifluously – it just sounds better!

However, this usage sometimes hints at a second meaning. By calling methods 'methodology', writers may suggest the conceptual baggage that comes with them. In this sense, 'methodology' means not so much the end use of a technique, but a grander scheme of ideas orienting researchers' work. This abuse of the word allows researchers to legitimate their choice of topic, methods and findings, by implicitly (and often explicitly) lining up an elaborate apparatus of justificatory literature. At best, this quickly tells the reader in which the camp researchers sit. If we are told that the writer has adopted a feminist methodology, or a constructivist methodology, we have some idea of the sets of values the researcher brought to the study, why it took a particular form, and how the interpretation was developed.

Most researchers say less about why they chose their topics than about their methods. In some cases, the research problem is taken as given, and the choice of method presented as flowing automatically from it. If we want to know rates of social mobility, a social survey is the only way of collecting data that can give a general representation of how much mobility is taking place across the country. We could, and do, use other methods to study social mobility – diaries, life histories, or semi-structured interviews (Payne 1987: 181–4) – but without a massive cost, these could not cover the number of people tapped by a sample survey.

Our example here neatly slipped in the starting phrase 'if we want to know . . .', but that is precisely what is problematic. If method does follow from the research question, what determines the selection of a research question in the first place? Even autobiographical accounts of doing research (e.g. McKeganey and Cunningham-Burley 1987) are vague about the real process of topic selection.

Most researchers find comfort in a congruence between personal orientations, conceptual frameworks, topics of study and methods chosen. Those interested in political change and public processes on a national scale (the older generation of sociologists in Britain were accused of being too closely tied to the political agenda of the post-war Labour Party) tend to be more comfortable with collective entities (classes); issues like power, wealth or problems of social welfare; and counting national rates at which things happen. Others with a more individualistic style favour topics like personal experience of identity (gender, ethnicity, sexuality, consumption), studied in smaller groups by qualitative methods. There are fashions even in academic research. Methods, and their associated research questions, do not float about in mid-air; methodology helps show how they are constructed from prior orientations and knowledge.

Key Words

collective entities
conceptual baggage
congruence
justificatory literature
methodological pluralism
problematic

Links

Positivism and Realism
Qualitative Methods
Quantitative Methods
Sampling: Questions of Size
Social Surveys

REFERENCES

General

Bell, C. and Newby, H. (1977) *Doing Sociological Research*. London: Allen & Unwin.

Payne, G., Dingwall, R., Payne, J. and Carter, M. (1981) *Sociology and Social Research*. London: Routledge & Kegan Paul.

Payne, G., Williams, M. and Chamberlain, S. (in press) 'Methodological Pluralism in British Sociology'. *Sociology*, 38 (1).

Examples

Hughes, J. and Sharrock, W. (1997) *The Philosophy of Social Research* (3rd edn). Harlow: Longman.

McKeganey, N. and Cunningham-Burley, S. (eds) (1987) *Enter the Sociologist*. Aldershot: Avebury.

Payne, G. (1987) 'Social Mobility'. In Burgess, R. (ed.), *Investigating Society*. Harlow: Longman.

Objectivity

Objectivity in social research is the principle drawn from positivism that, as far as is possible, researchers should remain distanced from what they study so findings depend on the nature of what was studied rather than on the personality, beliefs and values of the researcher (an approach not accepted by researchers in the critical, standpoint or interpretivist traditions).

Section Outline: *Objectivity and bias. Objectivity as orientation. Findings should not depend on who did the research. Early positivism: the detached 'scientific' view. Is neutrality actually conservative? Declaring values in 'qualified objectivity'. Are researchers aware of their lack of objectivity? Value freedom as an unachievable goal, at all stages of a project. Qualified objectivity; standpoint theory; credibility/transparency/ density in qualitative methods. Reliability and validity.*

Although the terms 'objectivity' and 'bias' are often used to refer to the same issues, it is helpful to reserve them for different dimensions of the problems they address. In this discussion, we shall use objectivity (or lack of it) to refer to questions of *research orientation and interpretation*, and bias to refer to *errors of procedure* (**Bias**). It is not possible to insist that this dichotomy is strictly maintained, particularly as we move from quantitative to qualitative research, but we shall at least be able to appreciate why and where the terms overlap (Hammersley 1996).

The case for objectivity is that readers need to feel confident that researchers have constrained their personal prejudices. Findings should not depend on who did the research, but on *what was there* to be found. In following a set of 'protocols' or standardised procedures, all relevant evidence will be reported, whether or not it sustained the researchers' hypotheses. Systematically applied protocols not only reduce the scope of the individual to distort the findings, but also, by being transparent, allow subsequent checking on the procedures. This aspect of objectivity is often called the **reliability** of the research.

Writing in an era dominated by the anti-intellectualism of the powerful churches, early sociologists like Comte and Durkheim stressed the special, 'scientific' nature of sociological knowledge. Social science's task is to discover what *is*, not what *ought to be*. Conviction statements – 'oughts' or 'shoulds' – are value judgements, which cannot be subjected to scientific test (**Positivism and Realism**). Value judgements belong in personal life, religion, morals or politics. In scientific research, they must be excluded. The researcher is a neutral observer rather than philosopher or social reformer. Value neutrality should be demonstrable in all theoretical statements and research practice.

This perspective loses the sense that researchers are human, over-optimistically seeing regulated protocols as a complete method of control. But sociologists are not technicians repairing a machine. Their feelings and evaluations are an integral part of their make-up, and cannot be neatly compartmentalised. Researchers are members of society, interacting with it. Where in the 'scientistic' model is there room for critical thought challenging the status quo, or for conceptualising alternative futures?

Those most vocal in rejecting a narrowly objective social science argue that one of sociology's tasks is to clarify what society is like, so that it can be changed 'for the better'. Positivist objectivity is not just unnecessary, but undesirable because it is inherently conservative. Without a clear set of values, it is impossible to define what is socially problematic, and what might be 'better'. For example, 'the rule of law' or 'social equality' are not the same as 'injustice or 'inequality'. Values help to show what should be researched, rather than preventing researchers from being rigorous in their research. By being honest and open about their values, actively disclosing them as part of their publications, they enable readers to take this 'qualified objectivity' into account in evaluating findings.

This assumes, of course, that the researchers are themselves aware of their own personal stances. Saunders argues that much British sociology consists of 'systematically distorted communication through which (left-wing) orthodoxies come to be perpetuated without anybody necessarily realising or intending it' (Saunders 1989: 3). However, his own conservative stance leads him to confuse the purely statistical concept of 'perfect mobility' (meaning random mobility) with other researchers' subjective judgements about what would be *ideal* rates of mobility (Payne 1992). Again, when the *Affluent Worker* study did not ask women about their political views, was this just unnecessary (as Goldthorpe (1994) claims) or a case of implicit sexist values (Hart 1994)? A third example of unconscious lack of objectivity falls under the heading of 'bias' in qualitative research. Payne (1996: 30, 22) is sceptical about researchers' claims of the 'apparent ease with which sociologists are accepted into communities', and the virtual lack of difficulty in including, evaluating and understanding 'those we dislike' among our informants. Declaring an interest or intention is no guarantee that the problem of objectivity has been tackled.

In accepting that complete objectivity is unobtainable (Abercrombie et al. 1988), most sociologists acknowledge that research is a collection of activities, in which the question of objectivity arises at several different points. Choice of topic, the theories brought to bear, how research questions are posed, kinds of data collection and analysis, and the construction of conclusions, are all stages where values can and do intervene. That is not to say that sociology must become merely selective, anecdotal or emotional. 'The impossibility of a completely value-free orientation goes without saying, but it does not follow that the ideal cannot be approximated to varying degrees' (Blalock 1984: 31).This involves sensitivity to the connections between values and procedures, and sound research practice.

This basic approach sustains three quite different philosophies of research. The first follows directly from the previous account. This acknowledges objectivity not as an absolute, but rather as a partially desirable, but limited and actually unobtainable, target. The intended outcome is to produce *reliable* and *valid* work. This entails properly implementing methods which are themselves basically neutral. At the same time, a visible value position is maintained, and indeed actively discussed, in order to display personal prejudices and preferences to the reader (Bell and Encel 1978; Bell and Newby 1977; Bell and Roberts 1984).

In contrast, a second approach places greater emphasis on the researcher's value stance. In **Feminist Research** both topic selection and the methods used are explicitly determined by the political stance of advancing the status of women. Here, 'value neutrality' is seen not just as conservative but as a device to disguise masculine power, including control over informants (Hammersley 1992, 1994; Ramazanoglu 1992). Rather than objectivity, subjectivity and involvement with the (female) informants are deliberately sought. If there is an objectivity, it is a uniquely feminist objectivity. The credibility of research findings lies not in rigid procedures aimed at controlling personal feelings, but in acceptance by other feminists and the women who have been informants. Indeed, personal feelings are for some feminists essential resources on which to draw in the research (Reinharz 1992; **Reflexivity**; **Auto/biography and Life Histories**).

The third approach, widely accepted in qualitative sociology (**Qualitative Methods**), shares with feminist research a concern that research findings depend on the researcher's interaction with those being researched. It follows that the researcher cannot stay detached and aloof, but is engaged in a personal and subjective process of mutual discovery with the informants. Because this occurs in a unique social setting, where the researcher responds to events as they happen, there can be no set protocols that could control for subjectivity, even if it were desirable. What matters is not neutrality but *credibility*: other researchers and those researched should be content with the interpretations advanced. Unfortunately, there are very few studies in which this 'inter-subjective reliability' is actually tested by comparing the independent judgements of more than one researcher (Gladney et al. 2003). In practice, most researchers appeal to transparency of detail and density in their fieldwork evidence as grounds for claiming the absence of unwarranted subjectivity.

In this view, the essence of good research is not that it should be neutral or distanced from its subjects, but that it should be reliable and valid. Reliability and validity are usually replaced by terms like 'transferability', 'dependability', 'credibility' and 'trustworthy' (**Reliability**; **Validity**). Although these are not grounded in fixed protocols, they draw on notions of appropriate procedures as the basis for confidence in research findings.

Key Words

positivist objectivity
protocol
qualified objectivity
value judgement
value neutrality
value stance

Links

Auto/biography and Life Histories
Bias
Feminist Research
Positivism and Realism
Qualitative Methods
Reliability
Validity

REFERENCES

General

Abercrombie, N., Hill, S. and Turner, B. (1988) *The Penguin Dictionary of Sociology.* Harmondsworth, Penguin.

Blalock, H. (1984) *Basic Dilemmas in the Social Sciences.* Beverley Hills, CA: Sage.

Gladney, A., Ayers, C., Taylor, W., Liehr, P. and Meininger, J. (2003) 'Consistency of Findings Produced by Two Multidisciplinary Research Teams'. *Sociology*, 37 (2): 297–313.

Hammersley, M. (1992) 'On Feminist Methodology'. *Sociology*, 26 (2): 187–206.

Hammersley, M. (1994) 'On Feminist Methodology: a Response'. *Sociology*, 28 (1): 293–300.

Hammersley, M. (1996) 'The Relationship Between Qualitative and Quantitative Research: Paradigm Loyalty Versus Methodological Eclecticism.' In Richardson, J. (ed.) *Handbook of Research Methods for Psychology and the Social Sciences*. Leicester: BPS Books.

Ramazanoglu, C. (1992) 'On Feminist Methodology'. *Sociology*, 26 (2): 207–12.

Reinharz, S. (1992) *Feminist Methods in Social Research*. Oxford: Oxford University Press.

Examples

Bell, C. and Encel, S. (eds) (1978) *Inside the Whale.* Sydney: Pergammon.

Bell, C. and Newby, H. (1977) *Doing Sociological Research*. London: Allen & Unwin.

Bell, C. and Roberts, H. (eds) (1984) *Social Researching.* London: Routledge & Kegan Paul.

Goldthorpe, J. (1994) 'The Uses of History in Sociology'. *Sociology*, 45 (1): 55–78.

Hart, N. (1994) 'John Goldthorpe and the Relics of Sociology'. *Sociology*, 45 (1): 21–30.
Payne, G. (1992) 'Social Divisions and Social Mobility'. In Burrows, R. and Marsh, C. (eds), *Consumption and Class*. London: Macmillan.
Payne, G. (1996) 'Imagining the Community: Some Reflections on the Community Study as Method'. In Lyon, E.S. and Busfield, J. (eds), *Methodological Imaginations*. London: Macmillan.
Saunders, P. (1989) 'Left Write in Sociology'. *Network*, 44 (May) 2–3.

Observation

Observation in a strict sense of simply watching people is little used in social research (except as an unobtrusive method) both because human behaviour is too complex to record in this way, and because it isolates researchers from what is being studied, so preventing participation or deeper exploration of understandings through conversation or interview.

Section Outline: *Observation and participant observation. Actions' meanings are not self-explanatory. Observation as a starting point. 'Active' observation: focused, systematic and recorded. Casing the joint. Unobtrusive observation: the difficulty of recording observations. Unstructured observation. Lack of control over events. Observation in the classroom. Selective perception. Structured observation: information overload. Sampling in observation.*

People coming new to social research are often surprised to learn that social scientists, and sociologists in particular, do not use observation very much as a method. An associated method, **Participant Observation** is more common, and this gives us a clue as to why simple, non-interventionist observation is less popular. In participant observation, the researcher takes on an active role within the social setting that is being studied. As well as watching, this facilitates listening, conversation, questioning and interviewing, so getting 'closer to life'. In practice, most 'observation' therefore includes listening as well as watching.

However, because sociologists are interested in meanings and explanations, observation alone cannot take them very far towards their goals. Human interaction involves speech, through which social life is negotiated and given meaning. In Max Weber's famous example, if we *observe* a man chopping wood, he may be preparing for his own fire; selling his labour to someone else; enjoying physical exercise or just keeping warm. It is not sufficient to observe the action, we need to *explain* it and *understand* its subjective meaning for the wood chopper.

Although, on its own, observation is of limited use, it can provide a starting point. For 70 years, the Mass Observation project has collected accounts of ordinary daily life from its amateur correspondents, so providing a national archive that can subsequently be inspected for patterns (*www.sussex.ac.uk/library/massobs*). Actions that we normally ignore or accept without thought, may take on a new significance if we watch them systematically and record their frequency, timing, regularity of sequence and participants.

Observation differs from the naturalistic looking and listening we use in our ordinary lives, where the processes of seeing and hearing are passive. Here, unless we are especially looking for something or someone, the visual images and sounds that we acquire are taken for granted, and we only actively notice the unusual. This does not mean that we go around bumping into people or objects, rather we respond (by avoiding, for example) without consciously seeing. For instance, can you remember how many people you saw when you last walked down a busy street? More importantly, can you describe them, who they were with, what they were doing and what they were saying? In contrast, observation as a research tool is *active* looking and listening: seeing, noticing, hearing and recording. It is 'structured' and 'systematic'.

Observational studies, in which the researcher's role is to record what is seen and heard without otherwise taking part in any activities, are termed *non-participant observation* (Polgar and Thomas 1991: 130–40). This type of observation includes both observations of small group activities and 'the community walk' or 'casing the joint'. There are few explicit descriptions of the latter but it underlies much of the more recent community-oriented fieldwork (e.g. Murray and Graham 1995). Usually at a preliminary or exploratory stage, researchers 'case the joint' to get a feel of the physical surroundings and how they impact on the social life of the community. (It can also be used as part of a mixed-method approach: to add more depth to **Community Profiles** or **Social Surveys**.)

This might lead to a more comprehensive study. A locality study of public health might count traffic flows to identify dangerous crossings, inspect parks for amounts of litter, broken glass and dog droppings, and record when anti-social behaviour – like the 'school run' or uncontrolled exercising of dogs – takes place. As in other research methods, even straightforward exercises like this require preliminary thought, planning, decisions on what data to collect, and piloting.

This approach could be unobtrusive, with the researchers looking like ordinary citizens on the streets and park (**Unobtrusive Methods and Triangulation**). This would imply that the observation could be accomplished by simply watching, without recording tools like clipboards or forms to complete. As a method, this allows researchers a degree of flexibility to 'follow the action', but in turn raises the problem of how to note down the complexity of activities for future reference (and the researcher's reactions to them: see **Fieldwork**).

Such 'simple' or 'unstructured observation,' as it is sometimes called, would have to be limited to simple objects, because of the problem of making accurate records. In the examples we have given of community walks, street surveys or park usage, it also raises the ethical question of whether people in public places have given 'informed consent' to be subjects of research, by virtue of appearing in the public gaze (**Ethical Practice**).

This suggests that observation works best where behaviour is repeated, in a fixed setting, by participants who agree to be observed (Collins 1984). It is more easily accomplished in a psychology laboratory than in a natural setting, where actors are free to 'do their own thing'. This helps to explain why observation has been more popular in education studies, where classroom observation can be conveniently performed, as in the ORACLE project (Galton and Delamont 1985; Stanworth 1983). Similarly, the activities and output performance of work groups doing repetitive tasks were observed in some of the Hawthorne experiments (**Hawthorne Effect**). However, even here, it is normal to combine observation with other methods, like **Ethnography**.

Observation is also limited to the researcher's pair of eyes: there is only so much that can be seen at any one time. Researchers also bring with them sets of social assumptions that determine what they *selectively perceive* among the complexities of what is going on around them. It is not unusual for observers to use a standardised form to record activities, because the form directs their attention to that part of the activity that most concerns the research project.

In one influential example of this 'structured observation', Flanders (1970) produced ten categories to analyse interactions between teachers and pupils (praises, asks questions, gives instructions etc.). Every three seconds, the observer ticks the category on a form (the 'observation schedule') which best describes the previous activity. However, this requires the observer to know the categories, make rapid judgements (some categories and many activities are complex), and continue to observe. The more thorough the analysis of activity, the more categories that are needed, and the more difficult observation becomes (Bell 1987: 88–98).

The particular features of observation require the researcher to have as wide a range of skills as those needed for asking questions. The researcher normally works alone and, thus, has sole responsibility for data collection. This requires the same unbiased or reflexive approach, adaptability, flexibility, recording accuracy and judgement as the interviewer role. It is highly likely that a researcher may have to record simultaneous events during fieldwork. People cannot be asked to repeat actions because they were missed. This requires creativity in the use of shorthand-like symbols and, inevitably, being selective. In making choices about what to record, a researcher must make decisions about the relevance of events to the central research topic.

Observation not only requires the researcher to record what is seen and heard but also, through theoretical sampling (**Grounded Theory**) and self-questioning, to develop, test and refine ideas that arise from the observations themselves. This process should also be recorded so that as full a processual account as possible is achieved. These accounts can then be scrutinised during post-fieldwork analysis with a degree of confidence.

Key Words

observation schedule
non-participant observation
participant observation
selective perception
unstructured observation

Links

Community Profiles
Ethical Practice
Ethnography
Fieldwork
Grounded Theory
Hawthorne Effect
Participant Observation
Social Surveys
Unobtrusive Methods and Triangulation

REFERENCES

General

Bell, J. (1987) *Doing Your Research Project*. Milton Keynes: Open University Press.

Flanders, N. (1970) *Analyzing Teacher Behaviour*. Reading, MA: Addison-Wesley.

Polgar, S. and Thomas, S. (1991) *Introduction to Research in the Health Sciences* (2nd edn). Harlow: Churchill Livingstone.

Examples

Collins, H. (1984) 'Researching Spoonbending'. In Bell, C. and Roberts, H. (eds), *Social Researching*. London: Routledge & Kegan Paul.

Galton, M. and Delamont, S. (1985) 'Speaking with Forked Tongue? Two Styles of Observation in the ORACLE Project'. In Burgess, R. (ed.), *Field Methods in the Study of Education*. Lewes: Falmer Press.

Murray, S. and Graham, C. (1995) 'Practice Based Health Needs Assessment: Use of Four Methods in a Small Neighbourhood'. *British Medical Journal*,1443: 8.

Stanworth, M. (1983) *Gender and Schooling*. London: Hutchinson.

Official Statistics

Official statistics are numerical data-sets, produced by official governmental agencies mainly for administrative purposes, including the Census, crime figures, health data, income and employment rates, as well as those based on government-sponsored social surveys.

Section Outline: *Governments publish quantitative data. Printed tables on wide range of topics. Recent availability of raw data. Advantages of official statistics: cheap; wide coverage; reliable; available. Disadvantages of official statistics: rigid; definitions; selective; sampling. The social construction of official statistics. Example: crime and criminal statistics. The state's view of what is important. Fiddling the official figures. Example: unemployment. Cicourel's critique. Excessive distrust of official statistics. Desktop computing revolutionises data access.*

In Britain, government departments routinely collect and publish quantitative socio-economic information covering England and Wales, and often Scotland and Northern Ireland as well. Some of these data are by-products of administrative procedures: e.g. annual statistics on crimes recorded by the police, or quarterly returns of unemployment rates. Others are based on large-scale **Social Surveys**: the Census (every ten years: Nissel 1987), the General Household Survey, or the Expenditure and Food Survey (replacing the earlier Family Expenditure, and National Food, Surveys).

These studies normally appear as printed summary **Contingency Tables** (e.g. the Office of National Statistics (ONS) publications: *Social Trends*; *Regional Trends*; the *New Earnings Survey* and Dorling's fascinating *New Social Atlas of Britain* (1995)). Browsing through your library's 'statistics', 'government statistics' or 'official statistics' sections will yield more on topics like health; education; work; households; ethnicity; transport; income; health and safety; social attitudes; industry; births, marriages and deaths, mostly as parts of a regular series covering many years. A list and further details of the major national studies can be found at www.data-archive.ac.uk/findingData/majorStudiesFulllist.asp. Harvey and MacDonald (1993: 61–9) also offer brief details with a helpful commentary. This includes some of the quasi-official surveys regularly conducted by academic researchers for the government, like the British Crime Study and the British General Election Studies.

The major studies are increasingly available as 'raw data' that can be re-analysed by researchers. Applications to download and re-analyse raw data (which are either free or very cheap) have to go through recognised academics. Undergraduates wishing to exploit these excellent resources for their dissertations (**Secondary Analysis**) need to approach their tutors.

There are at least ten main advantages in using official statistics. They are *already collected*, *cheap*, and *easy to obtain*. They usually consist of *large survey numbers* covering the *whole country* (**Sampling: Types of Sample**), and have been *collected to a very high technical standard* in the *same way* over *a period of years*, so that we can investigate changes in national rates of our target topic (**Quantitative Methods**). 'Official Statistics' are what they say: being 'official', they are generally accepted as credible, or at least credible within widely agreed and known limitations. They therefore *confer authority on users*. Some, like the Labour Force Survey, appear very soon after initial collection, and so are *up to date*. In a few weeks, researchers go from an original idea, to having produced a finished report on this year's social trends.

In some cases, official statistics are the only resource available, because of the scale of data-collection. Indeed, the privileged position of governments allows them to legislate to enforce organisations to collect data for them. For example, employers are required to report employment and production data to their governments in a standardised way across the European Union (see 'Eurostat': *www.europa.eu.int/comm/eurostat*). A spin-off is that this allows sociological comparison between nations and regions, even though this was not the primary purpose.

However, this optimistic assessment must be balanced by several practical difficulties. Like any **Secondary Analysis**, what is included and how the components are defined, are determined not by the researcher but by the original collection process. There may be changes in questions and coding definitions over time. Nor are all sample sizes sufficient to support investigation of sub-groups. Iganski et al. (2002), for example, report how their use of official statistics to study the changing socio-economic positions of minority ethnic groups was restricted by definitional changes in the Census, sample size in the General Household Survey, availability of the Labour Force Survey, and the occupational classification schemes in all three.

These kinds of problem are the most obvious examples of difficulties arising from *who* has collected the data, by means of *what processes*, and for what *original purposes*. Criminal statistics are usually taken as illustrating this most clearly. A crime has to pass several stages before it appears in the official statistics of 'crimes reported to the police'. It must be experienced or observed to happen; recognised to be a crime; and reported to the police: the police must then decide if it is on the national list of notifiable offences and worth investigating. Some crimes like rape are under-reported. Only about 40 per cent of reported 'crimes' are recorded (Mayhew and Maung 1992): workloads may be too high, the crime of little importance, or a caution deemed to be better than criminal proceedings.

Nor is the process consistent. Police forces respond to political and public pressures. They have a degree of discretion over what gets recorded (is the theft of milk bottles from a doorstep one crime or a separate crime for each bottle?). Government campaigns against particular 'crimes' ('yobbish' street behaviour in 2002–3) or media 'moral panics', like mugging or mobile phone thefts, result in greater police effort going into recording, re-classification of marginal activities as now falling into the relevant criminal category, and re-allocating forces to seek out these crimes. Their recorded number goes up. Efficiency drives and inter-force comparisons shift resources towards achieving measured outcomes (**Evaluation Studies**): crimes may be under-recorded, or over-recorded where they can be solved. The British Crime Survey, which samples the general public, reports a *fall* in crimes since 1997, whereas recorded crime shows an *increase*. The real fall is due to successful Labour government policies, whereas the rise is due to greater efficiency and consistency in recording reported crimes.

The fact that official statistics are produced by the state, in the interests of those who run and control it, is a problem. This led to many British sociologists, under the influence of work such as Hindess (1973), neglecting official sources during the 1970s and 1980s. The underlying problem remains: the state determines what is collected – and what is not. Data on taxation and extremes of wealth are scarce. Environmental damage is inadequately monitored or criminalised. Any one big fraud case (Maxwell, Guinness, etc.) steals more than the *total* annual value of thefts and burglaries (Levi 1993). What is regarded as worth monitoring, and how this is defined, are determined for us by those in power.

Between 1982 and the mid-1990s, Conservative governments changed the official definition of 'unemployment' over 30 times: unsurprisingly, the number of unemployed decreased! As one editor of *Social Trends* recorded,

> there has been great pressure on directors of statistics in departments to withhold or modify statistics, particularly in relation to employment and health, and professional integrity has forced some to threaten resignation (Nissel 1995).

Supported by politicians who do not want public scrutiny, civil servants guard information jealously. Both the public process, and academic research, depend on governmental statistical services operating with a degree of independence from our rulers.

However, in the 1960s, critics with a qualitative perspective began arguing that what gets treated as a crime depends on the day-to-day practices of policemen, lawyers and court procedures. These determine what is seen as criminal; crime and deviancy are in this sense socially constructed:

> rates of deviant behaviour are produced by the actions taken by persons in the social system which define, classify and record certain behaviours as deviant (Cicourel 1976: 135).

They should be seen as 'indices of organizational processes rather than as indices of certain forms of behaviour' (Kituse and Cicourel 1963: 137). The fallibility of official crime statistics was generalised, with some justification, to other official statistics. Rather than using them as evidence, it became fashionable to regard official statistics and the processes of their creation as *topics* of research.

Despite these considerations, the limitations of official statistics should not be exaggerated. While earlier critiques have given us a more sophisticated understanding of what lies behind such published 'social accounting', the utility of official statistics has since been rediscovered (e.g. Levitas and Guy 1996). The desktop computer has revolutionised availability and usage of government-produced data.

Key Words

deviancy
raw data
secondary analysis
series

Links

Contingency Tables
Evaluation Studies
Quantitative Methods
Sampling: Types of Sample
Secondary Analysis
Social Surveys

REFERENCES

General

Cicourel, A. (1976) *The Social Organisation of Juvenile Justice.* London: Heinemann.
Harvey, L. and MacDonald, M. (1993) *Doing Sociology.* Basingstoke: Macmillan.
Hindess, B. (1973) *The Uses of Official Statistics in Sociology.* London: Macmillan.
Kituse, J. and Cicourel, A. (1963) 'A Note on the Use of Official Statistics'. *Social Problems,* 11: 131–9.
Levitas, R. and Guy, W. (eds) (1996) *Interpreting Official Statistics.* London: Routledge.

Examples

Dorling, D. (1995) *A New Social Atlas of Britain*. Chichester: John Wiley & Sons.
Dorling, D. and Simpson, S. (eds) (1999) *Statistics in Society: the Arithmetic of Politics.* London: Arnold.
Iganski, P., Payne, G. and Roberts, J. (2002) 'Inclusion or Exclusion: Reflections on the Evidence of Declining Racial Disadvantage in the British Labour Market'. *International Journal of Sociology and Social Policy,* 21 (4–6):184–211.
Levi, M. (1993) *The Investigation, Prosecution and Trial of Serious Fraud*. London: Royal Commission on Criminal Justice, Research Study 14.
Mayhew, P. and Maung, N. (1992) *Surveying Crime*. London: Home Office Research and Statistics Department Research Findings No. 2, HMSO.
Nissel, M. (1987) *People Count*. London: HMSO (for OPCS).
Nissel, M. (1995) 'Vital Statistics'. *New Statesman and Society,* 27 January.

Participant Observation

Participant observation is data collection over a sustained period by means of watching, listening to, and asking questions of, people as they follow their day-to-day activities, while the researcher adopts a role from their setting and partially becomes a member of the group in question, as in doing ethnography.

Section Outline: *Blending in. Balance of participation and observation. Shift from observation to participation. Theoretical background of participant observation. Potential problems of fieldwork: making field notes; personal reactions; organising records; selectivity. The 'double shift'.*

There is an attractive commonsense about doing social research by watching (and listening to) other people going about their daily business. To avoid disrupting their goings-on, and drawing attention to ourselves as observers, we can *blend in by adopting a role.* If studying workers on a production line, we might get a job as an operative. If we want to explore medical treatment, the main roles available are nurse, doctor, patient, cleaner, ward auxiliary, porter, visitor, administrator and medical researcher. Some of these can only be adopted with professional qualifications. It is not surprising that those nurses who have gone on to become sociologists have done good health research.

Although this method of social research is called 'participant observation', the extent of participation varies, nor is the technique limited to observing (participant observation should not be confused with *participatory research*, which operates from the standpoint of emancipating and empowering the people being researched). Participation means playing a role, devoting energies to maintaining the pretence that the researcher is not really researching but in fact working/visiting/living there (e.g. Mac an Ghaill working as a teacher: see Devine and Heath 1999: 24–34). When the research can only be achieved by subterfuge (such as studying those who do not want to be studied, like fascists, criminals or religious fundamentalists (**Ethical Practice**)), the whole project depends on the continued maintenance of covert surveillance. However, most research is 'overt', with permission obtained in advance. Here, role-playing simply enables us to be unobtrusive. As people become used to the routine presence of the 'participant', he or she may more openly be seen to be doing research, for instance by making notes or asking direct questions.

Similarly, 'observation' means several things. Observation starts with ordinary and naturally occurring conversations. Questions based on feigned ignorance or misunderstanding follow; what a Scottish female colleague of the authors called 'acting the daft lassie'. Researchers soon initiate research-relevant topics, ask leading questions, frequently engage in what should properly be described as interviews, and entering into social relationships with the people being studied (see the **Hawthorne Effect**). Participant observation might better be called *participant listening*, because so much of 'social behaviour' is conducted through interpersonal communication (Grbich 1999: 121–35). Nor is the researcher restricted to listening: documents (**Documentary Methods**) can be read for background information, and formal interviews conducted with key informants (e.g. the managers of the production line mentioned in the first paragraph).

It is therefore conventional to represent participant observation as a continuum of activities stretching from *pure observation with no participation*, to *full participation* (Gold 1958; Junker 1960). At the observation end, researchers remain detached and uninvolved with the informants (**Observation**). At the fully participative end, researchers may identify with their roles to the extent that they lose their sociological perspective and capacity to analyse, temporarily abandoning their research objectives. In between these poles of the continuum lie positions of 'observer-participating' and 'participant-observing'. The former stresses the research over role-playing; the latter prioritises role-playing over researching (but also see Collins 1984).

Where the emphasis is on participation, the researcher is conventionally thought likely to be less analytical (but see Payne (1996) in **Community Studies**). Alternatively, the narrower the concentration on observation, the greater the probability that the researcher does not become sufficiently close to the other participants to learn about their world. With more recent shifts in research fashion towards ethnography and other methods that stress empathy and interpretation, 'pure' observation is now excluded from the participative framework (**Observation**; **Unobtrusive Methods and Triangulation**).

Participant observation is, then, not 'just commonsense'. It is implicitly based on a particular *theoretical perspective* of some complexity, which prioritises naturally occurring 'events' and the meanings that informants use in their interactions to make sense of these events (**Fieldwork**). It overlaps very closely with **Ethnography**, but with the added problems that it involves a challenging practical activity, both of the maintenance of role-playing, and of recording what takes place (Atkinson and Hammersley 1994).

Sociologists cannot instantly and simultaneously recognise a key event, describe it, analyse it in terms of its context, connect it to other events, reflect upon what it means for the research, and allocate it to its final position in the research report. These processes take considerable thought, extending over months of working and re-working the data. Events cannot be interrupted while the researcher steps out of role, pulls out a pad and takes notes, or thrusts a tape-recorder at an informant. But memory is notoriously fallible, and so some documentation must be made.

Documentation goes through four main stages. First, researchers make a conscious effort to *flag events mentally*, assigning a word, place or image as they happen. This helps re-start later recall. Second, at the earliest opportunity, they jot these cues down in a *temporary 'field note'*, expanding as much as possible in the circumstances. The key question researchers need to ask themselves at this point is whether the note being made will be sufficient to stimulate recall when a fuller account can be written out later. It is *always* better to write down more, rather than to trust to memory. All opportunities, like meal breaks, journeys between sites, being left in sole charge for a moment, having to do writing as part of the role played, or going for toilet breaks, have to be exploited. Ditton's well-known extensive use of the lavatory for this purpose evoked real concern from his co-workers about the state of his bladder (1973)!

The third stage comes at the end of the day, when a *full research note* must be completed from the jottings while memory is fresh. Care should be taken not to claim that statements are verbatim unless this is warranted. Particularly in the early phases of the project, it is important not to be too selective: it is not possible to be sure what will be relevant, as this will emerge and change as the fieldwork progresses. The more that is recorded, the better.

Field notes should also cover the participant's own personal reactions. Feelings, initial impressions, half ideas, possible leads, even admissions of tactical errors or things missed during the day, should all be included.

Fieldwork is a reflexive experience, researchers bringing themselves into contact with real-life social situations (**Reflexivity**). The researcher is part of the things being studied. The researcher's own reactions are an essential element of participation. Notes should not, however, be left as a stream of consciousness. They must be *organised and catalogued systematically* as they accumulate.

It is difficult to know what parts of any period of interaction are relevant. Initial confusion at the start of the project does normally give way to a more comfortable phase in which useful experience is gained. However, after a while, boredom sets in, with only routine, recognisable events taking place. Researchers must try to reduce their natural tendency to select only those parts which confirm their prior expectations. Accounts are often criticised for bias due to selectivity. Occasional dramatic events make good reading, but are un-representative of the low-grade, mundane activities that predominate. Data collection must be systematic and as comprehensive as possible.

That is by no means easy. Doing a job *and* doing research at the same time is a 'double shift'. Life in the field is unpredictable, which is a source of anxiety. Lack of control is frustrating: events cannot be made to happen, or people instructed to talk only about what interests the researcher. Having to stay in role is a strain, and not all researchers have a personality that makes fitting in easy. Despite its apparent attractiveness and the number of sociologists who use it, participant observation does not suit everybody, nor can everybody be good at it.

Key Words

covert
field notes
naturally occurring event
overt
reflexivity
role-playing
selectivity

Links

Community Studies
Documentary Methods
Ethical Practice
Ethnography
Fieldwork
Hawthorne Effect
Observation
Qualitative Methods
Reflexivity
Unobtrusive Methods and Triangulation

REFERENCES

General

Atkinson, P. and Hammersley, M. (1994) 'Ethnography and Participant Observation'. In Denzin, N. and Lincoln, Y. (eds), *Handbook of Qualitative Research*. Thousand Oaks, CA: Sage.

Gold, R. (1958) 'Roles in Sociological Field Observations,' *Social Forces*, 36: 217–23.

Grbich, C. (1999) *Qualitative Research in Health*. London: Sage.

Junker, B. (1960) *Field Work*. Chicago: University of Chicago Press.

Examples

Collins, H. (1984)'Researching Spoonbending'. In Bell, C. and Roberts, H. (eds) *Social Researching*. London: Routledge & Kegan Paul.

Devine, F. and Heath, S. (1999) *Sociological Research Methods in Context*. Basingstoke: Macmillan.

Ditton, J. (1973) *Part-Time Crime: an Ethnography of Fiddling and Pilferage*. London: Macmillan.

Payne, G. (1996) 'Imagining the Community'. In Lyon, S. and Busfield, J. (eds), *Methodological Imaginations*. Basingstoke: Macmillan.

Positivism and Realism

The approach of positivism to the social world in social research is similar, but not identical, to how the natural sciences approach the physical world, i.e. combining mainly deductive logic with empirical and predominantly quantitative methods in order to seek generally applying regularities, whereas realism assumes only the existence of a social world external to the researcher which can be accessed through the sense and reserach.

Section Outline: *Rejecting 'positivism'. Positivism: knowledge; reasoning and values. Realism knowing the* external world. *Interpretation: the* process *of knowing the social world. 'Natural science methods'. Deductive reasoning. Falsification and confirmation of hypotheses. Qualitative methods' hidden positivism.*

It became fashionable during the 1980s to 'reject positivism'. Articles appeared which did not offer a critique of positivism, but dismissed it in a sentence or two. However, positivism is not a simple or single concept. We can only cover some of its main features here, together with some of the alternative ways of looking at the world and researching it, like realism and constructivism. Positivism has been included precisely because it does confuse both those coming new to research methods, and many practitioners – even articles summarily rejecting positivism in fact often used some of its central elements. What they were actually rejecting was a caricature of positivism as a crude, quantitative and structurally deterministic method.

Positivism (or strictly, 'logical positivism') is one group of approaches to questions about the world, how we experience it, and how well the ideas we use to understand it express its actual nature (Williams 2000). In its earlier forms, positivism regards the world as being external to the observer, and consisting of 'phenomena' that can be observed. The observer makes up 'theories' that describe the phenomena, particularly describing the order in which events take place and making *testable predictions* about how that order will display itself in the future. Theories are improved through this testing against evidence (deductive reasoning).

'Knowledge' is our mental attempt to interpret what our senses tell us. We elaborate our interpretations by systematically collecting more information through our senses. This demarcates knowledge from feelings and belief, because belief is not based on what our senses tell us. We may *believe* in God, but we cannot experience God through our normal senses; not literally see, hear or touch God. Knowledge statements about the world must be consistent with our senses' experience of it.

We can identify three main aspects to this kind of positivism. It is *phenomenological*, because it distinguishes between an external world and the observer who experiences it. It is *empirical*, in that it uses observable evidence to establish 'knowledge'. It is *objective* in so far as it separates out 'scientific' knowledge acquired under specific practical procedures, from belief, values or feelings. We might add that it also favours regularity ('true' theories allow us to predict), measurement (only what we can observe and record – i.e. measure – is of interest), abstraction (it seeks 'laws' that can be applied generally), indifference to what is being observed (its procedural rules take priority, and feelings must be excluded) and political conservatism (there is no room for the beliefs, 'oughts' or 'shoulds' of radical critiques of the status quo).

We can compare this with two other broad approaches. 'Realism' is another group of approaches which also distinguish between observers and the world they observe. However, rather than seeing observable phenomena as being the totality of the real world, it accepts that less observable forces lie behind the phenomena. Whereas in positivism the purpose of theories is to describe/predict the phenomena, in scientific realism the purpose is to represent the *underlying real order* that we only observe as the phenomena.

Thus while realism is also phenomenological, it is less fixated on the empirical. It does not define the 'truth' of a theory as essentially its capacity to predict accurately. It is less exclusive of beliefs. Critical realism challenges the idea that scientific knowledge is the sole route to truth (Bhaskar 1989), and has been used to demonstrate that the natural sciences do not actually work in the simple way suggested by positivists (and indeed, by naïve critics of positivism in some sociological articles).

On the other hand, positivism and realism share a phenomenological basis, and our capacity to generate knowledge through systematic observation. An alternative strand to phenomenological thinking places greater weight on the *mental processes* that determine 'observation' and 'understanding'. The knowledge generated (i.e. our interpretation) is less clear-cut or independent of social circumstances. As humans, our minds develop through socialisation, we acquire culturally determined preconceptions in our thinking, and we learn how to make sense of both day-to-day social interactions and how 'scientific discourse' is constructed (e.g. why essays have to have bibliographies in a set form!). In this tradition, what matters is to empathise with those we study: 'understanding' or 'knowledge' is more to do with interpreting others' meanings than predicting or generalising (**Qualitative Methods:** Byrne 2002). In more extreme forms of the argument like social constructivism (Berger and Luckmann 1966), emphasis is placed on the way 'reality' is constructed and re-negotiated through social interaction. These positions draw on Husserl's writing, and in sociology, that of Schutz (**Ethnomethodology**).

Positivists are less comfortable with such views; natural scientists prefer to see their version of reality as a more direct reflection of the real world. Consequently, positivists and realists are often depicted as advocating the *primacy of the external world* rather than the *actor's interpretation* of it. Further, positivists are regarded as applying the basic methods of the natural sciences to studying social actions, both because of this primacy and because 'reliable knowledge' is solely dependent on the application of 'the scientific method'. The natural science methods in question are typically *quantitative*, involve testing of *hypotheses*, the search for *explanations and causes* which connect observations, and identification of '*laws*' or regular patterns from those observations.

The objection to scientific method in the social sciences lies in the nature of social life. Unlike inanimate objects studied by physical scientists, humans lead sentient existences outside the controlled conditions of the laboratory. Social life is less rigidly consistent, and subject to more factors, than elements in a chemistry experiment. It is therefore hard to make sociological predictions (i.e. express ideas as hypotheses), to discover 'laws', and even harder to know how far outcomes are the result of factors hidden from our view. Many of our sociological 'findings' show only that things are *associated*, i.e. usually happen together, not that they are causally linked in a one-for-one relationship (i.e. *more* working class children perform poorly in school, but *not all* of them: **Association and Causation**). If there are social regularities, they are subtle and dependent on circumstances, not something predictable in the abstract. The subject matter of sociology does lend itself to testing hypotheses.

When we speak of 'testing hypotheses' deductively, we do not mean 'proving' they are correct. If what we expect to observe from our prior hypothesis does happen, all this shows is that in the one particular case, the results were as expected. Another time it might not be so. Popper argued that we should instead seek disproof or 'falsification'. Just one negative set of findings means a hypothesis is untenable (provided that we have followed scientific method and formulated our hypothesis in a way that makes it falsifiable). This last point is part of what we meant earlier by positivism's 'values'. Researchers are obliged to operate by professional standards of scientific practice, and in particular to distinguish between their personal values and their research activities (**Feminist Research**).

While it is logically true that we can work by falsification, this is not what actually happens. The dominance of Newtonian physics was not marked by centuries of conscious attempts to falsify it, or eager anticipation of the day when it could be overturned. Scientists welcomed its principles as the basis for further work. Similarly, social scientists start with already accepted knowledge. Although in statistical analysis we may set up 'null hypotheses' (if we express our hypothesis as the opposite of what we really expect, and it is then falsified, our real hypothesis can still be accepted: **Hypothesis**), we normally operate on what Hempel calls *confirmation*. The absence of demonstrable falsification may not prove, but it does confirm, that our core hypothesis continues to be acceptable.

This applies to all sociological work, even that of those disavowing positivism. Sociological accounts implicitly say

> 'the external world is like this: if you in the audience study it in the same way as I have done you will come to the same conclusion'. This is at base a predictive exercise, and at various levels it is also an exercise in generalisation (Payne et al. 1981: 56).

It is not possible to work without some notion of regularities, and there is a danger that the positivist baby will be thrown out with the qualitative methods bathwater. Most legitimate concerns with interpretation need not eliminate all of the elements of positivism and realism. While there are subtle differences between philosophical positions, researchers actually slide between them during the process of doing research.

Key Words

confirmation
critical realism

deduction
falsification
hypothesis
induction
knowledge
laws
phenomenology
realism

Links

Association and Causation
Ethnomethodology and Conversational Analysis
Feminist Research
Grounded Theory
Hypothesis
Qualitative Methods

REFERENCES

General

Berger, P. and Luckmann, T. (1966) *The Social Construction of Reality.* New York: Doubleday.
Bhaskar, R. (1989) *Reclaiming Reality: A Critical Introduction to Contemporary Philosophy*. London: Verso.
Byrne, D. (2002) *Interpreting Qualitative Data*. London: Sage
Payne, G., Dingwall, R., Payne, J. and Carter, M. (1981) *Sociology and Social Research.* London: Routledge & Kegan Paul.
Williams, M. (2000) *Science and Social Science.* London: Sage.

Qualitative Methods

Qualitative methods produce detailed and non-quantitative accounts of small groups, seeking to interpret the meanings people make of their lives in natural settings, on the assumption that social interactions form an integrated set of relationships best understood by inductive procedures.

Section Outline: *Two traditions? Core issues: interpreting meanings; holistic; naturally occurring events; less abstract; small samples; detailed accounts; inductive reasoning. Advantages over quantitative methods. Techniques; philosophy and temperament. Conflicts between academics: USA and Britain. Methodological pluralism. Overlap of qualitative and quantitative methods.*

It is conventional to divide social research methods into two types: (a) qualitative or soft, and (b) quantitative or hard. This makes it easier to identify differences between approaches to research, in the form of a rough 'shorthand' way of talking about things. It provides a loose framework for linking specific techniques, like **Auto/biography and Life Histories**, **Case Study** or **Coding Qualitative Data**. We shall therefore use the distinction as a convenient way of exploring basic styles of research, although qualitative and quantitative methods *sometimes overlap* (e.g. Finch's (1989) use of sources in discussing family obligations).

The quickest way to gain a sense of qualitative methods is through examples. In this book for instance, there are sections on Community Studies, Ethnography, Feminist Research, Grounded Theory and Participant Observation. This is not an exclusive list: other references can be found in more general sections, such as Documentary Methods, Fieldwork, Levels of Measurement, or Methods and Methodologies (although not all of these are shown in the 'link list' at the end of this section).

Qualitative methods are 'especially interested in how ordinary people observe and describe their lives' (Silverman 1993: 170). It is an umbrella term covering different types of research. Almost all share certain features:

- The core concern is to seek out and *interpret the meanings* that people bring to their own actions, rather than describing any regularities or statistical associations between 'variables'.
- They treat actions as part of a *holistic social process and context*, rather than as something that can be extracted and studied in isolation.
- They set out to encounter social phenomena as they *naturally occur* (observing what happens, rather than making it happen).
- They operate at a *less abstract* and generalised level of explanation.
- They utilise *non-representative*, *small samples* of people, rather than working from large representative samples to identify the broad sweep of national patterns.
- They focus on the *detail* of human life.
- Rather than starting with a theoretical hypothesis, and trying to test it, they explore the data they encounter and allow ideas to emerge from them (i.e. using *inductive*, not deductive, logic).

Thus qualitative sociology focuses on how individuals interact, emphasising the interpretation of the meanings which each (including the researcher: **Reflexivity**) brings to the interaction and the way mutual understandings are negotiated. In this approach, there is no prior social order, or social structure external to the lived experiences of the actors, that predetermines outcomes. It makes little sense to seek general 'laws' of how 'society' works, because society is only the sum total of the many complex social situations that are going on at one time (Bryman 1988).

With social life being so intricate, and so dependent on circumstances, what would be the point of trying to reduce it to statistical simplifications? Social survey questionnaires cannot hope to catch the essence of social interactions. Only qualitative methods, with their detailed, flexible, sensitive and naturalistic characteristics, are suited to producing adequate sociological accounts. The term 'soft methods' suggests *subtlety*, not easy to do, whereas 'hard methods' does not mean more difficult, but less flexibility. The method follows from the kind of sociology adopted, which in turn incorporates a philosophical view of what the world is like, and how humans can know about it (**Reliability**; **Validity**).

Most sociologists would argue that the methods they use follow logically from prior intellectual understandings of the world (e.g. Seale 1999). These philosophical standpoints about what counts as 'social', and how it can be accessed, are rigorously developed. Research practice depends on pre-existing conceptual frameworks that have been carefully elaborated, and can be logically defended (this of course also applies to quantitative sociology). In some cases that draw heavily on phenomenological philosophy (**Positivism and Realism**) – like symbolic interactionism or ethnomethodology – qualitative methods are logically the *only* way to engage with the social world.

We can identify three elements here. One is research technique per se (**Participant Observation**; **Ethnography**, etc.). The second is the underlying intellectual understandings from which sociologists start. Other examples can be found in the sections on **Positivism** and **Ethnomethodology**. Third, debates over qualitative and quantitative methods reflect basic assumptions about free will and determinism: qualitative methods fitting more comfortably with those who stress the freedom of the individual to choose, and quantitative methods suiting those who tend to see human life as constrained and determined by external factors.

It would be easy to over-emphasise the logical consistency of philosophical orientation and methods used. The limited length of journal articles often means there is no room for such discussion, and the matter is left largely implicit. Platt's study of American sociology suggests that there has been a lot of post-hoc rationalisation of what were simple pragmatic choices: 'general theoretical/methodological stances are just stances: slogans, hopes aspirations, not guidelines' (Platt 1996: 275).

Two tendencies can be discerned. Currently, a commonly used method (to judge by what has recently been published in the main British journals) is discursive interviews with small numbers of informants (e.g. Solomon et al. 2002; Thomson et al. 2002). This might be called the soft version of soft methods, because little attempt is made to invoke substantial philosophical justifications for the research design, beyond a respect for complexity and sensitivity of social life and an attempt to represent the informants' views as they naturally exist.

The other tendency, an older tradition, adopts a hard version of soft methods, vehemently dismissing alternative approaches (e.g. Reinharz 1992; Stanley 1993). Academics trained to think consistently are naturally critical of views that they reject. For instance, quantitative sociologists have criticised qualitative methods as being 'unscientific' and a-theoretical (**Positivism and Realism**), open to subjective bias by the individual researcher (**Fieldwork**), and not open to inspection or replication. However, such attacks to a large extent merely reflect the history of academic institutions.

In the US, the early success of the University of Chicago's qualitative style of ethnographic sociology was later challenged by rival new departments espousing an alternative quantitative style. The emphasis placed on abstract theory and survey research by those like Parsons and Lazersfeld at Harvard and Columbia was due not only to their personal preferences as sociologists, but also to the tactic of competing academically against a discipline's leaders by embracing alternative stances.

The emergence of 'abstracted empiricism' and 'mindless number-crunching', as some critics called the new styles, was also facilitated by the extremist politics of the McCarthy Era. McCarthyism tolerated no questioning of the neo-Conservative version of the American Way of Life. Whereas Chicago had interested itself in the less advantaged in society, the new departments could appeal to the 'scientific' basis of statistical analysis, and the idea of social cohesion in functionalist social theory, so escaping accusations of 'Anti-Americanism'.

In Britain, neither qualitative nor quantitative sociology initially established itself as the dominant form in that way (Payne et al. 1981). If there was an older tradition to confront, it was an emphasis of abstract social theorising. Developing later (only after the Second World War was there more than one department of sociology), and with intellectual links to the Labour Party, British sociology used simple surveys alongside ethnographic methods to investigate social problems (Platt 2003). The creation of new sociology departments in the rapid expansion of Higher Education initially allowed space for any methodological disputants to co-exist.

Later on, in a rejection of both grand theorising (especially Marxist) and the focus on class-based social inequalities, a new generation of sociologists borrowed the dismissive (and often incorrectly applied) language of 'number-crunching' and 'positivism' (**Positivism and Realism**) from the US to challenge 'the old guard', and to legitimise their own feminist and ethnomethodological revolts. Attempts by the major research funding body, the Social Science Research Council (and its successor, the Economic and Social Research Council (ESRC)) to raise standards of numeracy provided a rallying point for resistance against alleged governmental interference with academic freedom.

By the mid-1970s, advocates of 'methodological pluralism' (**Methods and Methodologies**) called for quantitative and qualitative sociologists to co-exist. Methodological pluralism was basically a plea for tolerance. It did not demand that every sociologist must practise all kinds of methods. Pluralism is achieved by the sum total of output, rather than by each individual.

Some researchers with broad interests do however adopt a pragmatic approach, allowing the nature of the problem (the thing to be investigated) to dictate the techniques adopted for each study. This acknowledges that small-scale processes can best be studied qualitatively, whereas national patterns require quantitative methods. Preliminary exploration may best use 'softer' methods, in order to set up a more conventionally quantitative analysis as the next step. This pragmatism attempts to build on the strengths of both traditions rather than taking an exclusive philosophical stance.

It is also true that qualitative techniques draw on some of the stock-in-trade of what is normally regarded as quantitative methods. **Grounded Theory**, for example, uses both induction and deduction. Conversational analysis measures pauses in talk to the millisecond (**Ethnomethodology and Conversational Analysis**). Analysis of field notes involves content counting (**Content Analysis**). 'Qualitative research does imply a commitment to field activities. It does not imply a commitment to innumeracy' (Kirk and Miller 1986: 10). Reports based on qualitative methods often include statements about sample proportions, and can be written in such a generalising tone that it is hard to tell which tradition is being used (e.g. Jones 1999). For these reasons, while distinguishing between the two main 'schools' helps to clarify the different techniques, in practice too much can be made of the differences.

Key Words

ethnography
grand theory
holistic
inductive
McCarthyism
meaning
methodological pluralism

Links

Auto/biography and Life Histories
Case Study
Coding Qualitative Data
Content Analysis
Ethnography
Ethnomethodology and Conversational Analysis
Fieldwork
Grounded Theory
Methods and Methodologies
Participant Observation
Positivism and Realism
Reflexivity
Reliability
Validity

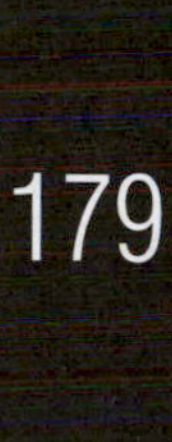

REFERENCES

General

Bryman, A. (1988) *Quantity and Quality in Social Research*. London: Routledge.

Kirk, J. and Miller, M. (1986) *Reliability and Validity in Qualitative Research*. Qualitative Research Methods Series, No. 1. London: Sage.

Payne, G., Dingwall, R., Payne, J. and Carter, M. (1981) *Sociology and Social Research*. London: Routledge & Kegan Paul.

Platt, J. (1996) *A History of Sociological Research Methods in America 1920–1960*. Cambridge: Cambridge University Press.

Platt, J. (2003) *The British Sociological Association: a Sociological History*. Durham: Sociologypress.

Seale, C. (1999) *The Quality of Qualitative Research*. London: Sage.

Silverman, D. (1993) *Interpreting Qualitative Data*. London: Sage.

Examples

Finch, J. (1989) *Family Obligations and Social Change*. Cambridge: Polity.

Jones, G. (1999) 'The Same People in the Same Places'. *Sociology*, 33 (1): 1–22.

Reinharz, S. (1992) *Feminist Methods in Social Research*. New York: Oxford University Press.

Solomon, Y., Warin, J., Lewis, C. and Langford, W. (2002) 'Intimate Talk Between Parents and Their Teenage Children'. *Sociology*, 36 (4): 965–83.

Stanley, L. (1993) 'Editorial Introduction'. *Sociology*, 27 (1): , pp. 1–4 (Special Issue on Auto/biography in Sociology).

Thomson, R., Bell, R., Holland, J., Henderson, S., McGrellis, S. and Sharpe, S. (2002) 'Critical Moments: Choice, Chance and Opportunity in Young People's Narrative of Transition'. *Sociology*, 36 (2): 335–54.

Quantitative Methods

Quantitative methods (normally using deductive logic) seek regularities in human lives, by separating the social world into empirical components called variables which can be represented numerically as frequencies or rate, whose associations with each other can be explored by statistical techniques, and accessed through researcher-introduced stimuli and systematic measurement.

Section Outline: *Two traditions? Core issues: regularities; variables; numerical values; statistical association; measurement stimuli; controlled measurement; external world. Large samples and deductive logic. 'Scientific knowledge'. Techniques, philosophy and temperaments. Fashions in methods. Methodological pluralism. Overlap of quantitative and qualitative methods.*

It is conventional to divide social research methods into two types: 'quantitative' and 'qualitative'. This makes it easier to identify differences between approaches to research, in the form of a rough 'shorthand' way of talking about things. It provides a loose framework for linking specific examples (see below). We will therefore use the distinction as a convenient way of exploring basic styles of research, although quantitative and qualitative methods *sometimes overlap* (e.g. Finch's use of sources in discussing family obligations (1989)).

The quickest way to gain a sense of quantitative methods is through examples. In this book for instance, there are sections on Contingency Tables, Hypotheses, Official Statistics, Questionnaires, Sampling and Survey Methods. This is not an exclusive list: other references can be found in more general sections, such as Fieldwork, Levels of Measurement, or Methods and Methodologies (although not all of these are listed in the 'link list' at the end of this section).

'Quantitative methods' is an umbrella term covering different types of research (Bryman 1988). In its simpler form, it consists of the counting of how frequently things happen (e.g. educational qualification levels among school leavers; attendance at doctors' surgeries; rates of divorce; proportion of national population living below the 'poverty line' (e.g. Dorling 1995; Kumar 1999: 226–40; Iganski and Payne 1999), and the presentation of these frequencies as summaries in tables and graphs (Frankfort-Nachmias and Leon-Guerrero 2000: 72–108). This can be extended by looking at how two or more factors seem to be connected, i.e. have associations (Rose and Sullivan 1993: 3–31) or to multivariate statistical techniques and mathematical models of social patterns (Sapsford 1999: 169–98; Schutt 1999).

Almost all forms of quantitative research share certain features.:

- The core concern is to describe and *account for regularities in social behaviour*, rather than seeking out and interpreting the meanings that people bring to their own actions.

- Patterns of behaviour can be *separated out into variables*, and *represented by numbers* (rather than treating actions as part of a holistic social process and context).
- Explanations are expressed as *associations* (usually statistical) *between variables*, ideally in a form that enables prediction of outcomes from known regularities.
- They explore social phenomena not just as they naturally occur, but by introducing *stimuli* like survey questions, collecting data by *systematic, repeated and controlled measurements*.
- They are based on the assumption that *social processes exist outside of individual actors' comprehension*, constraining individual actions, and accessible to researchers by virtue of their prior theoretical and empirical knowledge.

They often test theoretical hypotheses (i.e. using deductive not inductive logic), seeking regularities or 'laws' of social behaviour, but this approach is less common than often assumed by critics. Thus quantitative sociology focuses on those aspects of social behaviour that are most patterned and can best be quantified, rather than on highly fluid situations. The detail of social interaction and the meanings which individuals bring to the interaction are seen as lower-level and less important levels of explanation. This approach lays greater stress on prior social order or social structures external to the actors as contributing to the shaping of outcomes.

Most quantitative research therefore operates with less detail than qualitative methods, but with a wider scope and more generalised level of explanation. It utilises representative samples (**Sampling: Types**) to control for variations between people. Sometimes this is based on pragmatic decisions. For the basic frequencies about how many people experience certain conditions that feed into government policy (age groups, occupations, educational skills), we need accurate counts rather than highly sophisticated and detailed studies. It is much easier to use quantitative methods to identify national rates of, say, health or social inequality, or how such conditions relate to other social processes over say 40 years (**Longitudinal Studies**: Marmot and Wilkinson 1999; Payne and Roberts 2002) than to depend on and wait around for the face-to-face personal methods of qualitative research. Without a critical appreciation of numbers, the sociologist must struggle to engage with the forces of commerce, politics and other numerical disciplines that drive public life (Dorling and Simpson 1999; Payne 2003).

However, quantitative method is not just about pragmatics. It would be wrong to over-emphasise the idea that quantitative methods involve a concern just with 'social facts'. Much of the tradition is exploratory and through the use of **Attitude Scales** interested in 'meanings'. In its more positivistic formats (**Positivism and Realism**), researchers are usually seeking to test prior theoretical ideas (i.e. using deductive, not inductive, logic), and to produce results that can be expressed as 'laws' of social behaviour that are generally applicable.

This claim to scientific knowledge and expertise is one of the key features of quantitative social research. Its techniques are claimed to liberate researchers from personal bias and values, allowing the results to approximate to a distinctive 'truth'. The visibility of much of the technical process (sampling designs, questionnaires, code-books), and the potential this gives for subsequent replication of studies by other researchers, is used to substantiate a case that quantitative methods provide the basis for a social *science*. The objective knowledge of the quantitative sociologist is different from ordinary, everyday personal experience or beliefs. Research findings are both reliable and valid (**Reliability**; **Validity**). They are of a different nature than the interpretive observations of small-scale interactions that typify the work of the qualitative social researcher.

Most sociologists would argue that the methods they use follow logically from prior intellectual understandings of the world. These philosophical standpoints about what counts as 'social', and how it can be accessed, are rigorously developed. Research practice depends on pre-existing conceptual frameworks (Bryman 2001: 214–26) that have been carefully elaborated and that can be logically defended (this of course also applies to qualitative sociology). In some cases that draw heavily on the philosophy of logical positivism (**Positivism and Realism**), quantitative methods are logically the *only* way to engage with the social world. However, claims for such consistency are more often implicit: there is a big difference between a *tendency* for philosophical stance and method to hang together, and for it actually to happen consistently.

We can identify three elements here. One is research technique per se (**Social Surveys**, **Questionnaires**, etc.). The second is the underlying intellectual understandings from which sociologists start. Other examples can be found in the sections on **Positivism** and **Experiments**. Third, debates over quantitative and qualitative methods reflect basic assumptions about free will and determinism: quantitative methods suiting those who tend to see human life as constrained and determined by external factors, and qualitative methods fitting more comfortably with those who stress the freedom of the individual to choose.

It is therefore unsurprising that many sociological accounts vehemently dismiss alternative approaches. Academics trained to think consistently are naturally critical of views that they reject. For instance, qualitative sociologists have criticised quantitative methods as being superficial and failing to appreciate the complexity of social existence (**Ethnography**), falsely claiming to be value neutral, and treating the people being researched as mere objects (**Feminist Research**). However, such attacks also reflect the history of academic institutions, briefly illustrated in **Qualitative Methods**.

A glance at current sociological journals will show that American sociology is largely quantitative in style, and has been for many decades. In Britain, quantification was never so well established, and is currently the minority method of choice (Payne et al. in press). This has not prevented a great deal of conflict over research methods, leading some commentators to call for 'methodological pluralism', a plea for tolerance. This did not demand that every sociologist must practise all kinds of methods. Pluralism is achieved by the sum total of output, rather than by each individual.

Some researchers with broad interests do, however, allow the nature of the problem (the thing to be investigated) to dictate the techniques adopted for each study. This acknowledges that small-scale processes can best be studied qualitatively, whereas, say, national patterns require quantitative methods. This pragmatism attempts to build on the strengths of both traditions rather than taking an exclusive, philosophical stance. Preliminary exploration may best use 'softer' methods, in order to set up a more conventionally quantitative analysis as the next step, once basic hypotheses have been formulated and categories to be measured identified. On the other hand, many qualitative researchers find this denigrates their preferred style of research.

It is also true that quantitative techniques draw on some of the stock-in-trade of what is normally regarded as **Qualitative Methods** – and the reverse is also true. Question design needs to be extremely sensitive to the interpretation of phrases (**Questionnaires**). Conduct of **Fieldwork** involves interpersonal skills. There is no reason why quantitative approaches have to be restricted to questionnaires: they can also be used in **Observation** and **Key Informant** methods. While some of the more statistical styles of writing seem somewhat removed from qualitative methods, small-scale studies using simpler methods often move between quantification and interpretation, so that it is not entirely clear which tradition is being used (e.g. Werbner 2001). For these reasons, while distinguishing between the two main 'schools' helps to clarify the different techniques, in practice too much can be made of the differences.

Key Words

association
bias
deductive
measurement
objective

Links

Attitude Scales
Ethnography
Experiments
Fieldwork
Feminist Research
Key Informants
Longitudinal and cross-sectional Studies
Observation
Positivism and Realism
Qualitative Methods
Questionnaires
Reliability
Sampling: Types
Social Surveys
Validity

REFERENCES

General

Bryman, A. (1988) *Quantity and Quality in Social Research*. London: Sage.
Bryman, A. (2001) *Social Research Methods.* Oxford: Oxford University Press.
Kumar, R. (1999) *Research Methodology.* London: Sage.
Frankfort-Nachmias, C. and Leon-Guerrero, A. (2000) *Social Statistics for a Diverse Society* (2nd edn). Thousand Oaks, CA: Sage.
Payne, G., Williams, M. and Chamberlain, S. (in press). 'Methodological Pluralism in British Sociology'. *Sociology*, 38 (1).
Rose, D. and Sullivan, O. (1993) *Introducing Data Analysis for Social Scientists.* Buckingham: Open University Press.
Sapsford, R. (1999) *Survey Research*. London: Sage.
Schutt, R. (1999) *Investigating the Social World* (2nd edn). Thousand Oaks, CA: Pine Forge Press.

Examples

Dorling, D. (1995) *A New Social Atlas of Britain*. Chichester: John Wiley & Sons.
Dorling, D. and Simpson, S. (eds) (1999) *Statistics in Society: the Arithmetic of Politics.* London: Arnold.
Finch, J. (1989) *Family Obligations and Social Change.* Cambridge: Polity.
Iganski, P. and Payne, G. (1999) 'Socio-economic Re-structuring and Employment'. *British Journal of Sociology* 50 (2): 195–215.
Marmot, M. and Wilkinson, R. (1999) *Social Determinants of Health*. Oxford: Oxford University Press.
Payne, G. (2003) *Immobility, Inequality and 'Illiteracy'*. Paper presented to the Annual Conference of British Sociological Association, York.

Payne, G. and Roberts, J. (2002) 'Opening and Closing the Gates: Recent Developments in British Male Social Mobility'. *Sociological Research OnLine*, 6/6/4/payne.html..
Werbner, P. (2001) 'Metaphors of Spatiality and Networks in the Plural City'. *Sociology*, 35 (3):671–93.

Questionnaires

Questionnaires are the printed sets of questions to be answered by respondents, either through face-to-face interviews or self-completion, as a tested, structured, clearly presented and systematic means of collecting data (mainly in the quantitative methods tradition).

Section Outline: *Question format: simple, clear, understandable wording. Pitfalls: too general; double-barrelled questions; threatening; too complicated. Open and closed questions. Show cards. Question sequences. Filters. Self-completion.*

In survey research – probably the archetypal example of **Quantitative Methods** – everyone in the sample is systematically asked the same questions, in the same order in each interview and by each interviewer. This is in contrast to in-depth **Interviewing** (see also **Auto/biography and Life Histories**; **Unobtrusive Methods**). A list of topics to be included is converted into easily understandable and answerable questions, written down on a standardised form (the 'questionnaire'). Questionnaire design is a deceptively specialist skill, and best not tackled alone. A useful starting point for phrasing questions is the Question Bank (http://qb.soc.surrey.ac.uk). In designing the questionnaire, there are certain basic rules that should always be followed. These can be divided into pitfalls which you should avoid, types of questions and question order.

It has long been established that *questions must be easily understandable to all respondents* (Payne 1951). Each question should mean the same to everyone involved so that comparable answers are obtained. Thus the language used should be simple, non-technical and unambiguous. For example, a survey on eating patterns should not include questions about 'adequate nutritional requirements' or even 'a balanced diet', since some people would either not understand the terms used or interpret 'adequate', 'nutritional' or 'balanced' by their own standards. Instead, respondents might be asked what they ate during a particular day or their last meal. 'Ate' is better than 'consumed': always use the simplest vocabulary you can. *You* know what you mean, but will others?

This latter test applies to questions that are *too general*. For example, 'What do you think about this area?' might obtain a wider range of non-comparable answers such as 'not a lot' or a very detailed account of the history, environment and social life of the area (**Community Profiles**). Alternatives to such questions include using a list of statements that the respondent can agree or disagree with, or you might ask about specific features of the area separately. A general question is, however, useful as an introductory question to put the respondent at ease, rather than providing any data.

Questions that appear to expect a certain answer (*leading questions*) should not be used. Respondents are likely to agree with the sentiments expressed in such questions, believing there is a correct answer, rather than giving their own opinion. 'Youth crime is a problem in this area, isn't it?' would be better phrased as 'In this area, is youth crime a problem?' or, even better, 'In this area, which of the following do you think are the main problems?', followed by a list of possible problems. Note that qualifying phrases ('in this area') should come first in the question, to focus respondents before they tackle the more general issue of the main question.

A fourth common error is *combining two or more questions into one*, as for instance in 'Do you think there should be more recreational facilities and daycare centres for children and older people?' Here, you cannot know whether the answer is to 'recreational centres' or 'day-care centres', for 'children' or 'older people'. The question should become four separate questions.

Anything *threatening* or likely to arouse *anxiety* should be avoided by substituting indirect questions. A study of child abuse might therefore not ask about first-hand experience, but instead include questions listing a range of physical and mental abuses, to ascertain those that respondents thought most serious. People feel threatened or anxious about a range of topics, and if questions seem likely to intimidate, then a non-survey method could be considered.

Questions involving complex *knowledge, mental arithmetic* or that need *detailed memory recall* are particular sources of anxiety. They also produce a high proportion of factually incorrect answers. Thus, asking for the average age of people in a household would entail not only knowing everyone's ages, but also being able to *calculate averages in one's head*. Ask for the individual ages, and calculate the averages at the data analysis stage.

There are two main types of questions: 'open-ended' and 'closed'. Open-ended questions leave the answer entirely to the respondent, because the researcher either has little prior knowledge of possible responses, or feels that more detailed responses might add depth to the survey. For example, 'In this area, what do you think are the main health problems?' The layout of the questionnaire should leave sufficient space to record replies verbatim.

Most questions are likely to be phrased in closed format, offering a number of fixed answers from which respondents must choose. However, categories such as 'Other' or 'Don't Know' are included to cover all possible answers. The main advantage of closed questions is that they are easily classified at the coding stage, or even pre-coded on the questionnaire. The most common type are 'checklist' questions, offering several alternatives. For example, 'What is the main way you travel to work?: walk; cycle; bus; train; car; mixture of these; other'. Here, only one answer can be selected. Alternatively, the respondent may be allowed to select a fixed number of answers or as many as necessary: 'Which of the following foods have you eaten today?: bread; rice; pasta; potatoes; pastry; eggs; meat; lentils; beans fruit; vegetables'. Most 'attitude scale' questions offer a range of five possible responses to opinion statements (**Attitude Scales**: Oppenheim 1992).

Responses for some closed questions can be printed on 'show cards'. Each response is given a letter or digit, and respondents are asked to select their response to a particular question from a list handed to them, using that letter or number. This saves time and repetition when several questions have the same possible responses, the list is long, or sensitive questions are being asked, because the interviewer only has to read out the question and not the list.

The order of questions has an important influence on the answers. Generally, questions should flow into each other so that the rules of a normal conversation are followed. Sometimes, however, it is possible to 'hide' a question among other topics as a way of checking previous responses. The questionnaire's layout should not be crowded: it must be easy for interviewers to use, and 'instructions' (e.g. filters) differentiated from the question wordings to be read out.

Often respondents are only required to answer certain questions if they have answered a previous question in a particular way. This question is called a *contingency* or *filter question*. Clearly, to work, filter questions have to be closed. For example, you might want to ask questions about children only if respondents did have children. The filter would ask if they had children: if the answer was 'no', the interviewer's instruction would be to leave out the questions about children: 'IF NONE, GO TO QUESTION X'. – hence the term 'skip' or 'GOTO' questions. The other major instruction to interviewers is when to PROBE or PROMPT (**Interviewing**).

Most of these guidelines apply to *self-completion* questionnaires (including **Internet Polling**), but no question order can be guaranteed because respondents can choose their own order. Question wording is even more vital, and any filter instructions must be absolutely clear. The questionnaire must be brief, because respondents' attention spans are short. Both types of questionnaire are better suited to collecting 'factual' information than more subtle and complex social data, like interaction processes or full meanings. Their success relies heavily on careful design and full pre-testing, prior to going 'into the field' (**Social Surveys**). Equally, if the original concepts and insights are not intriguing, the results will disappoint: 'If we ask dull questions we shall get dull answers' (Sapsford 1999: 257).

Designing questionnaires looks simple but it is not. A good rule of thumb is always to work in pairs, and then to use a couple of friends or family members as guinea pigs (they will be your sternest critics!). Even some professional survey researchers sometimes produce seriously deficient questions: on the day this was written YouGov, the internet polling organisation, was running inter alia the following agree/disagree question:

Bologna in Birmingham, Madrid in Manchester; cities in continental Europe are a good example from which our towns could learn.

We might object:

1 What does the second and fifth word 'in' actually *mean*?
2 Do we all *know* Bologna/Birmingham/Madrid/Manchester, or already like/dislike them equally? How will this affect our response?
3 This is a *dual* question: what if we think Bologna 'yes', Madrid 'no'?
4 'a good example'? Of what? Bull-fighting? Cooked meats? Traffic? This is too general a question.
5 'towns': does this mean just Birmingham and Manchester, or other British *cities*, or smaller urban settlements? Can all 'towns' learn the same lessons?
6 Who is '*our*'?: Scots might not call Birmingham or Manchester 'our towns'.

Sadly, standards are not always beyond reproach.

This is often hidden because publishing conventions dictate that most published accounts do not include the questionnaires on which they are based – of course, in *qualitative* research, the questions are even more invisible, and therefore problematic. Questionnaire design is not just a technical matter: Savage et al. (2001) show how the type of question, and order of presentation affected the *conclusions* drawn in the Essex Class Survey (Marshall et al. 1989 – which includes the questionnaire). Among quantitative studies, the annual British Social Attitudes series (e.g. Park et al. 2002) is another good exception of including the questionnaire, and many questionnaires are available for inspection online from the UK Data Archive (www.data-archive.ac.uk). A useful test of your own understanding is to select an example on a topic which interests you, and to review the question wording and sequencing.

Key Words

closed questions
checklists
comparability
contingency question
filter question
leading question
open-ended questions
self-completion questionnaire
skip instruction

Links

Attitude Scales
Auto/biography and Life Histories
Community Profiles
Internet Polling
Interviewing
Quantitative Methods
Social Surveys
Unobtrusive Methods and Triangulation

REFERENCES

General

Oppenheim, A. (1992) *Questionnaire Design, Interviewing and Attitude Measurement.* London: Frances Pinter.
Payne, S. (1951) *The Art of Asking Questions.* Princeton, NJ: Princeton University Press.
Sapsford, R. (1999) *Survey Research*. London: Sage.

Examples

Marshall, G., Rose, D., Newby, H. and Vogler, C. (1989) *Social Class in Modern Britain.* London: Unwin Hyman.
Park, A., Curtice, J., Thomson, K., Jarvis, L. and Bromley, C. (eds) (2002) *British Social Attitudes: the 19th Report*. London: Sage.
Question Bank (2003) http://qb.soc.surrey.ac.uk.
Savage, M., Bagnall, G. and Longhurst, B. (2001) 'Ordinary, Ambivalent and Defensive: Class Identities in the Northwest of England'. *Sociology*, 35 (4): 875–92.
UKDA (2003) www.data-archive.ac.uk
YouGov (2003) *Special Feature Poll*, 1 August, www.YouGov.co.uk

Reflexivity

Reflexivity is the practice of researchers being* self-aware *of their own beliefs, values and attitudes, and their personal effects on the setting they have studied, and* self-critical *about their research methods and how they have been applied, so that the evaluation and understanding of their research findings, both by themselves and their audience, may be facilitated and enhanced.

Section Outline: *Reflexivity an underrated concept. Reflexivity for high professional research standards. Audit trails. Qualitative methods: personal reactions, feelings, doubts. Intellectual resource versus defensive audit. Positioning statements. Interacting with the setting. Self-critical awareness of own social skills. Limits of 'confessional accounts'. Writing with 'authority'.*

'Reflexivity is an immense area of comment and interest' (Denzin and Lincoln 1998: 394), but it receives little direct attention in many methods textbooks. The practice of researchers doing their research, and writing it up, *in explicitly self-aware and self-critical ways* is particularly important in qualitative research, where it feeds into debates about the 'validity' of research findings (**Qualitative Methods**; **Validity**). (This is different from 'reflexivity' in **Ethnomethodology**, which refers to how, when a pattern is perceived by members, it is used to interpret new situations, imposing definitions on novel experiences so that in turn 'evidence' is found in a form that supports the original pattern.)

The greatest variety and volume of commentary by researchers on their own work is to be found in qualitative work (e.g. Ladino 2002). However, at its most basic level, reflexivity is about maintaining high professional standards of investigation, which applies to all modes of social research. It may seem obvious, but good research depends on the selection and proper, systematic application of the right methods for the task in hand. The researcher is the *only* person who can ensure this happens. It means keeping each step under review, setting performance standards for oneself, thinking about how informants are reacting to being studied (**Unobtrusive Methods**), and constantly evaluating what is being achieved. Even highly competent or quantitative researchers need repeatedly to question their own practice, reflecting both on what they are trying to do, and on the progress of their work, so that they remain conscious of their research as a creative process, appropriately conducted.

Thus Huberman and Miles' call for 'regular, ongoing, self-conscious documentation' (1998: 201) in qualitative work could apply to other research methods. Any part of a project could be included, but they draw attention to decisions about sampling, operationalisation, data collection, analysis strategies (including any software used) and records of key evidence. It is on these that technical challenges to the findings might subsequently be mounted (i.e. validity questions raised: Hammersley 1992), or a replication study based. Lincoln and Guba (1985) and Schwandt and Halpern (1988) refer to such documentation as the 'audit trail'. However, perhaps because it takes more time to carry out, methodological audit is still not widely practised in this formal way.

On the other hand, it has become customary for fieldworkers to record not only their observations, but their own reactions to, and first interpretations of, those observations (**Fieldwork**; **Coding Qualitative Data**). This helps to keep the experiences alive, so that later analyses do not lose sight of their initial impact and intensity. The researcher retains something of the original emotional energy of events and encounters. Sanders refers to entries in his 'research diary' which start '*What a day!* This one starts off with an awful . . . case that pushes me to the limit' and '*It really strikes me* that [what I am doing now] is very different from any of the other research' (Sanders 1998: 195; 190: emphasis added). Later reports written in neutral, 'scientific', professionally detached and bloodless terms lose the highs and lows of the events on which they are based, so falsifying the record.

To use experience and reflection as a potential resource, researchers convert their rough observation notes at the end of each fieldwork 'shift' into proper records, adding the reflections in a clearly identifiable format. This should not become a mechanical process of note-making, because its main purpose is to stimulate fresh thinking about the research. Miles and Huberman suggest including feelings about informants; second thoughts about what their remarks meant; doubts about data quality; new hypotheses and ideas; and cross-referencing to and clarifying of previous events (1994: 66).

This emphasises reflexivity as an intellectual resource, rather than a defensive audit. Actively self-aware researchers not only produce more convincing research, but may also begin to question the very basis on which they started. Growing sensitivity to ethnographic methods provided grounds for a first generation of anthropologists to mark off professional studies from travellers' tales and colonial reports. Then, as the next generation continued to work reflexively, they began to doubt their elders' – and their own – practice. In **Feminist Research** reflexivity was seen as part of consciousness-raising. A woman's articulated subjectivity enabled her to reject methodological conventions that were intrinsically patriarchal. Thus reflexivity can move from being a resource in a given project, to being *a resource for a radical paradigm shift* of a more general kind.

Once researchers were no longer seen as 'free-floating scientists', separate from their projects, then their own values and personalities became matters of interest. 'Positioning statements' in article publications – e.g. 'I am a white middle class woman' – became a fashionable shorthand way to acknowledge the cultural starting point, and often political stance, that researchers brought to their research.

> The scientific observer is part and parcel of the setting, context and culture he or she is trying to understand and represent . . . scholars began to realize that the traditional problems of entrée or access to a setting, personal relations with the members of a setting, how field research data were conceived and recorded, and a host of other pragmatic issues had important implications for what a particular observer reported as the 'findings' (Altheide and Johnson 1998: 285).

In the ethnographic tradition (**Ethnography**), research is *situated* in specific settings, *relational* in its encounters with informants/members, and *textual* in the dual sense that it has first to be read/interpreted by the researcher, and then communicated via a written document. These elements interact with each other and the research method. They come together in the person of the researcher, who must remain centre-stage if an authentic account of the research process is to be achieved.

This in turn raises the question of how effectively has the research act been accomplished? As Grills reminds us, research is not simply an intellectual exercise: our personalities and social skills are crucial. Informants

> may be much more attentive to the various qualities of the researcher (e.g. trustworthy, humorous, friendly, open, and non-judgemental) than they are to the purpose of the research, consent forms, or credentials (1998: 12).

In reflecting on these elements, researchers began to include commentary in their own publications, and to write directly about doing research in order to demonstrate issues of wider practice. Following the lead of anthropologist Clifford Geertz (1973), these cautionary tales or 'confessions' have come to show how research is a messy, complicated business, full of inter-personal problems and anxieties often unhinted at by the clean and tidy world of the textbooks. Through self-criticism, their manifest function is to offer help to other, particularly inexperienced, researchers (e.g. Bell and Newby 1977; Payne et al. 1981: 181–252).

The 'telling it like it is' tradition has itself been criticised (even by Geertz himself (1988)). At its worst, it deteriorates into personal self-discovery, of more interest to the writer than the reader. There may be no lesson to convey: all we are offered is narcissistic, self-indulgent introspection. By definition, it is not possible for unconscious biases to be brought out. Far from holding up the research process to further examination, apparent self-criticism can be presented so as to convince readers that the researcher was right all along. Confessional accounts can be exercises in self-justification, lending 'authority' to the author's version of reality (Seale 1999).

As a number of post-modern critics have shown, 'authority' in writing is a more general issue. The use of the editorial 'we', impersonal/passive verbs, formal structures to presentation and argument, bibliographic references and other academic writing conventions are signals of the writer's claim to competence and expert knowledge (undergraduates please note!). It is not clear to us why anybody should do research and then *not* claim that the findings have some special significance, but that is a problem for the post-modernists. What is more important is that in practising reflexivity, researchers help not only their own understanding, but that of readers too. All writing has a readership in mind, and reflexive writing should aim at assisting the reader to handle problematic elements and, in turn, to reflect upon them.

Key Words

audit trail
confessional account
relational
research diary
setting
situational
textual

Links

Coding Qualitative Data
Ethnography
Ethnomethodology and Conversational Analysis
Feminist Research
Fieldwork
Qualitative Methods
Unobtrusive Methods and Triangulation
Validity

REFERENCES

General

Altheide, D. and Johnson, J. (1998) 'Criteria for Assessing Interpretive Validity in Qualitative Research'. In Denzin, N. and Lincoln, Y. (eds), *Collecting and Interpreting Qualitative Materials.* London: Sage.

Denzin, N. and Lincoln, Y. (eds) (1998) *The Landscape of Qualitative Research*. London: Sage.

Geertz, C. (1988) *Work and Lives: the Anthropologist as Author.* Stanford, CA: Stanford University Press.

Grills, S. (1998) (ed.) *Doing Ethnographic Research*. London: Sage.

Hammersley, M. (1992) *What's Wrong with Ethnomethodology?* London: Routledge.

Huberman, M. and Miles, M. (1998) 'Data Management and Analysis Methods'. In Denzin, N. and Lincoln, Y. (eds), *Collecting and Interpreting Qualitative Materials.* London: Sage.

Lincoln, Y. and Guba, E. (1985) *Naturalistic Inquiry.* Beverly Hills, CA: Sage.

Miles, M. and Huberman, M. (1994) *Qualitive Data Analysis* (2nd edn). London: Sage.

Schwandt, T. and Halpern, E. (1988) *Linking Auditing and Metaevaluation*. Newbury Park, CA: Sage.

Seale, C. (1999) *The Quality of Qualitative Research*. London: Sage.

Examples

Bell, C. and Newby, H. (1977) *Doing Social Research*. London: Allen & Unwin.

Geertz, C. (1973) *The Interpretation of Cultures.* London: Fontana.

Ladino, C. (2002) 'You Make Yourself Sound So Important'. *Sociological Research Online*, 7 (4). *http:*//www.socresonline.org.uk/socresonline/7/4/ladino.html

Payne, G., Dingwall, R., Payne J. and Carter M. (1981) *Sociology and Social Research*. London: Routledge & Kegan Paul.

Sanders, C. (1998) 'Animal Passions'. In Grills, S. (ed.), *Doing Ethnographic Research*. London: Sage.

Reliability

Reliability is that property of a measuring device for social phenomena (particularly in the quantitative methods tradition) which yields consistent measurements when the phenomena are stable, regardless of who uses it, provided the basic conditions remain the same.

Section Outline: *Credibility of research findings. Reliability in quantitative methods. Repeatable, consistent measuring. Validity: are measurements measuring the right things? Example: student status. Replication. Example: social mobility. Reliability: 'temporal'; 'representative'. Tests for reliability. Reliability in qualitative methods. Dependability. Internal and external validity. Plausibility; credibility. Little research on qualitative reliability as practice. Greater interest in validity.*

There is little point in research unless we can believe its results. 'Believing' in this context means having rational grounds for arguing that the accounts produced accurately reflect the nature of what we studied. It is by 'recourse to a set of rules concerning knowledge, its production, and representation' that it is possible to assert that we were 'faithful to the context and the individuals it is supposed to represent' (Denzin and Lincoln 1998: 414). In particular, we need to substantiate the research 'instruments' or 'measures' that we have created – and applied (see **Ethical Practice**).

The terms 'research instruments' and 'measures' indicate that this issue is more actively debated in quantitative methods than in qualitative styles. If we wish to transform social action into 'quantities', this obviously involves constructing 'mechanisms' to do so. Do the measuring mechanisms work? However, as we shall see, qualitative research shares an interest in demonstrating credibility, although it approaches this problem differently.

There are two main questions about credibility of research. The first addresses whether we would get similar results if the study were repeated. The second question is more challenging: even if the same results were obtained, would they be *right*, i.e. have we actually measured what we needed to look at, in a way that accurately captures its characteristics? The first question is about *reliability*, the second about *validity* (dealt with in a closely linked section, **Validity**). The two are often confused (for people who like mnemonics, REliabity is about REpeatability). This is because the validity aspects of the way we handle measurement (**Levels of Measurement**; **Indicators and Operationalisations**; **Attitude Scales**) are indeed related to the technical aspects of measuring reliability.

Reliability is about being confident that the *way* data were gathered could be *repeated without the methods themselves producing different results*. Suppose we were to interview you every three months while you are a student, in a study of students' attitudes to higher education. We might check each time whether you were still a student: 'Are you still enrolled as a full-time student?' It is unlikely that you would misunderstand, or say you were not a student, because this question is clear.

We would therefore have an accurate picture of your student status in each interview. Each time we used the question, it would produce the same result. It would be a reliable measure of your status (and conversely, if your status changed, it would discover that too).

But what if we asked 'Are you studying?' or 'What are you doing these days?' You might answer that you were still a student. However, you might plausibly say you were not studying just now (student life is not all work!) or that you were working in a bar (i.e. as a part-time job to pay your way through university). Our two looser questions might not consistently produce the answer that you were a student. These two questions are not a reliable way of gathering data.

Most research does not re-interview like this. More typically, one wants to be sure that all respondents understand questions in the same way, or that if other researchers were to repeat the study with the same instruments (questions, definitions, sampling, data collection like **Social Surveys** or **Internet Polling**), they would find similar results. Repeated studies are called 'replications', but whereas in natural science experiments are frequently repeated as part of the process by which findings are accepted, relatively few sociological studies are directly replicated.

One exception was the social mobility studies of England and Wales (Goldthorpe 1987) and Scotland (Payne 1987). Using very similar questionnaires and coding, within two years of each other, these two sample surveys independently found much the same rates of mobility. There was slightly less mobility in Scotland, as expected given its smaller middle class. Thus although the results were not identical, it can reasonably be said that the data were collected in a *reliable* way.

If we assume for the moment that what is being studied is itself stable, consistent and measurable (something which many qualitative researchers would deny about social phenomena), then we seek reliability of two main kinds. '*Temporal reliability*' (like our student example) requires that we get the same answer at different time-points. Of course, if what we are studying has a time pattern, such as time of day/night in the case of shopping or travel behaviour, or seasonal variation in leisure activities, then we would not expect uniformity. '*Representative reliability*' requires that findings from other similar samples will be basically the same as those for the original study: in other words, that we can plausibly generalise from our study.

There are several ways of checking for reliability. We can divide our respondents' data into two halves, to see if there are any unexplained differences ('split halves' method). We can repeat the research with the same sample to be sure the findings do not change ('test/retest'). Or we can include two or more measurements of the same thing, and compare the results ('inter-item' checking, often part of attitude scale construction).

These checks make good sense in a quantitative framework where the emphasis is on standardisation and control in data collection. This emphasis follows from philosophical stances seeking to discover general patterns believed to exist in society (**Positivism and Realism**). Such patterns are regarded as stable, accessible with suitable research instruments, and based on data simplified and extracted from its original setting (**Quantitative Methods**). For some, like Denzin and Lincoln (1998), claims to correct knowledge are implicit statements about superior knowledge and power to control.

This illustration highlights how the philosophical assumptions play into everyday research practice. For qualitative researchers, reliability takes a different form as a problem, because of their different philosophical starting points (Shipman 1997). They see social action as being far more complex, and having its true character both in its detailed complexity and in the specific setting in which it naturally occurs. Thus 're-studying' is less possible (indeed, probably impossible: Marshall and Rossman 1989) and likely to discover new features. Social life is not repetitive or stable, and so our research perceptions of it cannot be entirely consistent.

Instead of seeking uniformity, qualitative research offers a conscious openness to alternative, innovative methods. Alternative approaches help to eliminate serious inconsistencies. Similarly, the tradition of **Reflexivity** (briefly, exploring the researcher's own experience of engaging with the research process and participants: **Qualitative Methods**) sets up a discourse among researchers about how the research was done, and whether it is reliable. By confronting the researcher's own reactions and shortcomings, and comparing what different techniques have produced, plausibility and coherence emerge from dialogue and experience (**Objectivity**).

Lincoln and Guba (1985) suggest that rather than seeking 'reliability', a better term would be 'dependability', indicating the more general question of whether the results of one study are likely to occur again. This is what Lecompte and Goetz (1982) call 'external reliability', although they see it as more problematic, due to the variations between any two settings or methods used. They also propose the test of 'internal reliability': do researchers on the same project agree on interpretations? Other quantitative researchers, such as Hammersley (1992), Mason

(1996) and Silverman (1993), treat reliability, plausibility and credibility more in line with quantitative approaches. They see 'evidence' as having a crucial role in interpretative sociology: 'like all scientific work, it is concerned with the problem of how to generate adequate descriptions of what it observes' (Silverman 1993: 170).

However, Gladney et al. (2003), who compared how two independent teams analysed open-ended interviews, report being able to find only one other such study of qualitative reliability (Armstrong et al. 1997). Althoug most qualitative researchers are less exercised about reliability, it is generally agreed that quantitative research is better at handling reliability on a practical level. These differences in emphasis apply not just to reliability, the question of whether the *way* we identify things leads to the same thing *always* being so identified. They also apply to the issue of validity, i.e. whether when we identify something, we have actually got hold of the *right thing* (**Validity**).

Key Words

dependability
external reliability
internal reliability
replication
representative reliability
research instrument
split halves test
temporal reliability
test/re-test

Links

Attitude Scales
Ethical Practice
Indicators and Operationalisations
Internet Polling
Levels of Measurement
Objectivity
Positivism and Realism
Qualitative Methods
Quantitative Methods
Reflexivity
Social Surveys
Validity

REFERENCES

General

Denzin, N. and Lincoln, Y. (eds) (1998) *The Landscape of Qualitative Research*. London: Sage.

Hammersley, M. (1992) *What's Wrong with Ethnography?* London: Routledge.

Lecompte, M. and Goetz, J. (1982) 'Problems of Reliability and Validity in Ethnographic Research'. *Review of Educational Research*, 53: 32–60.

Lincoln, Y. and Guba, E. (1985) *Naturalistic Inquiry*. London: Sage.

Marshall, C. and Rossman, G. (1989) *Designing Qualitative Research* (2nd edn). London: Sage.

Mason, J. (1996) *Qualitative Researching.* London: Sage.
Shipman, M. (1997) *The Limitations of Social Research* (4th edn). Harlow: Longman.
Silverman, D. (1993) *Interpreting Qualitative Data.* London: Sage.

Examples

Armstrong, D., Gosling, A., Weinman, J. and Marteau, T. (1997) 'The Place of Inter-Rater Reliability in Qualitative Research'. *Sociology*, 31 (3): 597–606.
Gladney, A., Ayers, C., Taylor, W., Liehr, P. and Meininger, J. (2003) 'Consistency of Findings Produced by Two Multidisciplinary Research Teams'. *Sociology*, 37 (2): 297–313.
Goldthorpe, J. (1987) *Social Mobility and Class Structure in Modern Britain.* Oxford: Clarendon Press.
Payne, G. (1987) *Employment and Opportunity.* London: Macmillan.

Sampling: Estimates and Size

Sampling is the process of selecting a sub-set, of people or social phenomena to be studied, from the larger 'universe' to which they belong, which process in the case of probability or representative samples is based on the statistics of probability theory but can be reduced to a simple look-up table to decide how big a sample is needed.

Section Outline: *Confidence in estimates. Estimating proportions. Confidence intervals. Levels of confidence. Sample size depends on need for precision and correctness, not size of 'universe'. Limits to gain in increasing sample size. Look-up table for sample size. Reporting estimates: conventional approach.*

Most quantitative sociological research relies on fairly low **Levels of Measurement** and so is more concerned with *proportions* within, and simple counts of, variables. While some more advanced methods do draw on the means (averages) and more sophisticated calculations of variables, more commonly it is proportions in variables in the 'universe' that we are actually trying to estimate with our sampling (**Sampling: Types**). How can we know how good are the estimates based on our samples?

An alternative way of asking essentially the same question is 'How large a sample do we need to be confident about our findings?' Decisions about the size of probability samples are determined by *resources*; planned *analysis* methods; and the *variability* of the universe from which a sample is being drawn, as well as statistical principles (**Sampling: Questions of Size** – and also availability, if we are doing **Secondary Analysis**). To understand the latter, we need to engage in a little statistical calculation *(if you want to skip the stats, go to the last two paragraphs of this section: if you feel more comfortable about statistical treatments, see e.g. Frankfort-Nachmias and Leon-Guerrero (2000: 443–64))*.

The most useful formula for calculating sample size is: size = $pqZ^2 \div E^2$. Here, p means our 'guess' at the proportion in question, and q is (100 – p). The guess of p can be based on previous studies, or pilot work. If we do not have such guidance, p is usually set at 50 per cent because this is the worst case, requiring the largest sample. If we are wrong in this estimate of 50 per cent, it will only mean that we have decided on *too big a sample:* at least nobody can accuse us of having an unreliably small sample.

We can demonstrate this by simple arithmetic. When p = 50 per cent, the value of pq is 50 × (100 – 50) = 2500. If the real value of p were 40 per cent, pq would drop to 40 × (100 – 60) = 2400. The same applies if the real figure for p were 60 per cent: the results are just the mirror-image of 40 per cent. The further p is from 50 per cent (i.e. the more wrong our worst case guess is), the lower pq becomes. You can test this out by calculating various values of p for yourself. The bigger the value of pq in the upper half of our equation, the larger the overall sum comes out to be for the sample size. As the value of pq declines, so sample size declines.

The other factors in the formula are Z, the 'level of confidence' we want to set, and E, the 'confidence interval'. E is the more straightforward, being the amount of imprecision or error we can accept. If we want to be accurate within a range of, say, 10 per cent (5 per cent either side of the 'true' figure) then the worst deviation from the true proportion that we can accept is 5 per cent. In this case we enter E = 5. The more precision we want, the smaller the confidence interval, and so the value of E is reduced. Within the formula, the effect is to increase the size of the sample.

Z, the level of confidence, means the probability that our estimates (within the range of their confidence intervals) will turn out to be correct. If we want to be sure we are right 19 times out of 20, we set E at 1.96. If we need to be more certain, say 99 per cent of the time, we set the level of confidence at 2.57. The higher the level of confidence required, the larger is Z and so the bigger the sample. (Readers familiar with statistics will recognise that in a 'normal distribution', 95 per cent of cases lie within plus or minus (1.96 × the standard deviation) of the measurement in question. The theory behind our level of confidence is that a very large number of samples would produce a normal, binomial distribution of estimates. The variation of sample means (in a large number of samples) around a universe mean is called the standard error of the mean).

It should be noted that the formula does not include any term for the size of the universe from which we are sampling. Sample size depends on estimated proportions, precision and confidence levels, not on the universe. It is worth stressing this point by referring again to the standard deviation.

The amount that cases vary in the universe on any variable is its standard deviation, the value of which we do not know. We can none the less use an estimate to calculate the 'standard error' by means of the formula SE = $\sigma \div N$, where σ is the estimated standard deviation and N is the sample size. The bigger the sample size, the smaller the standard error (the sample variation from the universe mean). However, because we take the square root of the sample size, an increase in size has a limited effect.

Suppose sample size N was 100: its square root is 10. If we increase sample size to 1,000 (by a factor of 100), it does not reduce the standard error by 100 times, but by its square root, 31.6. Similarly, to halve the standard error, the sample size must increase fourfold. Alternatively, for every step increase in sample size (say, each extra hundred) the standard error reduces at a smaller rate. After a certain point, the required amount of increase in sample size becomes uneconomic.

If you have any difficulty in following these calculations, there is an even simpler method to decide sample size. Using a different calculation method, Krejcie and Morgan (1970) provide a look-up table which, for the same worst case proportions (50:50) and the same 95 per cent confidence level, gives sample sizes for different sizes of universe.

Table 4 *A look-up table for sample sizes from different sized universes*

Universe	Sample	Universe	Sample	Universe	Sample	Universe	Sample
10	*10*	100	*80*	1,250	*294*	6,000	*361*
15	*14*	200	*132*	1,500	*306*	7,500	*366*
20	*19*	300	*169*	2,000	*322*	10,000	*370*
30	*28*	400	*196*	2,500	*333*	15,000	*375*
40	*36*	500	*217*	3,000	*341*	20,000	*377*
50	*40*	600	*234*	3,500	*346*	30,000	*379*
60	*44*	700	*248*	4,000	*351*	40,000	*380*
70	*59*	800	*260*	4,500	*354*	50,000	*381*
80	*66*	900	*269*	5,000	*357*	75,000	*382*
90	*73*	1,000	*278*	5,500	*359*	1,000,000	*384*

Source: adapted from Krejcie, R. and Morgan, D. (1970)

Thus Hunt's sample is *statistically* inadequate, whether regarded as being *one* church from 50, or 50 *respondents* from 1,500 attenders at that church, or from the national universe of 170,000 (2002: 151). On the other hand, Clarke's sample of 4,023 households is highly likely to sustain generalisation to his four cities (and indeed the whole country (2002: 553).

We can now tackle our original question, 'How can we know how good are the estimates based on our samples?' The answer is that we set the limits (confidence interval and level) in advance, as part of the sample design. If all of our statistical assumptions are correct (and it should be remembered that that is not certain), we know the precision and confidence of our results. In the absence of stated confidence levels and intervals (and conventionally these are not reported for sample statistics in sociology), the safest assumption is that the spot figures given were based on the 50:50 estimate of proportions and 95 per cent confidence levels.

Key Words

confidence interval
confidence level
normal distribution
standard deviation
standard error
variation

Links

Levels of Measurement
Sampling: Types
Sampling: Questions of Size
Secondary Analysis

REFERENCES

General

Frankfort-Nachmias, C. and Leon-Guerrero, A. (2000) *Social Statistics for a Diverse Society* (2nd edn). Thousand Oaks, CA: Sage.

Krejcie, R. and Morgan, D. (1970) 'Determining Sample Size for Research Activities'. *Educational and Psychological Measurement*, 30: 607–10.

Kumar, R. (1999) *Research Methodology*. London: Sage.

Examples

Clarke, C. (2002) 'Budgetary Management in Russian Households'. *Sociology*, 36 (3): 539–57.

Hunt, S. (2002) '"Neither Here nor There"'. *Sociology*, 36 (1): 147–69.

Sampling: Questions of Size

Sampling is the process of selecting a sub-set, of people or social phenomena to be studied, from the larger 'universe' to which they belong, determined by a balance between resources available; anticipated techniques of analysis; how much variation there is believed to be in the universe; and the level of precision needed in estimates to be made about the universe on the basis of data from the sample.

Section Outline: *How big a sample? Non-probability samples. Samples from 'universes'. Trading off resources, planned analysis techniques, and variability of universe's components. Example: student elections. Stratified samples. Cluster samples. Estimates: correctness not the same as precision.*

The most frequently asked question in sampling for **Social Surveys** is 'How big a sample do we need?' The answer depends on the type of sample (**Sampling: Types**), the *resources* at our disposal, and what *quality of information* we want from the sample. It is partly a technical statistical question, but actually less so than most people believe.

'Non-probability sampling', like quota samples, can be cheaper than 'probability sampling', but we can attach less confidence to its findings. A probability sample is better for making estimates about the 'universe' from which it is drawn. We take a small sub-set ('sample') from a bigger set (the universe or population) because we want to *estimate something* in that universe/population. (Confusingly, population and universe in this sense are *statistical* terms, not ordinary nouns meaning people or the whole of creation. We therefore prefer 'universe' because it is more distinct from the human subjects of social research, and reminds us to include things like **Content Analysis** or **Documentary Methods**). While the size of a probability sample is related to the accuracy and precision of the universe estimates we want to make (Hoinville et al. 1982: 55–89), size is determined less by statistical principle than three other pragmatic considerations. These are: *resources*; planned *analysis* methods; and the *variability* of the universe from which a sample is being drawn.

Resources includes all aspects of what is available to do the fieldwork on the sample. Contacting a member of a sample costs money, takes time, and involves people to do the work. One of the implicit attractions of the experiment for social psychologists is speed and cheapness. If large sums of money are available, one can hire assistants to work quickly. A researcher working alone (e.g. a student) can obviously do less than research teams with large field-forces of interviewers (**Interviewing**; **Social Surveys**). When time is of the essence, (as it normally is) even large-sale projects cannot go on for ever, collecting more data from some huge sample.

Researchers inevitably work to a fixed resource budget, trading off their instinct for a large sample with the realities of what they can afford. While costs do change, currently the data collected from, say, a national sample of 3,000 people, processed into computer-readable format, would cost about £40 per person sampled (€58, or $65). The biggest factor in determining sample size in social science is budget: other things being equal, the smaller the resources, the smaller the sample.

The planned *method of analysis* is also important. Here we mean not the qualitative/quantitative divide (**Methods and Methodologies**; **Grounded Theory**) but differences *within* quantitative research.

Sometimes, the research questions are very specific, with a small range of factors influencing the main focus. Here, a small sample would be sufficient. However, if we plan to use several important variables, each with several possible values, then we risk subdividing our data into ever smaller slices.

For instance, social mobility studies commonly use seven social classes of origin and seven social classes of destination in their analysis. This produces a 7 × 7 contingency table (**Contingency Tables**), dividing the sample into roughly 50 slices (or 'cells'). If we split the data into four cohorts, each with three levels of educational qualification, we now have 50 × 4 × 3 = 600 cells. A sample of 3,000 would give us an average of 5 people in each combination of these four variables, even before we looked at any other issue, like explaining voting behaviour. Some cells would actually have no cases in them. Several common analytical techniques function poorly with empty cells. The more we plan to subdivide our sample data on analysis, the bigger the sample needed.

This problem presents itself in another form in connection with the *variability* of the population. If the people in the population are all very like one another, the population is said to be 'homogeneous'. If we are studying female university graduates who have had children, we would be studying a much more homogeneous population than the general public. If asked their views, it is likely that there would be more agreement among our target group than among the general public, because the latter includes men, children, women who have not given birth, and less educated women.

Even if the specification for the sample tries to eliminate unwanted cases, some of our target variables will still genuinely have a wide range of values. For instance, if we were mainly interested in education per se, there are many different levels, types of qualifications and educational institutions to take into account. On the other hand, in a simple (student) project to explore *gender* effects in *voting* preferences between *two candidates* running for Student President, education would be unimportant. Here, there are two key variables, both with a narrow range of variability. There are only two candidates, so voters must vote for one or the other, or not at all, giving only three values. The number of genders is also two. The population consists of the students of a single university. In this example, for the level of analysis, there is little variability. The greater the anticipated variability, the bigger the sample needed. It would not matter greatly how successful such a study was in predicting the election result, or showing gender differences: being a student project, resources would be more important than statistical accuracy.

Variability is relevant to two special cases of random sample design. In one, 'stratified sampling', the sample is divided into 'strata' or proportions to reflect more accurately the distributions in the universe (urban/rural; North/South, etc.), and drawn separately. In the other, sampling locations are concentrated to make fieldwork easier and cheaper. Because *more* respondents are drawn from these *fewer* 'clusters', this is less reliable because there may be localised variability (Kumar 1999: 158–60). Hunt (2002: 151) clustered by sampling 50 people attending the biggest church (1500) in a national congregation of 170,000 members. Clarke (2002: 553) clustered his national sample into four major cities. A technique called sampling 'proportionate to probability' seeks to balance the chances of a location being chosen, and the chances of being chosen within the locality, so that overall probabilities of being sampled remain the same as in a simple random sample.

Most quantitative researchers want to make statements about the universe which are both 'probably correct' and 'precise' (Sapsford 1999). These are not the same thing, depending as they do on statistical theory (**Sampling: Estimates and Size**). Estimates can be more or less likely to be *correct* ('Our estimates are likely to be good ones, close to the real universe value, *19 times out of 20*', or '*99 times out of hundred*'). Here, correctness is a statement about the *likelihood* of our estimate being close to the real universe value.

Estimates can also be more or less *precise* ('From our sample we estimate the figure for the universe lies somewhere *between 20 and 30*', or, with a great degree of precision, 'the figure for the universe lies somewhere between *20 and 24*'). Here, precision is a statement about the range within which we estimate the universe value to lie. For further discussion of the implications of this distinction, see de Vaus (1991) or Frankfort-Nachmias and Leon-Guerrero (2000).

Giving a *precise* estimate is not the same as being sure that the estimate (however precise or imprecise) is close to the real figure in the population. Although it is commonsense to think that the more precise we are, the bigger margin of error for correctness we ought to leave, precision and correctness are two different things. We do normally take them together, but they come from different parts of the statistical processes we use to decide sample size (see **Sampling: Estimates and Size**).

Decisions about sample design, in particular about sample size, involve a consideration of all four of the factors discussed here, and the needs of one will be traded off against the needs of the others. Few publishers allow space for researchers to report a complete explanation of sampling, so this usually remains invisible. The range of solutions chosen, and how they are reported (or not!) is illustrated by comparing Clarke's careful random sample in his account of household budgets in Russia (2002: 553–4) with the total absence of any information in Crawford's work on sports fans (2003).

Key Words

correctness
population
precision
resources
universe
variability

Links

Content Analysis
Contingency Tables
Documentary Methods
Grounded Theory
Interviewing
Methods and Methodologies
Sampling: Estimates and Size
Sampling: Types
Social Surveys

REFERENCES

General

Frankfort-Nachmias, C. and Leon-Guerrero, A. (2000) *Social Statistics for a Diverse Society* (2nd edn). Thousand Oaks, CA: Sage.
Hoinville, G., Jowell, R. and Associates (1982) *Survey Research Practice*. London: Heinemann.
Kumar, R. (1999) *Research Methodology*. London: Sage.
Sapsford, R. (1999) *Survey Research*. London: Sage.

Examples

Clarke, C. (2002) 'Budgetary Management in Russian Households'. *Sociology*, 36 (3): 539–57.
Crawford, G. (2003) 'The Career of the Sport Supporter'. *Sociology*, 37 (2): 219–37.
deVaus, D. (1991) *Surveys in Social Research* (3rd edn). London: UCL Press.
Hunt, S. (2002) '"Neither Here nor There"'. *Sociology*, 36 (1): 147–69.

Sampling: Types

Sampling is the process of selecting a sub-set, of people or social phenomena to be studied, from the larger 'universe' to which they belong, in one of several ways so as to be either non-representative (based on simple convenience or choice of particular illustrative cases) or representative (based on probability theory to make the cases more typical of the universe from which they have been selected).

Section Outline: *All research is based on samples. Time; place; availability. Qualitative methods sampling: purposive; theoretical; snowballing; non-representative. Quantitative methods sampling: probability samples. 'Randomness': chances of being selected for a sample from a universe. Sample frame requirements. Sample/universe 'fit': weighting. Quota sampling and its limitations.*

It is not possible to study *everything*. Inevitably, social researchers work on small sub-sets of the social phenomena that interest them. If we collect data this month, or this year, we take a 'time sample' from longer processes. This may be no more than accidental, taking what is available at a convenient time and 'place': access to a local research setting or a case study becoming possible when researchers' workloads permit them to go into the field. Other studies use time more rigorously, selecting the study period to representative events at other times.

Thus hospital patients and their visitors might be interviewed every day of the week for a period of weeks, to eliminate the atypical peculiarities of any one day or short stays. We might similarly sample on the basis of 'place'. Study periods or sites are usually taken to be typical of a longer or wider process, or a repeating sequence (a study of Christmas shopping could be typical of Decembers, but not the whole year). When there are seasonal or longer-run patterns, timing is crucial to knowing about the whole sequence.

Qualitative Methods focus on the specific, and its meanings, not explaining wider processes. Some qualitative researchers deny the possibility of generalisation (e.g. Guba and Lincoln 1994) and others have raised serious doubts (e.g. Hammersley 1992), but Williams has suggested that limited, careful moderatum generalisations are possible (2000). The *who* of 'who are picked' inevitably plays into the *what* of 'what is discovered'. People and events are deliberately selected because they are interesting or suitable, rather than being representative.

This 'purposive sampling' picks its sub-set for a particular, non-statistical purpose (for other types, see the list in Sarantakos 1998). For example, we deliberately select **Key Informants** because they are *not* typical: they know more about the community or organisation than other people. In **Grounded Theory**, theoretical concepts are tested against the fullest possible range of conditions. Such 'theoretical sampling' is selective, not representative. 'Snowball sampling' starts with a few informants, who pass researchers on to other individuals whom they personally know (Lupton and Tulloch 2002). Snowballing ends when there are no more people to add, or extra people add no useful information, or when researchers run out of time. The quality of the sample depends on the starting point, and strength, of the network.

Quantitative Methods attach more importance to *generalising* our sub-set findings to the larger set (or 'universe': **Sampling: Questions of Size**) from which the sub-set was selected. Samples are designed to resemble the universe on a smaller scale, representing the universe's features. Designs draw on the mathematics of probability theory; hence their correct name, 'probability samples'.

Probability samples are often called 'random samples'. 'Randomness' is actually a mathematical concept, implying that each element in a set is unconnected. Lists of 'random numbers' have been constructed with this property. To random sample, we should number every unit in our universe, and then draw the sample using random numbers, a very time-consuming process which is seldom used. The word 'random' is a source of confusion: informants, individually selected to represent our universe, often mistakenly think they have been picked for no special reason (chosen at random) and that anybody else will do. Whereas in **Experiments,** conditions are controlled to eliminate extraneous factor, in probability sampling they are controlled by ensuring that they are *included in the same proportions* as in the universe.

The most accurate basis for generalising is where we know that every person or social phenomenon in the relevant universe had an *equal probability of being sampled*. Strictly speaking, we need to know that probability (e.g. one chance in a thousand), which cannot take the value of zero. Because every unit had the same chance of being sampled, our sample should be a miniature version of the universe, resembling it in all but scale.

To achieve this, we first need a *list* of the items that make up the universe, from which to count the size of the universe, and select our named units for the sample. This 'sampling frame' should be *up to date, accurate, complete* and *suitable* for our purpose. A two-year-old telephone directory would *not* be up to date, would not accurately cover people moving house and keeping their old numbers, would be incomplete due to those with ex-directory numbers or without landline telephones, and therefore unsuitable for accessing, say, highly mobile, young or very poor people (**Internet Polling** and **Telephone and Computer-assisted Polling** raise particular problems of sampling).

Good lists ('sampling frames') for **Social Surveys** of the general populations are rare. The register of electors (the 'electoral roll') has been widely used, but this also has limitations of coverage of transient people (and has become extremely expensive to obtain for large areas). Sampling by addresses or post codes has become popular: addresses change more slowly and are updated more quickly than the register's list of people.

Such neat solutions are not always available. 'Hidden populations' – like Asian women workers or criminals not on any official list – may not volunteer to come forward. In such cases, alternatives to random sampling have to be employed, whatever the final method of data collection (Devine and Heath 1999: 45–52; Lee 1993; Williams and Cheal 2001). This raises problems of knowing how far our non-random sample is representative, but that does not mean that the question can be ignored. Brannen and Nilsen (2002: 533–4) used focus groups in their study of young people, but carefully explain what participants were like, and how their co-operation was obtained.

In contrast, when we have collected data from our representative sample, we can usually compare some of its key characteristics with what we already know about the universe. If we are sampling the general population, we want the proportions of genders, age groups and locations in the sample to be close to those of the population, as known from other studies like the Census. The closer the sample and the universe, the more confident we can be that findings for one can be generalised for the other. This equivalence is not inevitable. Even if we have escaped technical errors (**Bias**), we may still be unlucky, in that our correctly drawn sample might none the less have been an atypical one (**Sampling: Estimates and Size**). As we will not have interviewed everybody in the sample, we might have an unrepresentative part of our original sample.

One solution is to adjust the sample data by weighting. If we have too few cases of some kind, we can include those cases we do have more than once in our data. Suppose that we had only half the younger informants we required. We could take data obtained for those younger people we did contact, and include them twice, thus weighting them up to the right proportion. This of course assumes that our data on those we *do* have are basically the same as for those we *do not* have, and that the correction is better than the original error. Many opinion polls regularly use this method, because their data collection would otherwise have systematic biases. For instance, some adjust their aggregate voting intention data, giving more weight to informants who are actually likely to vote. This is *weighted probability sampling.*

A third type of widely used sample is the '*quota sample*'. Informants are selected in the *proportions* known to be present in the universe: gender, age, class, locality etc. Some samples use the dimensions separately, but better designs make them 'interlock'. Thus we would not be satisfied with the right gender balance on its own, and the right age distribution on its own, but would want the right age distribution for each gender. Obviously we can only design quotas when we first know the universe characteristics. Quota sampling is much quicker and cheaper than a proper probability sample, and if well conducted can give good results. However, it is not a probability sample, strictly defined (see above), and for technical reasons this limits which statistical methods that can be used in its analysis.

Another objection to quota sampling is lack of control over whom interviewers select to 'fill' their individual quotas. Each interviewer's quota consists not of named people or addresses, but only numbers of the general categories. For example, a quota of 12 might be '7 women, 5 men; 4 manual workers, 5 professional/managerial workers, and 3 not in paid work; 6 aged over 45 and 6 under'. The interviewer is free to pick informants that fit (MacFarlane Smith 1972: 45–52). The danger is that interviewers select those easiest to contact, or who seem friendly and approachable, whose answers may not be representative (**Interviewing**).

Early selections are easy, but become progressively harder. Almost anybody will fit the first 3 interviews, but the final cases might be constrained to be a female manual worker aged less than 45, or an older professional man. It may be impossible to obtain suitable interviewees. The temptation for the interviewer to fiddle the selection increases.

Even honest interviewers may misjudge ages or social classes, or just pick 'friendly' people. Quota sample tend to under-represent those in the lower classes, who work in the private sector, or are very poor or very rich. They over-represent women with young children and members of large households. It is difficult to prevent this, because fieldwork supervision is more difficult. When each interviewer's quota is combined, the sample should resemble the characteristics of the universe. If there has been poor interviewer selection, this will not be achieved. Indeed, however well achieved, cautious statistically minded sociologists will not wish to utilise the data in any sophisticated ways (Kumar 1999: 148–58).

Key Words

interlocking quotas
probability sample
purposive sample
quota sample
sampling frame
snowballing
theoretical sampling
weighting

Links

Bias
Experiments
Grounded Theory
Internet Polling
Interviewing
Key Informants
Qualitative Methods
Quantitative Methods
Sampling: Estimates of Size
Sampling: Questions of Size
Social Surveys
Telephone and Computer-assisted Polling

REFERENCES

General

Guba, E. and Lincoln, Y. (1994) 'Competing Paradigms in Qualitative Research'. In Denzin, N. and Lincoln, Y. (eds), *Handbook of Qualitative Methods.* London: Sage.
Hammersley, M. (1992) *What's Wrong with Ethnography?* London: Routledge.
Kumar, R. (1999) *Research Methodology.* London: Sage.
Lee, R. (1993) *Doing Research on Sensitive Topics*. London: Sage.
MacFarlane Smith, J. (1972) *Interviewing in Market and Social Research*. London: Routledge & Kegan Paul.
Sarantakos, S. (1998) *Social Research* (2nd edn). London: Macmillan.
Williams, M. (2000) 'Interpretivism and Generalisation'. *Sociology*, 34 (2): 209–24.

Examples

Brannen, J. and Nilsen, A. (2002) 'Young People's Time Perspective'. *Sociology*, 36 (3): 513–37.
Devine, F. and Heath, S. (1999) *Sociological Research Methods in Context*. Basingstoke: Macmillan.
Lupton, D. and Tulloch, J. (2002) '"Risk is Part of Your Life"'. *Sociology*, 36 (2): 317–34.
Williams, M. and Cheal, B. (2001) 'Is There Any Such Thing as Homelessness?' *European Journal of Social Science Research*, 11 (3): 239–54.

Secondary Analysis

Secondary analysis is the re-analysis of either qualitative or quantitative data already collected in a previous study, by a different researcher normally wishing to address a new research question.

Section Outline: *Data-sets are never fully used. Re-use for new purposes. Access to published or raw data? Archive sources of data-sets. Secondary analysis for student dissertations. Data-sets: suitability and re-defining measurements for new concepts. Are data-sets available? Secondary analysis in qualitative methods: ethics; the person in the setting.*

Because of time and other career pressures, no study analyses every aspect of the data collected. This creates opportunities for other researchers to re-examine and re-use data from previous studies. Sometimes a data-set is re-analysed to develop the original topic, such as Payne's re-calculations from the main Nuffield Mobility Study table (2003). More typically, the second use of the data-set is for a different purpose than its original intention. Oral histories of Welsh miners, for example, have been re-used to explore theories of social capital, while employment data have been re-analysed to investigate the socio-economics of racism (Bloor 2002; Iganski et al. 2001: **Documentary Analysis**; **Official Statistics**).

The term for this is 'secondary analysis', meaning the use of data, collected in one project, in a second study. This goes beyond just quoting from a publication, reproducing tables essentially as they appear in the original document, or cross-referencing something as a source. To qualify as secondary analysis, the data must be used as if the second researcher had collected them, i.e. *evaluated in detail, re-processed,* and placed as evidence in *an argument that is different* from the first study (Dale et al. 1988). The great attractions of secondary analysis are that already collected data are so quickly to hand, with virtually no fieldwork cost. On the other hand, we are restricted to the quality of the original research: for instance, it there have been technical errors in data collection (**Bias**), we cannot normally correct for them retrospectively.

Data availability has been crucial in the changing status of secondary analysis. There is a great difference in accessibility between hand-recorded interviews still stored in dusty piles of old questionnaires, and a coded, cleaned and categorised data-set downloaded over the internet. In the past, whole sets were not released, while new tabulations were not provided, or took so long and cost so much to extract that it was uneconomic. Researchers were largely dependent on adapting published tables, which could to some extent be manipulated, but fell far short of the full set of raw data (i.e. for each respondent, individual responses to each question) ready to be processed into whatever format needed. In the mid-1970s, a secondary analysis study of industrial convergence theory involved re-coding the occupation tables from five Censuses by hand and calculator, collapsing the more detailed classifications from 1921 into the smaller units used in 1971 (Payne 1977). This took the researcher two months to complete, before any real analysis could start.

Today, official sites e-mail data-sets at little or no cost. For instance, modern Census data are now available to use 'on every researcher's desktop'. This influences what is processed in what order, the structures in which data are held, and the technical media of their 'publication'. While not all data are released ('small area statistics' are adapted to prevent identification of anyone contained therein), geographical boundaries, age groupings, detailed social class categorisations, etc., can largely be chosen by the researcher.

Major studies now copy their data to a central archive on completion of their first analysis. Indeed, Britain's main funder, the Economic and Social Research Council (ESRC), makes this a condition of its research grants. Data-sets and coding documents describing their format are held at the UK Data Archive (www.data-archive.ac.uk and archive-userservices@essex.ac.uk), part of the national Economic and Social Data Service (ESDS) set up in 2003 to co-ordinate holdings of archived records. The Archive does not run a data-processing service, but does make data-sets available, at a very low cost, to bona fide researchers. Other parts of ESDS hold data on **Longitudinal Studies**, government surveys (**Official Statistics**) qualitative and historical data (qual@essex.ac.uk and hds@essex.ac.uk) and international comparative surveys. Electronic catalogues list the variables and sample sizes, facilitating choices from among the original studies.

A wide range of statistical information is available for comparative purposes at the international level. Of particular relevance are those produced by EUROSTAT for the European Union; the World Health Organization; and the Organization for Economic Co-operation and

Development (OECD). All produce statistics relating to health and social conditions on an annual basis (for example, the OECD's *Annual Health Data*). In addition, ad hoc reports are produced frequently. All of these sources are listed at the organisations' websites on the internet (**Internet and Other Searches**).

These resources offer an excellent prospect for undergraduate dissertations. No student preparing a thesis could collect and process thousands of interviews. Indeed, the data have often been collected by highly competent interviewers, described, and made professionally acceptable through academic publication. Their quality can be demonstrated by the fact that well-established findings have already come from them. Speed, cheapness, quality and legitimacy are readily on offer, obtainable from ESDS through one's supervisor.

However, secondary analysis dissertations come with three 'health warnings'. A few departments retain dissertation assessment regulations that award marks for data collection per se, so not giving full credit for using archived sources: this should be checked in advance with one's supervisor. Second, the focus of a secondary analysis thesis shifts to the *ideas* being explored, and the data *analysis* (because there are no marks to gain from *data collection)*. The re-analysis has to be well handled if good marks are to be obtained. Third, and here we return to a problem faced in all secondary analysis, the data really must be capable of supporting the new uses planned.

As with official statistics, each study has involved a series of operational definitions and practical procedures. When re-using data, we need to ensure that the samples are large enough and representative of the people or organisations that interest us. When studies talk about, say, children, households, inner cities, migrants or religiosity (topics selected from a recent journal), do these things mean what *we* mean by the same words? Formal records like coding instructions are often incomplete: the original team shared implicit knowledge. We also need studies that included all the factors we want to explore. This limits what we can re-analyse, and how confident we can be about our new findings.

To take one example in more detail, Iganski et al. (2001) wanted to know how the position of British minority ethnic groups had changed since the 1960s. There had been several individual sociological studies, but these used inconsistent definitions and did not cover the whole country. Nor were there repeated government surveys providing all the answers. The biennial General Household Survey had good questions but for samples too small to give estimates without potentially large sample error (**Sampling: Estimates and Size**). The Census had a very large sample but asked about 'country of birth', so mis-allocating expatriate whites and British-born members of the ethnic minorities. The annual New Earnings Survey had questions about jobs, industries and incomes, but no ethnicity data. The quarterly Labour Force Survey (LFS) became the main source, but because of its sample size, surveys had to be merged, and only five ethnic groupings could be considered. The LFS income data were unreliable, so it was necessary to substitute employment categories, following the LFS's use of the Registrar General's 'socio-economic groups'.

This illustrates how even in quantitative research, secondary analysis encounters difficulties. In qualitative research, where secondary analysis is still relatively new, there is less agreement about what can be justified. The participants did not agree to the secondary analysis: is re-use ethical? In one sense, secondary analysis is an **Unobtrusive Method,** but of course the original research may have been highly intrusive. If the data depended on the unique interaction of the original researcher with people and events (**Qualitative Methods**), how can a subsequent analyst claim access to that original understanding (Hammersley 1997)? Again, the archived format matters: simple re-analysis of interview transcripts or recordings may be possible, but these probably require re-coding. Even more work is involved in re-processing field notes or original observations, but these seldom survive in easily intelligible form. These practical problems help to explain the still limited use of secondary analysis.

Key Words

coding
ESDS
legitimacy
operational definition
raw data
tabulation

Links

Bias
Documentary Analysis
Ethical Practice
Internet and Other Searches
Longitudinal and Cross-sectional Studies
Official Statistics
Qualitative Methods
Sampling: Estimates and Size
Unobtrusive Methods and Triangulation

REFERENCES

General

Dale, A., Arber, S. and Proctor, M. (1988) *Doing Secondary Analysis.* London: Unwin Hyman.

Hammersley, M. (1997) 'Qualitative Data Archiving: Some Reflections on Its Prospects and Problems'. *Sociology*, 31 (1): 131–42.

Examples

Bloor, M. (2002) 'No Longer Dying for a Living'. *Sociology*, 36 (1): 89–104.
Iganski, P., Payne, G. and Roberts, J. (2001) 'Inclusion or Exclusion? Reflections on the Evidence of Declining Racial Disadvantage in the British Labour Market'. *International Journal of Sociology and Social Policy*, 21 (4–6): 184–211.
Payne, G. (1977) 'Occupational Transition in Advanced Industrial Societies'. *Sociological Review*, 25 (1): 5–39.
Payne, G. (2003) 'Size Doesn't Matter'. *International Journal of Social Research Methodology*, 6 (2): 141–57.

Social Surveys

Social surveys collect mainly quantitative but also qualitative data from (usually representative) samples of people, by means of their verbal responses to uniform sets of systematic, structured questions presented either by interviewers or in self-completion questionnaires.

Section Outline: *Current status of survey research. Surveys involve standardisation, a sample and codifiable data. Types of social survey. Hypotheses and operationalisation. Pre-tests and pilots. Sample designs and workloads. Interviewer training and briefing. Contracting out the fieldwork. Pre-fieldwork checks. Interviewing, fieldwork management and response rates.*

Social surveys are one of the most widely used social science tools, and through market research and opinion polling, have become recognised parts of contemporary life. Within their own frame of reference, properly conducted surveys are effective means of collecting data (although other paradigms reject surveys out of hand: **Methods and Methodologies**; **Feminist Research**). However, misuse by less than scrupulous lobbyists has helped to discredit them, while social researchers more concerned with interpreting meanings than explaining wider social patterns have chosen other methods (**Qualitative Methods**). Confidence in survey results depends both on the integration of good practice across a series of components (Hoinville et al. 1982), and the application of the method to appropriate purposes (**Quantitative Methods**). In this section, we concentrate on the former, presenting the survey as a sequence of tasks.

Social surveys typically involve three characteristics. They *collect data in a standardised way* from a *sample* of respondents, enabling the data to be *codified, normally into quantitative form*. There are several types of survey: face-to-face interviewer surveys, telephone and internet surveys (**Interviewing**; **Telephone and Computer-assisted Polling**; and **Internet Polling**); and self-completion surveys (**Questionnaires**). They share the same basic steps, differing only in the importance of specific issues. For instance, questionnaire design is even more important for self-completion surveys, because no researcher is present to help informants having problems to answer the questions. Sampling and response rates are more problematic in electronic surveys. Face-to-face surveys can encounter difficulties with interviewing and, in larger studies, with managing a field-force of interviewers (MacFarlane Smith 1972: 52–71). The scale of such large studies contrasts with the **Case Study** method, and most qualitative work.

Survey research frequently starts with a theory to be tested in the form of hypotheses (**Hypothesis**), or more often, an idea to be explored as a step towards greater theoretical clarification. Indeed, the starting point should probably be whether a social survey is the right thing to do. Is it the best method and is it 'do-able' (Sapsford 1999: 10)? Theories and ideas need to be expressed in terms of *operational definitions*, by means of which data can be collected. Operationalisation begins as an intellectual process, leading to draft measurements and questions. For example, 'ethnicity' needs to be refined into a list of ethnic groups, and one or more questions to enable the categorisation of respondents into those groups. For some purposes, five broad groupings might suffice in Britain (e.g. White, Indian, West Indian, Pakistani-Bangladeshi, and 'Other': Iganski et al. 2001). In other countries, these groupings might be different. For more detailed research, smaller groups might need to be identified: Chinese, West African, and East European (Abbott and Tyler 1995: see also **Indicators and Operationalisations**).

The draft questions are collected into a preliminary questionnaire which is 'pre-tested' and 'piloted'. Pre-testing typically checks basic formats on a few people chosen for convenience (colleagues, friends), whereas piloting should involve a miniature version of the study, using a realistic sub-sample and working through coding to produce at least a draft set of coding instructions (the 'code-book'). Piloting should reveal whether the questionnaire, including its layout and instructions, 'works' to produce the information that is wanted. **Attitude Scales** require even more preparatory development.

While the **questionnaire** is being readied, the sample can be designed and drawn (**Sampling: Types**). As well as drawing the complete list of potential respondents from the sample frame, targeted names or addresses for face-to-face interviews are divided into suitable *workloads for interviewers*. This will be determined by whether the interviewers can work throughout the day, or only in the evenings, how many interviewers are available, the travelling times involved in the geographical spread of the survey, and the time each interview will take to complete.

It will also be necessary to obtain and train the interviewers. In some cases, experienced and highly skilful interviewers will be available, who need only to have the specific features of the study explained to them. In other cases, more basic training may first be required (McCrossan 1991). This should be workshop-based and include:

- general principles of surveys (samples, types of questions);
- confidentiality;
- truthfulness;
- presentation of self and personal appearance – tidy but not too smart;
- how to gain co-operation and trust;
- the importance of reading the questions exactly as they are worded;
- prompting and probing techniques;
- accuracy in recording answers;
- personal protection and safety;
- essential items to carry: identity card, covering letters, telephone numbers, addresses of respondents, folder, blank questionnaires, maps, pens and pencils, show cards;
- issues relating to the particular survey: preferably a handbook should be prepared. Interviewers should be taken through the questionnaire and also have time to conduct some trial interviews.

Not all researchers have ready access to a team of interviewers, or want the responsibility of managing them. This is therefore often 'contracted out' to a market research company, with its field-force of experienced personnel. In fact, interviewers normally work part-time for several companies, accepting commissions through self-employed 'supervisors' whom they know personally. A cheaper compromise, where possible, is to contract directly a supervisor. If farming out the data collection is being considered, it is normal to ask for cost quotations from several companies prior to entering into a contract.

Some companies specialise in social research, and offer a full range of services, from questionnaire design, through interviewing, to delivery of a pre-analysed electronic version of the data. While there are some well-regarded firms (acknowledgements in the literature identify which they are), *contracting out is no guarantee of successful fieldwork*. Not all researchers wish to hand over control in this way, or more likely, can afford the cost of doing so.

Even in smaller surveys, where one researcher completes all the interviews, it is important that *all* of the preparatory stages are completed. For example, an identity card or letter is essential to gain access to justifiably nervous respondents. In area surveys, the local police service should be notified (not least, this gives potential respondents an independent method of checking on interviewers). If the respondents constitute a special category (ethnic group, gender, class) will the interviewer(s) be easily able to gain *access* and establish *rapport*? The timing of interviews (in terms of the day, week and season) should be carefully planned. If there is more than one interviewer, quality controls will be needed: prompt inspection of completed questionnaires, and a sub-sample postal check that respondents were actually interviewed as claimed.

Researchers are often anxious about refusals to be interviewed and failure to achieve a good response rate. It is true that face-to-face interviews (and even more so, **Telephone Polling**) are more intrusive than, say, re-using **Official Statistics** or other **Unobtrusive Methods**. However, for most topics, only a *very few* people will refuse to be interviewed if the survey is conducted correctly (see Devine and Heath 1999: 107–28 for a discussion of 'sensitive' topics). If a 'first refusal' is given, interviewers should attempt to find out the reason (**Interviewing**). It might be they called at an inconvenient time, in which case a more suitable time should be arranged. Other reasons include fear, respondents' worry about their views becoming known, or that they feel that they do not know anything about the topic. The interviewer should attempt to reassure them. Two further attempts/re-calls are normal, the last by a different (and preferably more experienced) interviewer. In postal surveys, follow-up mailings to non-responses should go out 10 days and 20 days after initial mailing. Incentives (small gifts like a pen or a lottery ticket) are usually made to encourage response.

No survey has a 100 per cent response rate. People move away or die, or the address or person is unknown. Standardised procedures have been developed to tackle these problems. If people have died, moved out of the area, cannot be traced, or if the address or person is unknown, a replacement is made. (It is usual to draw up a list of substitutes/reserves when you select your sample.) These are not counted as non-response.

High response rates depend on *good record-keeping* and *prompt intervention*. As a rule of thumb, 70 per cent is an adequate response rate in face-to-face operations, although 80–85 per cent is a better target. In self-completion and postal surveys, 33 per cent is more typical, although for topics of particular relevance for the respondents, 60 per cent should be expected. What matters is not the proportion of non-responses, but whether the sample of achieved responses *resembles the original sample* (**Sampling: Questions of Size**).

Key Words

field-force
hypothesis
operational definition
pilot
pre-test
response rate

Links

Attitude Scales
Case Study
Feminist Research
Hypothesis
Indicators and Operationalisations
Internet Polling
Interviewing
Methods and Methodologies
Official Statistics
Qualitative Methods
Quantitative Methods
Questionnaires
Sampling: Types
Sampling: Questions of Size
Telephone and Computer-assisted Polling
Unobtrusive Methods and Triangulation

REFERENCES

General

Hoinville, G., Jowell, R. and Associates (1982) *Survey Research Practice.* London: Heinemann.

MacFarlane Smith, J. (1972) *Interviewing in Market and Social Research*. London: Routledge & Kegan Paul.

McCrossan, L. (1991) *A Handbook for Interviewers* (2nd edn). London: HMSO (for OPCS).

Sapsford, R. (1999) *Survey Research*. London: Sage.

Examples

Abbott, P. and Tyler, M. (1995) 'Ethnic Variation in the Female Labour Force'. *British Journal of Sociology*, 46 (2): 339–53.

Devine, F. and Heath, S. (1999) *Sociological Research Methods in Context*. Basingstoke: Macmillan.

Iganski, P., Payne, G. and Roberts, J. (2001) 'Inclusion or Exclusion? Reflections on the Evidence of Declining Racial Disadvantage in the British Labour Market'. *International Journal of Sociology and Social Policy*, 21 (4–6): 184–211.

Telephone and Computer-assisted Polling

Telephone polling, still probably the dominant data collection method in commercial research, uses special sampling and usually computer techniques to administer quantitative survey interviews at a distance, and is one of several electronic aids for the social researcher.

Section Outline: *Attractions of telephone polling. Most common method in USA, less so in Britain. Sampling: Random Digit Dialling. Other technological innovations: multiple dialling; CATI; CAPI; 'watches'. Mobiles and answer-phones. Interaction in phone interviewing. Contacting the 'right' person. Ethics of intrusion. Shifts to internet polling?*

Interviewing people over the phone sounds quite a good idea. The researchers can stay in one place, and save time and money on chasing up the addresses of the people whom they wish to interview. Supervision of those asking the questions is easier because they are all together, and a supervisor can be on hand to answer any queries. Longer interviews might not be suitable over the phone, but for shorter sets of questions such as opinion polls (often needing rapid completion to meet media or political party deadlines), everyday technology provides a handy solution.

One of the major exponents of telephone surveys offers evidence that by the 1980s in America, telephone polling was the most common single method, with nearly four in ten of completed interviews done over the phone (Frey 1989: 35–6). This figure does, however, include both academic social research and market research. Completion rates (**Social Surveys**) of between 60 per cent and 70 per cent were being quoted, almost as high as in face-to-face interviewing. The Federal Committee on Statistical Methodology advocated even greater telephone use in research.

> Today, the telephone survey is the dominant and most popular survey technique. Most commercial, and academic survey research, whether it be national, regional, or local, is conducted by phone (Frey 1989: 9).

Telephone polling has not been such a feature of research practice in Britain, for several reasons. Phone ownership was widespread in the States at an early stage, with 83 per cent of households having a phone by 1970 and reaching 97 per cent by the mid-1980s. In Britain, the spread of the telephone started later, was slower and only reached 75 per cent in the late 1980s, and 95 per cent a decade later. A combination of cheaper local billing conventions, competitive supply companies and the greater affluence of Americans, made phone calls relatively much cheaper in the States. The upshot of lack of penetration and higher costs in Britain was that a phone-friendly culture was much slower to emerge. Whereas most Americans seem content to answer telephone polls, between only one in six and one in four Britons called at random currently agree to participate (Kellner 2003; Sparrow 2003).

Telephone polling was also inhibited by two features of British academic social science. The social survey tradition in British social research has always been fairly weak, so there was less impetus for innovation in survey techniques. This ran in parallel to a widespread sensitivity to social inequalities. It was generally held to be the case that phone ownership was heavily skewed towards well-off people. Non-subscribers, who would be missing from any telephone sample, tend to be the more poorly paid, unemployed, inner-city renters, with low education and, particularly in America, members of ethnic minorities. People recently connected or with ex-directory numbers again differ from the rest of the population. Telephone samples therefore raise *serious problems of drawing representative samples.*

American telephone polling tackled this problem in two ways. First, as household coverage was much higher, there were fewer people omitted. Second, researchers soon discarded traditional telephone directories as the sampling frame, in favour of listings of the 'banks' of numbers allocated to an area by phone companies. By selecting or varying individual numbers 'at random' (**Sampling: Types**), even unlisted subscribers could be included. This Random Digit Dialling (RDD: see Frey 1989: 91–104) meant that statistically representative samples could be quickly and cheaply achieved, as well as being large enough to allow for discounting non-residential business phones (Lavrakas 1986). (Of course, listings of the *members* of an organisation could only be obtained with the agreement of that organisation.)

Later developments combine this with multiple dialling facilities in which several numbers are simultaneously called until one answers, whereupon the others disengage. This reduces waiting time and therefore costs (transposing the irritation of unwelcome calls that ring off onto potential respondents). Calling is handled by the software: interviewers no longer select the numbers they ring. Nor do they even need to direct the interviews: computer-assisted telephone interviewing (CATI) software provides one question at a time to be read out, and an automated coding and key stroke entry system to log the responses (**Interviewing**). Supervisors can monitor performance directly, so controlling work rates and accuracy in classic call centre mode. Examples are QPSMR, Bellview or Surveycraft. An (optimistic) description of what can be achieved with CATI can be found on various market research web-sites.

The idea of computer-assisted interviewing and telephone communication has also spread into the fieldwork for personal interviews – 'CAPI'. Responses entered into laptop computers, are downloaded, often via a modem and telephone link, for rapid central processing. Each question appears on the screen: there is no paperwork. The software ensures that filters are correctly followed (**Questionnaires**). Interviewers can be directed by the software to work through the questionnaire in a much more precise way, requiring less expertise and training. Respondents themselves can enter answers to sensitive questions directly. Another recent technological innovation is the 'electronic watch': rather than interviewers *asking* what radio stations have been listened to, or respondents writing it down in a *diary*, members of a sample wear a small device which *directly monitors* all listening. Conventional methods say talk Radio 4 has about 10 million listeners, and music Radio 2 some 13.2 million, whereas the 'watch' reports Radio 4 with nearly 18 million, and Radio 2 with 15.2 million (*The Guardian* 2003). One interpretation of these findings is that older conventional methods of data collection are invalid.

However, rapid developments in telephone polling were slowed by other new technological phenomena that complicated the picture; principally the mobile phone and answer-phone. Mobile phones became commonplace in Britain at a much more rapid pace than in America, partly owing to a different telecommunications technology, and partly owing to the weakness of the previous phone system. The classic *Survey Research by Telephone*, published only 15 years ago (Frey 1989) does not once mention mobile phones. Whereas phone polling had taken off in the States on the basis of telephone directories, the British shifted with great rapidity to a system effectively of unlisted numbers of variable length held by competing companies. Without a sampling frame of phone numbers (**Sampling: Types**), it is not possible to draw a representative sample of the population using RDD. Even when numbers are called, they are increasingly intercepted by answer-phones and filtered out as unwelcome.

Where telephone interviews are completed, many of the same good practice guidelines for other kinds of survey research apply (for a good comparison of methods, see Schutt 1999: 254–69). However, there are particular problems with telephone interviews. Attention spans on the phone are shorter, and complicated material cannot be presented in printed format, as in other methods. The interviewer is not present to see non-verbal behaviour, such as confusion over questions or indifference. Alternatively, this lack of physical presence can be taken to mean that respondents are less likely to react to an interviewer's appearance (e.g. ethnicity or age) and feel safer in a more anonymous 'relationship'. Either way, the interaction is atypical of everyday life (*pace* the conversational analysts: **Ethnomethodology and Conversational Analysis**).

A further problem is that the person answering the phone may not be the right person to interview (who is first to answer the phone in your household?). Additional sampling stages have to be applied over the phone to achieve balanced age and gender profiles. In organisations, offices are often explicitly designed to filter out unwelcome calls, so that targeted calling to managers can be very difficult.

In terms of both a busy work setting and the home environment, phone calls can be highly intrusive. The telephone reaches directly into the living room: like calls selling double glazing, its unwarranted entry is an unethical intrusion into people's private lives. It is not surprising that, as we have seen, in Britain the refusal rates are probably fifteen times higher than in face-to-face interviewing (American claims for telephone interviewing confuse the comparison by taking different bases for response rates: Frey and Oishi 1995).

The other challenge to the telephone poll is **Internet Polling.** Although this shares many of the same problems of access, representative sample and intrusion, its advocates are optimistic about its potential. Home computers are still much less common than landline telephones (about half of all homes own a PC), and internet samples need weighting to correct for under-representation of women, older people and the working class. Even with weighting, internet respondents tend to be several percentage points more progressive and liberal than the population as a whole.

At the time of writing, anxieties about telephone polling are growing, even in America (but see Bourque 2003). Former President Clinton's polling adviser, Stan Greenberg, is on record as predicting that 'there's going to be a crash between what's happening in the country and what's picked up on the phone'. Whit Ayres, a leading pollster for the Republicans, is quoted as saying:

> I can't fathom 20 years from now the telephone remaining the primary means of data collection. The industry is in a transition from telephone data collection to internet collection (Kellner 2003).

The decline in telephone polling is being driven by several factors, including declining administration cost differentials. However, differences between it and rival technologically assisted methods, not least on questions of **Reliability** and **Validity** which are central to social research, have yet to be settled.

Key Words

CAPI
CATI
filters
phone-friendly culture
RDD
representative samples
weighting

Links

Ethnomethodology and Conversational Anaysis
Internet Polling
Interviewing
Questionnaires
Reliability
Sampling: types
Social Surveys
Validity

REFERENCES

General

Bourque, L. (2003) *How to Conduct Telephone Surveys* (2nd edn). Thousand Oaks, CA: Sage.
Frey, J. (1989) *Survey Research by Telephone* (2nd edn). London: Sage.
Frey, J. and Oishi, S. (1995) *How to Conduct Interviews by Phone and in Person*. Thousand Oaks, CA: Sage.
Lavrakas, P. (1986) *Telephone Survey Methods.* Newbury Park, CA: Sage.
Schutt, R. (1999) *Investigating the Social World* (2nd edn). Thousand Oaks, CA: Pine Forge Press.

Examples

Bellview CATI (2003) www.bellviewcati.com
Kellner, P. (2003) 'For the Record'. *The Guardian*, 12 February: 19.
QPSMR CATI (2003) www.qpsmrcati.ltd/qpsmr_cati.htm
Sparrow, N. (2003) 'Why Internet Polls Have a Liberal Bias'. Letter to the Editor, *The Guardian*, 13 February: 23.
Surveycraft CATI (2003) www.infocorp.co.uk
The Guardian (2003) 'R4 to the fore – or is 2 still No 1?' 29 May: 21.

Unobtrusive Methods and Triangulation

Unobtrusive methods, which extract data from physical sources, or from groups and individuals without them being aware that data are being extracted or modifying their behaviour because they know they are being studied, are often used in multi-method triangulation as alternative data sources against which research findings on a particular topic can be cross-checked.

Section Outline: *'Non-reactive methods'. Addition to survey research, not replacement. Multi-method approaches. Triangulation and its forms. Methodological pluralism. 'Less reactive methods'. Physical records. Field notes, secondary analysis and psychological experiments not really unobtrusive. Examples of clever indirect methods. Participant observation. Issues of ethical practice. Reporting unobtrusiveness.*

Unobtrusive methods is the collective term for ways of gathering data without intruding into the lives of the people being studied. Their advantage is that they do not disturb the naturally occurring processes that are the subject of the research. In particular, because the informants are not aware of the research that is going on, their behaviour and self-descriptions are not modified by the researcher's presence or activities (Lee 2000). Other names for these techniques are 'non-reactive' or 'indirect' methods.

While advocates of unobtrusive approaches (e.g. Webb et al. 1966) were not opposed to survey research, they drew attention to its limitations as a means of tapping into the actual behaviour and belief systems of respondents. Rather than rejecting the survey, they proposed that data could also be gathered *by using additional techniques*, so that a better picture might be gained from several sources. Non-reactive measures would enable researchers to 'shore up reactive infirmities of the interview and questionnaire' (Webb et al. 1966: 174).

The purpose was to improve the way social science concepts were defined, represented empirically and so better understood. Concepts like racism, sexuality or even kinship, for example, might not be accessed fully by interview questions as the sole measure. Respondents are believed to be less reluctant to admit in public (i.e. to interviewers) that they take racist stances, have unconventional sexual preferences or do not visit their parents often.

The presence of an interviewer modifies their reported position, because they *react to being under scrutiny*. They might withhold socially unacceptable views; act the way they think researchers want to study; become self-conscious about audio-recorders; respond to questionnaires in a routine fashion (e.g. answering 'no' to all similar questions: **Questionnaires**); or just modify activities to accommodate the presence of a researcher in a confined space. Measuring anything inevitably changes it (**Hawthorne Effect**). What matters is what informants might otherwise actually do and believe, not how they act and what they say when they know they are being 'watched' (Speer and Hutchby 2003). Invisible methods help to constrain this problem, and the results from them can be compared with those found by conventional survey techniques (**Social Surveys**).

Using several methods would offer complementary measures of concepts, and a comparison between them would yield both a more rounded and accurate set of measurements. The employment of several methods is called 'triangulation', a term borrowed from land surveying based on two points. Denzin (1970, 1978) advocates using different perspectives ('theoretical triangulation'); data-sets ('data triangulation'); research workers ('investigator triangulation'); studies ('in-method methodological triangulation'); and methods of data collection ('between-methods methodological triangulation'). Combinations of these types of triangulation are called 'multiple triangulation' (Denzin 1970: 472). The more extensive the triangulation, the more confident we can be about the findings (**Reliability**; **Validity**).

Triangulation is a special case of 'methodological pluralism', a perspective that argues for an end to disputes about 'the best method' and the use of the 'most suitable methods' for the tasks in hand (**Methods and Methodologies**). Webb's between-methods triangulation emphasises adding new insights that non-reactive methods bring to survey research. However, it applies more generally: 'Every data-gathering class – interviews, questionnaires, observation, performance records, physical evidence – is potentially biased' (Webb 1970: 450). Unobtrusive methods do not prioritise qualitative research over quantitative research: rather they add *less reactive* measures to *more reactive* ones.

We can distinguish between 'indirect methods' involving no face-to-face encounters, and 'less reactive methods' which, while involving contacts, minimise the unintended effects of the researcher's presence. The most important of the standard methods in this respect is documentary analysis (**Documentary Methods**). Documents produced *before* the research cannot have been influenced by the research itself (although diaries and 'personal' papers are often produced with an eye to posterity and public reputation: **Auto/biography and Life Histories**). To varying degrees, documents are unrepresentative, incomplete, inaccessible and unreliable: each method has its own limitations.

The other major indirect method is **Content Analysis**. This has most of the same strengths and weaknesses of documentary analysis, with the added benefit that it is cheap, most frequently applied to published sources, and its source materials are easy to check. However, content analysis of field notes – the most common method of 'coding' – is a *direct* method because the data have previously been collected by researchers in face-to-face research settings. Similarly, social psychology experiments in which subjects are not told *in advance* what the experiment is testing, because this would bias the outcome, are only partially less obtrusive.

A parallel caveat applies to **Secondary Analysis**, where data collected for one purpose is later re-analysed for another. Clearly, secondary analysis of previous research studies could not count as less reactive, even though the reactivity would have been in the primary research. Indeed, most primary sources like official statistics involve face-to-face data collection, as do most 'social indicators' (**Indicators and Operationalisations**).

Examples of direct and most ingenious methods include Mosteller's examination of wear and tear on library reference books to see which sections were most used and so intellectually important (quoted in Webb 1970). Journalists and market researchers sort through household garbage to investigate consumption patterns. In both cases, it was physical objects that were studied, not people. Using such physical traces is a well-established tradition in archaeology for information about lifestyles, religious practices and social hierarchies). Campbell et al. (1966) monitored lecture theatre seating patterns to infer inter-racial attitudes among student groups. This did involve **Observation** of people, but without social interaction.

The availability of pre-existing objects, and the researcher's lack of control over them is a limitation. An alternative less reactive method is 'contrived observation,' where the researcher introduces a stimulus without the research being obvious. Bryman (2001: 165–6) gives the example of leaving a ladder against a wall and observing how many people walk under it, as a measurement of superstitions. More common is **Participant Observation,** where the researcher attempts to blend in so that respondents will get used to the researcher's presence.

As in these last two methods, unobtrusive research raises ethical problems because respondents have not given their informed consent (**Ethical Practice**). Denzin (1970: 447) casually dismisses this, saying that the researcher knows best if subjects 'would be harmed or discredited . . . I place the ethical matter in the observer's hands'. In other words, Denzin advocates a stance that many scholars would find *unethical*, but transfers to the individual researcher, as the sole judge, the full responsibility for the potentially unethical practice. However, simply improving the quality of research is a poor basis for unethical procedures.

Employing several measures, some of which are less intrusive, should not be confused with a simplistic commitment to studying what occurs 'naturally'. Hammersley and Atkinson (1995) argue that both qualitative and quantitative traditions seek to learn about the way the world would operate regardless of whether it is being studied. Both, in their own ways, build on situations where the research process has little, and known, impact, and where variations in procedures and researchers are minimised. But this does *not* mean that naturally occurring events can only be studied in ways that do not disrupt them (despite many qualitative writers prioritising this), or that they have to be studied in a covert way. The purpose of multi-method approaches is to understand *how* the data collection changes things, or in other words to handle the inevitable processes of reactivity. By systematically exercising **Reflexivity**, researchers scrutinise

> why they did what they did and its consequences, both methodological and ethical . . . they make explicit for their readers how their research was done, and their own role in producing the findings (Hammersley 2003: 344–5).

Key Words

contrived observation
field notes
naturally occurring
physical traces
reactivity
reflexivity

Links

Auto/biography and Life Histories
Content Analysis
Documentary Methods
Ethical Practice
Hawthorne Effect
Indicators and Operationalisations
Methods and Methodologies
Observation
Participant Observation
Questionnaires
Reflexivity
Reliability
Secondary Analysis
Social Surveys
Validity

REFERENCES

General

Denzin, N. (ed.) (1970) *Sociological Methods.* Chicago: Aldine.
Denzin, N. (1978) *The Research Act*. Englewood Cliffs, NJ: Prentice Hall.
Hammersley, M. (2003) '"Analytics" are No Substitute for Methodology'. *Sociology*, 37 (2): 339–51.
Hammersley, M. and Atkinson, P. (1995) *Ethnography: Principles in Practice.* London: Routledge.
Lee, R. (2000) *Unobtrusive Methods in Social Research*. Buckingham: Open University Press.

Webb, E. (1970) 'Unconventionality, Triangulation, and Inference'. In Denzin, N. (ed), *Sociological Methods.* Chicago: Aldine.
Webb, E., Campbell, D., Schwartz, R. and Sechrest, L. (1966) *Unobtrusive Measures: Nonreactive Measures in the Social Sciences.* Chicago: Rand McNally.

Examples

Bryman, A. (2001) *Social Research Methods*. Oxford: Oxford University Press.
Campbell, D., Kruskal, W. and Wallace, W. (1966) 'Seating Aggregation as an Index of Attitude'. *Sociometry*, 29 (1): 1–15.
Speer, S. and Hutchby, I. (2003) 'From Ethics to Analytics'. *Sociology*, 37 (2): 339–51.

Validity

Validity, which can take several forms, refers to the capacity of research techniques to encapsulate the characteristics of the concepts being studied, and so properly to measure what the methods were intended to measure.

Section Outline: *Justifying findings. Reliability and validity. 'Representations' of concepts in quantitative research. Internal and external validity. Example: occupations and gender in social mobility. Validity: predictive; pragmatic; concurrent. Validity of findings in qualitative research: trustworthiness; credibility; transferable. Ecological validity. Confirming findings.*

There is little point in research unless we can believe its results. 'Believing' in this context means having *rational grounds* for arguing that the accounts produced accurately reflect the nature of what we have studied. It is by 'recourse to a set of rules concerning knowledge, its production, and representation' that it is possible to assert that we were 'faithful to the context and the individuals it is supposed to represent' (Denzin and Lincoln 1998: 414). In particular, we need to substantiate the research 'instruments' that we have applied (**Ethical Practice**).

Research instruments are the ideas, concepts and techniques of data collection and analysis that researchers use to make sense of the social world. These abstract mechanisms are only approximations, or representations, of the actual phenomena that interest us. Two key questions need to be asked of them. First, do they yield *consistent* results (**Reliability**)? Second, do they capture the essence of what they are intended to represent – do they have 'validity'?

If we want to explore, say, religious beliefs and secularisation, do church attendance rates give an adequate picture? Do IQ tests measure 'intelligence' or prior learning experience and the cultural values inevitably 'built into' the tests? (**Indicators and Operationalisations**). If 42 per cent of people actually use recreational drugs, is that what our research finds? When residents distinguish between those with long connections with a place, and more recent arrivals, will concepts like 'local' and 'incomer' fully reflect how residents think and feel?

Most types of validity question can be grouped under a measure's 'internal' or 'external' validity. '*Internal validity*' deals with a study's own logic: does it achieve what it sets out to do? Its operational definitions must reflect a fully developed conceptual framework, and its conclusions be plausibly defensible. If associations are claimed between phenomena, it should be clear that no unstudied phenomena intervened (**Association and Causation**). '*External validity*' refers to the *limits of generalisation* that operationalisation imposes. A study's findings might validly apply to all men, but not to women (the social mobility example below). It might sometimes be sufficient to measure industrial relations unrest solely by 'days lost' in strikes, but this would not do in other contexts, because it fails to include 'go-slows', absenteeism or worker sabotage (for more detailed examples, see Hammersley 1998: 90–109).

A good quantitative example is social mobility analysis. Measurements of *class* mobility have used groups of *occupations*. There has been considerable *theoretical* debate over how well occupational groups can represent the class system (e.g. Marshall et al. 1988). *Empirically*, there are questions about which occupations should be grouped together, and about how we should deal with those who are 'not working': young people still in training or education; married women not in paid employment; those working part-time (however defined); workers who are temporarily or long-term unemployed; those who are disabled and unable to work; people who have taken early retirement; very rich or privileged people who have never had to work; people with more than one job; and those whose 'jobs' are part of the black economy. Only when we have decided on all of these (which some estimates put as high as half of all male 'workers' and three-quarters of all women), can we decide how far occupational group *validly* represents class membership (Payne 1987).

When sociologists have talked about rates of 'class mobility', they imply that they are describing the experiences of all working-age adults, but their conclusions have usually been based on samples of men. It was assumed that female mobility was either the same as male mobility, or that women's mobility did not matter because their class behaviour could be as well approximated from that of their husband's occupation, as from their own. The question of validity turns on whether male and female mobility is very similar (which it is not), and how closely wives resemble their husbands in class behaviours (which depends on the behaviours chosen for examination) (Payne and Abbott 1991).

How well does mobility analysis perform on validity tests? 'On the face of it', our mobility measures could be improved: they lack 'face validity' because not all the obvious questions have been asked about the logical connections between class, work and gender. They also lack 'content validity', because they have not covered all known forms of mobility, particularly female mobility. They perform poorly on 'construct' or 'measurement validity', because what they have measured ('rates of male movements between occupational groups') is a *limited representation of the theoretical phenomenon that was meant to be measured* ('adult class mobility': **Levels of Measurement**).

In empirical terms, there are three possible validity tests in **Quantitative Methods**. The most demanding is '*predictive validity*', which requires us to predict in advance that if one thing happens, so subsequently will another. The validity of our measurements is justified by the results of our study being as anticipated (of course, such predictions also involve a theoretical element). The simplest test of empirical validity is to check all of the procedures to ensure that they contain no obvious errors or flaws (or **Bias**): this is referred to as *'practical'* or *'pragmatic validity'*. A third test is whether the results produced in one piece of research are similar to previous findings. However this 'concurrent validity' test is really about **reliability** (or consistency) of measures, rather than whether research has captured the true essence of the subject being studied (Hammersley 1998: 58–70; 78–90).

Apart from those who adopt a fairly extreme phenomenological stance (**Ethnomethodology**), most qualitative researchers are equally concerned with most aspects of validity, although their vocabulary differs. For example, the external test of comparing one study's conclusions with other studies is usually called 'cumulative validity'. 'Argumentative validity' refers to the internal consistency: the plausibility of the way evidence and conclusions are presented.

Lincoln and Guba (1985) have identified four aspects of 'trustworthiness' in qualitative research (**Qualitative Methods**: see also Lecompte and Goetz 1982; Kirk and Miller 1986). 'Credibility' and 'transferability' are basically the same as internal and external validity in quantitative methods. 'Confirmability' questions the degree of what quantitative researchers would call 'observer bias' (**Objectivity**; **Reflexivity**). 'Dependability' addresses the general applicability of results, and is actually a test of **Reliability**.

It is generally agreed that qualitative research handles most validity issues more effectively than does quantitative work. Although qualitative research is less concerned about generalisation (Shipman 1997), its concern for the *details* of the setting observed, as they naturally happen in their unique social context, together with close and repeated observation of this, all help to capture the essence of what is being studied. Testing interpretations back with the informants ('communicative validity'), and seeking participation and equality in the research process (**Grounded Theory**; **Feminist Research**) contribute to the same ends.

Cicourel (1982) calls this capacity of research findings to make sense in their natural setting, for the people concerned 'ecological validity'. Because qualitative research aims to interpret subjective meanings, it counts for little that other kinds of validity may be satisfactory, if ecological validity is not achieved. The results of laboratory experiments may enable predictive hypotheses to be made, but people do not live their lives in laboratories.

'The "goodness" of qualitative research' has to be worked at and *demonstrated*. Miles and Huberman set out a range of 'tactics' for 'confirming' findings (1994: 262–79). These essentially boil down to ensuring that the potential strengths of qualitative methods have been achieved, and potential weaknesses avoided.

> Qualitative analyses can be evocative, illuminating and masterful – and wrong. The story, well told as it is, does not fit the data . . . The phenomenologist chuckles, reinforced in the idea that there is no single reality to get 'right' – but cannot escape a sneaky feeling that, in fact, reasonable conclusions are out there somewhere (ibid.: 262).

Key Words

confirmability
construct validity
ecological validity
external validity
face validity

internal validity
reliability
trustworthiness

Links

Association and Causation
Bias
Ethical Practice
Ethnography
Ethnomethodology and Conversational Analysis
Feminist Research
Grounded Theory
Indicators and Operationalisations
Levels of Measurement
Objectivity
Qualitative Methods
Quantitative Methods
Reflexivity
Reliability

REFERENCES

General

Cicourel, A. (1982) 'Interviews, Surveys, and the Problem of Ecological Validity'. *American Sociologist*, 17: 11–20.

Denzin, N. and Lincoln, Y. (eds) (1998) *The Landscape of Qualitative Research*. London: Sage.

Hammersley, M. (1998) *Reading Ethnographic Research* (2nd edn). Harlow: Longman.

Kirk, J. and Miller, M. (1986) *Reliability and Validity in Qualitative Research*. Beverly Hills, CA: Sage.

Lecompte, M. and Goetz, J. (1982) 'Problems of Reliability and Validity in Ethnographic Research'. *Review of Educational Research*, 54: 31–60.

Lincoln, Y. and Guba, E. (1985) *Naturalistic Inquiry*. London: Sage.

Miles, M. and Huberman, M. (1994) *Qualitative Data Analysis* (2nd edn). London: Sage.

Shipman, M. (1997) *The Limitations of Social Research* (4th edn). London: Longman.

Examples

Marshall, G., Rose, D., Newby, H. and Vogler, C. (1988) *Social Class in Modern Britain*. London: Unwin Hyman.

Payne, G. (1987) *Mobility and Change in Modern Society*. London: Macmillan.

Payne, G. and Abbott, P. (eds) (1990) *The Social Mobility of Women*. London: Falmer Press.

Visual Methods

Visual methods cover all uses of images, with or without accompanying words, such as photographs, video, film, television, or hand-drawn artwork, whether pre-existing or generated as part of the research process, as data for social research purposes.

Section Outline: *Reluctance to use visual methods. Visual illiteracy. Film as complex of lived encounters. Pre-existing images; elicitation images; visual records; visual reports. Video for ecological validation. Issues of ethical practice. Selectivity and distortion. Reactivity to the camera. Technical competence with the camera. Making and editing a video. Photography and artwork as elicitation devices. Interpretation and the researcher's constructed version of reality.*

Apart from social anthropology's films of exotic customs, the social sciences have always been disciplines that deal in words and numbers. Little use has been made of visual images, either moving or still. As Prosser (1998) shows, the usual reason given is that *making* images involves distortions by the maker, and *seeing* the images depends on the viewer's cultural interpretations. Despite some recent expressions of interest (e.g. Banks 1995; Payne 1996; Foster's excellent illustrations of Docklands (1999) and Bolton et al. 2001), the dominant opinion is that

> images are so complex that analysis is untenable. There is little attempt to point to solutions to these issues or *identify parallel problems within word-oriented research* (Prosser 1998: 99; emphasis added).

Most sociologists are 'visually illiterate', showing little sign of considering use of visual images. Even in **Qualitative Methods**, with the emphasis on the details of interaction,

> images are another neglected source of data for field research . . . In societies where television is central to leisure . . . we have become lazy with our eyes. Thus what we see is taken for granted and our first thought tends to associate social research with what we can read (texts, statistics) or hear (interviews, conversations) (Silverman 1997: 70).

And yet, film in particular has 'the same mix of transparent obviousness (often absent from data) and impenetrability (often abundant in data) that forms of lived encounter also possess' (Nichols 1996: 8). Despite their problems, the continued under-use of video and photography seems almost perverse.

Images fall into four main research categories:

1 Pictures already made by other people for their own purposes , e.g. family 'snaps'; illustrations in publications, works in art galleries) can be interpreted as our topic of research ('semiotics': see Rose 2001).
2 We can work collaboratively with informants, using image-making and images as a way of eliciting information (Harrison 1996).
3 We can make our own images to record what is taking place during our research (**Fieldwork**).
4 Finally, images can be used as an addition to words in communicating our findings.

Here we shall concentrate on making visual records in the field.

The recording of overt observations by video and photography can provide very rich data to supplement note-taking or as data in their own right. This is particularly useful when you are presenting your results. As advocated in collaborative work and in grounded theory (**Feminist Research**; **Grounded Theory**), one test of the process is to share the product with the original informants: 'ecological validation'. Our own experience of videoing showed us the emotional impact of the anxiety this generates, the informants' interest, and their ultimate pleasure that we had faithfully represented their way of life (Payne and Payne 2002).

Before using cameras you must, of course, ensure that everyone is agreeable. Complete informed consent is, however, virtually impossible in a busy street or other public place (**Ethical Practice**). Here, commonsense and sensitivity are important, especially in subsequent use of the images in any presentation.

Willingness to be filmed is an example of how only some items get recorded. Even where everybody agrees to filming, visual images are the inevitable result of the *subjective selectivity* of the person recording them (Lomax and Casey 1998). Your reasons for selecting events should be noted in your research diary, both at the time and in any later editing. At another level, selectivity happens in that research takes place at one historical point: images capture the style and feel of an era, and remind us that research soon gets out of date (Payne 1996).

Nor are images to be regarded as automatically credible. The camera *can* lie. Famous images like flag-raising in Iwo Jima, or American Civil War battlefields, were artificially composed. The researcher has a duty not to misrepresent, but faces the difficulty of not always knowing in advance what would be representative. It is important to be aware that visual images are no more 'objective' than more traditional observations.

Further, people often behave differently when they know that they are being filmed. However, if filming is done unobtrusively – but with consent – people do get used to it: for instance, we tend to take for granted the CCTV cameras in shops and town centres. Bottoroff's study of nurse–patient interactions installed cameras a month *before* the start of data collection (1994). The actual observations were complemented by interviews (Grbich 1999).

Before using cameras, you should ensure that you are technically competent to use them. This applies to 'throwaway cameras' used in collaborative projects, as well as to digital photography (which has greatly speeded storage and access) and modern camcorders. For video, you also need to have some knowledge of *basic filming techniques*.

First, you should ensure that you get the correct light balance. Artificial lighting is different from outdoor natural lighting, and very strange results can be achieved if the wrong setting is selected. Second, you should make sure that you can hold the camera steady, especially when zooming or panning. Here, a tripod, although expensive, is useful. Third, do not move the camera or your position too often – let what you are filming move, not you.

If you are going to edit the tape for display to others, you should make a 'story board'. Even with the recent availability of PC editing software, editing takes a considerable time (up to ten times the running time of the original tape) and you should allow for this in your research plan. You should also take longer sequences of events than you think you will need, to improve the technical quality of the editing (these days, we all expect 'broadcast standard' of production, not 'home movies'!).

When videoing, and in any subsequent editing, you must be aware that you are *selecting* cases and *constructing* a story. Are you choosing 'good' or 'typical' shots? How far will you 'narrate' the 'story' in the order in which it occurred naturally (including the mundane bits) or re-order it and select the more 'dramatic' events? These decisions should all be recorded in your researcher's diary.

Photographs are far easier and cheaper to take and use than video. In addition to taking photographs yourself, you might consider asking different groups or individuals to make their own photographic record. These visual accounts can provide very rich data on personal visions that cannot be collected by any other method. Also, they could be exhibited as both a visual history of the area or group and as a focus and 'memory jogger' for oral accounts of community life (Blaikie in press).

Visual methods are particularly appropriate for involving children and teenagers. In a primary school evaluation, pupils photographed places in the school that they felt good or bad about, combining images with explanations of their feelings (Schratz and Steiner-Löffler 1998). The *Draw and Write* technique for school health education programmes developed from research on language development (Wetton and McWhirter 1998). Children were asked to make annotated drawings of what they did to make and keep themselves healthy. Although the analysis was mainly of the written accounts, later analysis of the drawings showed children had a broader definition of health than just 'not ill'.

The examples of video and children's art again remind us that images are selected, constructed and interpreted. They are not simple 'givens' to be taken at face value. None the less, their potential has still not been fully exploited. It is not yet clear whether software for image analysis will help this process (e.g. 'Atlas ti'). There is nothing so powerful as simple video editing to bring home to researchers that they re-construct reality – not just with images but in every word they *write*. That should not incapacitate us, but rather empower us to greater self-awareness in the practice of our craft. With due care in the analysis, particularly of moving images (Banks 2001), the potential for connecting images to more conventional written sociology is tremendous (Smith and Emmison 2000).

Key Words

collaboration
ecological validation
elicitation
image
story board
subjective selectivity
visually illiterate

Links

Ethical Practice
Feminist Research
Fieldwork
Grounded Theory
Qualitative Methods

REFERENCES

General

Banks, M. (1995) 'Visual Research Methods'. *Social Research Update No. 11*. Guildford: Department of Sociology, University of Surrey.

Banks, M. (2001) *Visual Methods in Social Research*. London: Sage.
Grbich, C. (1999) *Qualitative Research in Health: an Introduction*. London: Sage.
Prosser, J. (1998) 'The Status of Image-based Research'. In Prosser, J. (ed.) *Image-based Research*. London: Falmer Press.
Rose, G. (2001) *Visual Methodologies*. London: Sage.
Smith, P. and Emmison, M. (2000) *Researching the Visual*. London: Sage.

Examples

Atlas ti (2003) www.scolari.co.uk.
Blaikie, A. (in press) *Scottish Lives in Modern Memory*. Edinburgh: Edinburgh University Press.
Bolton, A., Pole, C. and Mizen, P. (2001) 'Picture This: Researching Child Workers'. *Sociology*, 35 (2): 501–18.
Bottoroff, J. (1994) 'Using Videotaped Recordings in Qualitative Research'. In Morse, J. (ed.) *Critical Issues in Qualitative Research Methods*. Thousand Oaks, CA: Sage.
Foster, J. (1999) *Docklands*. London: UCL Press.
Harrison, B. (1996) 'Every Picture "Tells a Story"' In Lyon, S. and Busfield, J. (eds), *Methodological Imaginations*. Basingstoke: Macmillan.
Lomax, H. and Casey, N. (1998) 'Recording Social Life: Reflexivity and Video Methodology'. *Sociological Research Online*, 3 (2). http://www.socresonline.org.uk/socresonline/3/2/1.html
Nichols, B. (1996) 'What Really Happened: the Ax Fight Reconsidered'. *Media International Australia*, 82 (November).
Payne, G. (1996) 'Imagining the Community'. In Lyon, S. and Busfield, J. (eds) *Methodological Imaginations*. Basingstoke: Macmillan.
Payne, G. and Payne, J. (2002) *Coigach Life*. Achiltibuie: CCHG (video).
Schratz, M. and Steiner-Löffler, U. (1998) 'Pupils Using Photographs in School Self-evaluation'. In Prosser, J. (ed.), *Image-based Research*. London: Falmer Press.
Silverman, D. (1997) *Interpreting Qualitative Data*. London: Sage.
Wetton, N. and McWhirter, J. (1998) 'Images and Curriculum Development in Health Education'. In Prosser, J. (ed.), *Image-based Research*. London: Falmer Press.